The Chosen People Seen from the
Backdrop of the Hebrew Scriptures

How should "Chosen" be seen in a Critical Time from a
Critical Mindset within an Age of Political Correctness?

We could call it *The Choice*

One Goy's Perspective

Mike,

May you know Yeshua's Shalom & May he
bless you and your family

Bill

William A. Parker

William A. Parker

Scripture quotations, unless otherwise indicated, taken from the Holy Bible, New International Version. Copyright © 1973, 1978, 1984 by International Bible Society. Used by permission of Zondervan Publishing House.

Scripture quotations i.e. Psalm 51:5[7] show the non-Jewish version numbering system first, as Psalm 51:**5**; while Psalm 51:5 **[7]** shows the different numbering system found in most Jewish versions. When this occurs the Jewish numbering is placed inside brackets, as shown above.

Instead of speaking of a reference in the following way: Exodus, chapter 6, verse 1, I have used the following reference style, i.e., Exodus 6:1 to shorten the space required for the book and make it consistent. There is no intention to provoke disrespect.

Writing formats teach a protocol for quotations. I use another format but want my readers to know "my" rule. True quotes are given with double quotation marks. When a "quote" suggests what someone might say, single quotation marks help readers accurately distinguish between a direct and indirect quote. Scripture marked with single quotations marks, i.e., 'Yes, I was completely full of sin from birth.' is my own paraphrase of the noted Scripture.

All definitions taken from The Strong's Concordance are used with permission as follows: Taken from *The New Strong's Exhaustive Concordance of the Bible* by James Strong, LL.D, S.T.D. Copyright ©

Contents

Contents (Continued)

Foreword

William Parker weaves a beautiful portrait of what it means to be Chosen, synthesizing truths from the Hebrew Scriptures with beautiful literary style. He then takes those truth strands and blends them beautifully with New Covenant (Testament insights, painting a picture for all serious believers of Scripture to appreciate, enjoy and savor. His book is clearly written for anyone seeking to drink deeply from the Scriptures.

Barri Cae Seif, Ph.D.

Author, theologian

Dedications

I want to first and foremost dedicate this book to the Jewish People. Without them, their God and their Scriptures, I would not know God, His Word or myself. I truly appreciate the blessings they have been to this world and to me personally. Their almost innumerable, positive and, in many instances, lifesaving contributions are breathtaking.

Second, I want to thank my departed parents. It was their love of God and the Jewish People that gave me the first desire to know more of God and His Chosen People. Their lives were shining lights on a hill for all to see.

Third, I want to thank my wife, Lola, with whom I've traveled along on the road of life for forty years. She has blessed me with her life, love, determination and quiet tenacity for all these years, in the sunshine as well as the rain. Her life has always been one of service to others.

Fourth, I thank my four kids, who could ask for any who exude life and love. I am indebted to them for their love and many of the life-lessons learned. It was these lessons that drew me closer to God and helped teach me love.

Fifth, I thank my siblings. Growing up with brothers and sisters helps one prepare for life. If you can survive siblings you should be able to survive life. I am blessed by each of their personalities and temperaments; they have taught me much over the years and continue to do so.

Sixth, I owe a big thank you to Marcia Adams and Jolie Barrios who drew the pictures on the front cover and last page. And also to Nate Parker for the Cover Design.

Seventh, I also owe a great deal to my brother Tim, who helped tremendously with punctuation and clarity.

I also owe a big thank you to Barri Cae for her encouragement to publish this book in the first place. She and her desire for truth has been an inspiration to me.

Preface

The fact of a Goy (Gentile) attempting to write something meaningful concerning the topic of being the Chosen People, while writing to Gentiles and especially Jewish people in general, will be seen in many different ways. Some will see it as being pretentious or arrogant. Some will see it as just more Gentile deception. Still others may see this as just more bad ink about the Jewish people. But I hope you see it differently.

The truth of the matter is that I feel compelled to write, and not from any of the above perspectives. I certainly don't want to show the superiority of the Gentile, nor of the Christian perspective. From my viewpoint it is we, as Gentile Christians, who should shoulder much of the burden for the evil that was perpetrated against the Jewish people for much of the Common Era. It was our arrogance and lack of love and respect for our fellow man that brought about so much suffering to the Jewish people over the centuries. In these events we were the infidels, brute beasts, and house of Satan. We were ones in the wrong.

Yes, I realize some Gentile Christians and others helped the Jewish people during the dark, dark days of Nazi Germany. However, the help was far too little. The vast majority of Christendom did nothing to help; in this way, the Church failed to love its neighbors as themselves and to bless the Chosen People of God. If you disagree with my assessment, I hope you will look up the history of these events for yourself; you may find yourself enlightened.

There is nothing I can do to undo all the ugliness that transpired against Jewish people down through the centuries but I would like to offer a new start. Can we take a fresh look at history – Jewish history in general – by beginning all the way back at the story of the great Hebrew named Abraham and bringing it all the way forward to our current day and time? This is why I am writing. I want to offer a new, hopefully non-antagonistic perspective to

Jewish as well as Gentile minds, hearts and ears. Travel with me as we look at what the Hebrew Scriptures have to say, starting with the Lord's friend, Abraham. As we travel, I hope and believe we will be able to see some things in a fresh light.

I have a heart of gratitude toward the Jewish people and owe them a great deal. Without their Scriptures, I would not know myself nor would I have understanding of the Lord. It is with awe that I read these Scriptures and see how the Lord preserved a people for Himself through all the centuries of hatred, hardship and loss. I am still in awe, as I continue to see the Lord's faithfulness of his promise to Abraham, to make his descendants a blessing to the whole earth. My love and respect for the Lord's Chosen People grows with time even as my desire is to share the trust of Abraham and truths of Messiah with the Jewish people.

Introduction

The word *Chosen* in regards to the nation of Israel and the Jewish people has been seen in many ways down through the centuries. Today, I believe the understanding of this term and its implications are all but lost to most. More so than at any time, I believe the meaning of the term needs to be understood in its entirety. In my estimation, misunderstanding of this term and its specific Scriptural designations led to European ghettos, pogroms, expulsions, forced conversions, the Spanish Inquisition and the Holocaust among other evils.

After the Holocaust, the tide of public opinion towards the Jewish people changed. This change resulted in a homeland for both the Palestinians and the Jewish people. Now, however, once again the tide of public opinion is waffling backwards against the Jewish people and their homeland. Anti-Semitism is on the rise in Europe, the United States and around the world. It is because of these very issues that I want to reexamine this specific topic of being *The Chosen People.* I want us to examine this topic and its ramifications using the writings of Moses and the Prophets of Israel, specifically using the perspective of the Hebrew Scriptures or Tanakh (Old Testament for Gentiles).

I want to posit three main points using these very same Scriptures. These points are: **One**, God's choice of Israel through Abraham was specific, not arbitrary. **Two**, Israel's mission to the world has three goals, which are to reflect God's holiness, be priestly intercessors, and proclaim God's glory (all prophetic realities). **Three**, the coming of Messiah brings life from the dead for Israel and provides the unmasking of truth for all of humanity.

Within the backdrop of these three facts is something that's too often missed. What people miss is this; God's choice of Israel provides blessing for Israel as well as for all the rest of us. His choosing of Israel allows for the inclusion of all humanity through the forgiveness of sin, under God.

Today, trust in God and His Hebrew Scriptures has fallen on hard times because people don't believe in them. There are, however, good reasons for trusting in God and His Scriptures; I state two reasons here. The first reason for believing both God and His Scriptures is this: the state of Israel and its people have recently fulfilled ancient prophecy. Prophecy has been fulfilled in this way: no other ancient people have ever returned to their ancestral home after an almost 2,000 year diaspora. This return happened just as the prophets of Israel predicted, thousands of years earlier. My second reason for believing God and His Scriptures is this: the Jewish people have not only returned but also regained their ancient language. This regaining of language is another thing that has never happened to a people before, after an almost 2,000 year diaspora.

God Begins Choosing

1st Choice

'Why all this fuss over an offering to the Lord in the first place,' Cain asks no one in particular. 'There's no way that I'm going to buy a lamb from my kid brother; God will just have to settle for what I'm good at. I'll give him some of my fruits and vegetables. Yea, I know Dad told me how important an offering is and how it needs to come from the heart. He even harped on the issue of giving the Lord the first and best. But there really can't be that much to it; I think Dad's just a little paranoid after the Garden-and-Curse episode and all. Well, I'll do my duty and bring an offering, but I'm definitely not going to get any blood on my hands; and that's that; I'm also not going to lose any sleep over it.'

In the cool of the day, just outside of Eden's entrance, Cain is in no mood to be bothered. 'I have to finish my duty,' Cain says, remembering what he had just finished an hour or so before. He had picked some apples from his orchard, even tossing in some wormy ones he found on the ground, 'It doesn't matter which ones,' Cain tells himself, 'and besides they can't be used for food anyway.'

Cain was, after all, just offering these apples and some vegetables; it wasn't as if they needed to be the best. These apples and vegetables, of course, weren't first fruits. They were just some of his fruits and vegetables which he didn't even want. He was, after all, the one who had toiled, and he had birthed this fruit by the sweat of his brow. Now that his picking had ended and his fruit and vegetables were in the basket, Cain brought his basket of fruit and vegetables right to the outside of Eden's Gate, making sure to keep a safe distance away from the flaming sword of the cherubim. He hastily dusted off the altar and dumped his fruit and vegetables on top. Now his duty was done and his offering was complete. 'The Lord of the first fruits should be pleased,' Cain muttered to himself as he left.

Earlier that morning we find Abel in the midst of a daydream, while thinking of his offering. 'I can't believe it,' Abel tells himself while watching his favorite lambs play. 'Look at those guys jump and kick. It seems like only yesterday that I watched their births,' Abel remembers. 'Come over here, I have something to tell you,' Abel calls out to Babe, Danny and Herbie. These three are never far from his side. Abel asks his three favorite lambs, 'Do you know what today is? Yep, that's right, today is the day for sacrifice. One of you special guys will give it your best, and your all! I'll bet you guys know all about it, don't you? I've talked about this day of sacrifice so often, lately.'

As Babe lies next to him, Abel reaches over and rolls him over while he runs his fingers through his coat. 'There's no doubt about it, Babe,' Abel says, 'you're definitely one fine lamb specimen.' 'Look at this' Abel tells himself, remembering the vicious kick grumpy old Ed, his oldest ram, had delivered to Babe a couple weeks earlier. 'It's just as I thought,' Abel tells Babe, 'this leg of yours hasn't quite healed. Let's give it some more time,' Abel tells him as he rubs his ears.

Not to be outdone, Danny gently butts Abel to get his attention. 'Okay fellow,' Abel tells him, 'I haven't forgotten you; let's see how you're doing young man.' With that, Abel begins inspecting Danny. 'You're some specimen too,' Abel says, 'you're neck-and-neck with Babe for lamb runner-up. But look at this,' Abel tells Danny, 'your eye still needs more time to heal; you just had to try to protect Babe from Ed didn't you? Well, it's a good thing that you pulled back just in time to miss the full impact of his head butt. Just the same, he still nicked your eye and it's going to take a little while for it to completely heal.' With that Abel gently lays Danny back down on the grass.

'Now, let me take a look at you young fellow,' Abel says to Herbie. 'You know what, you're a little bit bigger than your two friends; those midnight snacks must have paid off.' As Abel runs his fingers and hands through Herbie's coat, he tells him, 'Herbie,' he says, 'You are definitely the best lamb-prospect of them all. 'You know,' Abel continues, 'the Lord always deserves the best, that's one thing Dad and Mom always made sure I knew. Well, you're the best little guy,' Abel tells Herbie, 'and you know what that means, yep, you guessed it; you're going to be presented as the spotless lamb to the Lord.'

Even though Abel says it with pride, thinking of what will happen next brings tears to his eyes. Abel can't help but remember all the nights that Herbie kept him company. Herbie has been so much more than an animal to Abel. 'You've been my companion and friend,' Abel tells him. As Abel picks Herbie up, he tells him, 'Let's go, my friend,' Abel says. With that, they set off to "the altar of sacrifice."

Entering the outskirts of the Garden, in fact, right on the heels of Cain's exit, his kid brother Abel comes in carrying his offering. 'I love the Lord, and I love giving him my best,' Abel says to himself. 'But this one really hurts,' he says, while thinking of the loss that Herbie's death will bring.

Abel arrives at the altar and begins his preparations. Abel gathers the necessary wood and arranges it on the altar after thoroughly cleaning the altar off. After tying Herbie's legs, he gently places the lamb he loves on top of the wood. As tears begin to fall, Abel swiftly and precisely slits Herbie's throat. 'Lord, I'm bringing you my best offering,' Abel says, choking on his tears. 'Thank you Lord for always giving me and my family your best,' Abel prays as he cuts the fat off the meat and sets it aside to sacrifice later. 'You are worthy, Lord,' Abel whispers, remembering the stories his mom and dad told him.

As Abel quickly though meticulously cuts the meat, he remembers one story in particular – the one of his parent's sin in the Garden. Abel remembers how God atoned for them and covered their shame. With that remembrance, Abel once more declares aloud, 'Lord, you are worthy. Lord, you killed an animal in our place and shed its blood for our atonement. But's that's not all, Lord, you didn't leave my parents simply forgiven, you covered their shame with the animal's skin. Yes, you are worthy,' Abel once more slowly and thoughtfully whispers.

'How did you do it,' Abel asks the Lord? 'How could you, a perfect God, kill an innocent animal in the place of my parents? They were the ones who sinned; they had been in the wrong. Yet, in spite of their rebellion against you, you sought them out and you chose to buy them back through the shedding of the blood of innocence. You are an amazing God' Abel tells the Lord. 'And I'm honored by your love and your grace.' With that, Abel bows down and worships his Maker and Lord; tears and blood flow down together.

It's within the book of beginnings, B'resheet (Genesis) chapter four, that we've encountered our above narrative and God's first lesson on choice. The word used here for God's choosing is *respect* and within this narrative we encounter two offerings. The first offering is brought by Cain. The second offering is brought by his brother Abel.

Genesis 4:3-5 speaks of how these offerings were viewed by the Lord. The Lord had *respect* for Abel's offering. But the Lord did not have respect for Cain's offering. Why? The Hebrew definition for respect in these verses means to gaze, inspect, consider, and to show compassion.

In other words, the Lord carefully considers or receives Abel's offering. The Lord, however, was not impressed with Cain's offering in the least. Lest we think this choice of the Lord is arbitrary, we encounter Genesis 4:7 in this narrative. In this verse the Lord tells Cain if he does what is right then he will be accepted. This verse speaks of the fact that all was not well with Cain and his offering. Why? What had Cain done wrong? Let me show you a vivid picture of what went wrong with Cain and his offering below. We need to understand that the attitude of the worshiper is extremely important.

Genesis 4:3-4 answer the "Why questions" for us in this narrative. We see in verse 4 that Abel brought the Lord the first or best of his flock. Cain, however, only brought the Lord some of his fruit and vegetables. The reason Cain's sacrifice was not accepted and Abel's was accepted is that Abel offered the first and best. What Cain offered was not first or best. Abel, by his actions shows that he holds the Lord's word in high regard. At this point, however, Cain is the opposite of his brother Abel.

In Cain's offering we see the reflection of the heart of one who sees no need for the blessing of God. This may also show us that Cain's offering came from a stingy heart. Within these few verses we encounter the Lord's first lesson on choice. Our first lesson instructs us in how we should obey. We have learned that obedience alone is not enough for acceptance from God. <u>Obedience must come from giving Him our first and best, and giving it from a heart of trust</u>. However, there's more to this narrative than we may realize.

Eve, upon the birth of her firstborn son, Cain, believed he was the one who would be the Seed – Chosen by God – to bruise the serpent's head. I refer back to God's pronouncement at the end of Genesis 3 concerning Adam, Eve and the Serpent. But what Eve desired was not to be, as we have seen within this narrative; God's choice was Abel. Both of these themes – <u>giving God the first and giving Him our heart</u> – are discussed in great detail within the pages of Scripture. We will also discover many times humanity's choice is not the same as God's choice.

2nd Choice

Enoch was not going to waste one more day, he told himself. 'Lord, I know that you walked in the Garden in Eden with Adam and Eve, talking with them as your friends. Will you walk with me?' Enoch asked. 'I want to know you myself. I'm not content to just hear about you from others.'

'What's that?' Enoch asked, amazed to hear someone speaking. After all, he had been walking alone with no one around. But there it was again; yes, it was an answer to his question, and the answer was coming from the Lord. 'Yes, I'll walk with you,' the voice replied. 'Just as you walk with me,' the Lord answered. With that short reply began Enoch's and the Lord's daily chats of discovery and friendship. There was nothing in his life that Enoch looked forward to more than his daily encounters with the Lord.

On one day's walk, the Lord explained every aspect of a killer whale, from their emotional makeup to their vast diet and everything in between. It was during one of these walks over their 300-year journey, as Enoch was speaking to the Lord, that he suddenly found himself in the Lord's presence and no longer walking on earth.

In Genesis 5, in four short verses, the Lord chooses Enoch over the rest of Seth's descendants. Verse 24 tells us the reason He makes this choice. Here, the Lord receives Enoch to Himself, because Enoch *walked* with God. This man walked with God for 300 years and because of this relationship, the Lord took him. Can you imagine Enoch's life? Enoch did what we hadn't seen done since the days of Eden – with Adam and Eve – he walked with his God. Enoch made the choice to engage the Lord in relationship day after day.

Our second lesson on choice shows us that God not only desires to have a relationship with His creation but His desire is to have a very personal and up close encounter with us. We see this in the narrative of Adam and Eve, where they walk with God in the cool of the garden. What is this walking and talking that the Lord, Adam, Eve and Enoch experience?

Walking with the Lord entails listening to, believing, trusting in and respecting God's word. The opposite end of this spectrum encompasses one who does not follow God or those who oppose God. Later in the Scriptures, walking with the Lord is called Walking in the Way, the Way of Righteousness and also Walking in the Light.

<u>Walking with the Lord</u> is another theme to wind its way like a cord through the Scriptures.

3rd Choice

Noah well remembered the day. He heard the Lord's voice after Japheth's birth, his third son. Long ago saddened and repulsed by his neighbor's lack of regard for anyone or anything, including even God himself, he had heard the Lord.

Here's how that day began. Noah, as usual, prayed to the Lord. Let's pick up the conversation as the Lord tells him, 'I'm grieved by humanity's continual and wanton sin. Noah, because of the world's sinful perversity, I've chosen you and your family to preserve My Name in the earth. I'm going to bring judgment on this entire evil generation. You must tell your family, friends and neighbors that judgment is coming and they must repent to be saved. As you speak about repentance, they must see the urgency and finality of your call. So, as you're speaking, you and your family must build an ark.'

As a result of this encounter with the Lord, Noah's carpentry skills would never be more sharpened than over the next 120 years. No, Noah didn't hear his neighbor say, 'Do you mind getting the ark out of my driveway, I have to get to work,' as Bill Cosby's *Noah* rendition goes. But he did have to endure reproach and unjust hatred. Noah, after all, tried desperately to get his generation to repent and turn back to God. For 120 years he talked with them, asking and pleading with them to reconsider their lives and beliefs. Even Noah's best boyhood friend, Jared, refused Noah's pleas.

The rain comes down in one torrent, and Noah is thankful God shut the ark's door. Even now, Noah's heart is filled with grief as he remembers the last time he pled with his friend Jared, asking and begging him to repent before it was too late. Noah remembered how Jared gradually changed over the years. When he was young, Jared wasn't too bad but he was definitely the only one who was always right, at least as far as he was concerned. Jared wouldn't even entertain the thought someone else's opinion or idea mattered. And as Jared grew older, his life grew progressively worse. In fact, on Noah's last visit, only days before the deluge began; Noah tried desperately to get him to understand the truth, but it was no use.

It had been such a depressing 120 years, not one of his friends or neighbors had listened to his pleas to repent, even as they saw Noah's huge ship continue to grow in size toward its completion. 'Jared,' Noah had pleaded, 'You must really listen to me this time! Repent and ask God to change you. Time is winding down, and the 120 years are about to end.' But Jared refused Noah's advice, 'Look, Noah,' he said, 'I'm better than most. Anyway, it was your God who made me how I am.' Even though Noah continued to plead with him, it was to no avail; he just couldn't get Jared to see God's goodness and graciousness, or the fact that he needed to repent before it was too late.

Within Genesis 6 we've encountered God's third choice. As we saw, the man of God's own choosing is Noah. This man stands in stark contrast to all the rest of earth's population. Why? The answer is simple; Noah found grace in the Lord's sight. Noah stood in stark contrast to the rest of humanity as their hearts were continually wicked. The word *grace* used here has the idea of a Superior, one like an Army Commander, bending down to show kindness or favor to one of lower rank, let's say a Private. However, this is not an arbitrary choice, as we see from verse 9.

We can see the Lord made this choice due to Noah's <u>walking in truthful integrity and righteousness</u>. Our third lesson on choice deals with two more important themes from the Scriptures – righteousness and truth.

4th Choice

Now picture our fourth encounter found in Genesis 9, as the narrative consists of Noah and his sons, Shem, Ham and Japheth. This narrative that comes on the heels of the Great Deluge shows us that, contrary to what we might think, sin and wickedness aren't destroyed even though Noah's wicked generation is completely wiped out. This should tell us something of the enormity and all-encompassing character of sin, or what some call the sinful inclination. We can see this more vividly in the Noah/ Ham/ Canaan narrative below.

With the deluge all but a forgotten memory, Noah and his family have started well to rebuild their lives and vocations. Noah, no longer a carpenter or sea captain, now takes care of a vineyard. In fact, after an abundant harvest of grapes, he has tasted a little too much of his final product. He sleeps off his drunkenness in his tent. The next morning, lying inside his goatskin tent, Noah awakes to the heaving of his stomach and the continual pounding of his head. 'So this is what it's like to have a hangover,' he thinks.

Thinking back to early morning, right before his wife left the tent, Noah barely remembers his first groggy awakening moment. Now Noah asks himself, 'Was there someone else here with me early this morning. Wait a minute,' he says, 'wasn't that Ham just leaving my tent?' With that, Noah passes back out in his stupor.

Noah's wife, having already viewed the carnage, had gone to get the person responsible for what happened to her husband Noah. The responsible one was her grandson, Canaan. While she is on her way, she runs smack dab into her son, Ham. She hurriedly escorts him back to his Dad's tent. 'Look at what your son Canaan has done to your father,' she tells Ham. As they both leave the tent Ham responds to her, 'I'll go and deal with my son.' An eerie cloud hangs over what occurred.

Walking a short way, Ham encounters his brothers Shem and Japheth and tells them their father Noah is lying naked in his tent after his encounter with Canaan. Upon hearing of this tragedy, Shem says to Japheth, 'Let's get a blanket and cover our father up.' While walking backwards these brothers, without even looking at their father, drop the blanket over their father's naked body.

Whatever happened in our above narrative, one thing is sure: it involved Noah's grandson, Canaan. A sexual sin appears to have been committed. Notice Canaan is named explicitly in Genesis 9:25-27 as the culprit. From the pages of Scripture, we know of one prevalent sexual sin within the region of Canaan many years later. This sin is primarily practiced in four towns.

Again, as we saw above, Shem and Japheth distinguish themselves from Ham by their righteous actions. Notice in Genesis 9:20-23 when Shem and Japheth come upon their father, they walk backwards to cover their father's nakedness without looking. Though implicit, our Why-answer of choice once again comes from the backdrop of the _righteous choice_ of the individual. Our fourth lesson on choice points to our ability to choose righteous action and its great importance to the Lord.

Have you noticed that all of these noble choices have been made or approved by the Lord himself, not by the human actors within these narratives? This is an important point we will get back to later.

Even with the deluge a distant memory, humanity still hasn't overcome their sinful inclinations, including the desire to worship other gods instead of the one true God. Shortly after the flood, most of humanity is worshipping multiple gods. It's within this idolatrous backdrop that the man Abram emerges. Even Abram's own father and family were idol worshippers.

5th Choice

Abram had long wondered and spent countless hours in thought concerning just exactly whom and what represented God. He found it hard to believe some stone-like substance, no matter how costly, could be deity. 'Besides,' he reasoned, 'No stone cares about me or my existence. How you can appease or please an inanimate object, no matter how beautiful? Only a Being Who is beyond humanity – one of tremendous power, intellect, and love can truly be God!' At least that's what Abram had grown to believe.

Abram told himself, 'These petty, insipid and contradictory gods of my family simply won't do!'

Shortly after making this decision, Abram had his first encounter with God who told him, 'Abram, you are right in your thinking. A god that humans make is really no god at all. These idols have no power, voice, intellect or love at all. They can do absolutely nothing for those who worship them. Abram, I'm calling you to take an adventure with me. This adventure will require you to leave your family, friends and country and to travel to a land I will tell you about during our journey.'

After Abram's father dies, he takes his nephew Lot, their combined families, servants and livestock, and begins his journey of discovery. Abram travels on, day after day, based solely on God's word. Even though his God-journey began quietly, it eventually made Abram "God's friend." He was a man of powerful faith which showed through his actions of trust.

Now we've come upon our fifth encounter and choice of God; this one brings us to the Father of the Hebrews, Abram in Genesis 12. The human actor, Abram, acts positively towards the Lord's direction as he responds obediently. Abram chose to obey the Lord and follow Him alone, contrary to the idolatrous culture and decisions of his father and ancestors. Like Abel's, Abram's obedience speaks volumes, as David's does later.

Once again the Why-question is answered implicitly, seen within Abram's actions of obedience based on his own choosing. Later in Genesis 18, we run face-first into the explicit reason behind the Lord's choice. This explicit reason, found in verse 19, says Abram will ensure that his family follows the Lord and His Ways. We graphically experience the truthfulness of this above statement later on in Genesis 22.

Our fifth lesson on choice again speaks of <u>individual choices of righteousness</u>, <u>relationship with God</u> and all of this comes from <u>within the truth of God being One</u>.

In Abram's faith-journey comes a son miraculously born to him and his wife, Sarah while they are 100 and 90 years old respectively. Their son, Isaac, would also learn what it is to walk with the Creator, the only God, his father's friend and constant companion. Is this really possible? Can a man and God walk, talk and love together? This was sure true of Isaac's dad and mom, and would prove true of him as well.

In Genesis 17 we encounter the Lord's sixth choice that is the man called Isaac. God chose this particular son of Abram over all the rest. His choice is the one promised to Abram when he is 99, Isaac, the yet-to-be-born son.

At this point, Abram is a 99 year old man, not a young lad by anyone's imagination. Our narrative in Genesis 17 takes place 13 years after Ishmael's birth to Abram and Hagar. Abram thoroughly enjoyed his role as Dad to Ishmael. Abram may not have spent every waking hour with Ishmael but, to friends and servants, it seemed like it. These two were inseparable. They took long trips together to see sights, slept under the stars, watched and experienced all the wild animals, and constantly talked together about everything, including the one who had finally blessed this man, Abram with a son.

No father was prouder or happier to be a Dad than Abram; he had waited so long to see this day. Being a Dad was one of life's greatest enjoyments. Listen in as we experience one of these father-and-son walk-and-talks for ourselves.

Abram had just told himself, 'Yes, there's not much better under the sun than being a Dad and enjoying your son.' 'Lord, I'm so thankful that you've blessed me with Ishmael,' Abram had told the Lord earlier that morning. That reminded Abram of something he wanted to talk to Ishmael about. 'Ishmael,' Abram said, 'Remember how we've talked about the Lord's promise to me and my descendants to bless all the peoples of the earth? Remember, that I left my families' country and their gods to follow the Lord, even when I wasn't sure where I was going? Let me tell you, Ishmael, those were not easy days. I was just beginning to learn the ways of the Lord and follow him as my God. All my relatives worshipped idols, and each had their own household image of their god.'

'Eventually, we ended up here in the land of Canaan, the land the Lord told me about before I left my family to follow him. The Lord promised me a son, and even though it took over ten years for you to be born, it was definitely worth the wait. You've been my pride and joy, Ishmael; now, with you here, my life has been revived. Ishmael, you are my promised heir and you will inherit all of my estate. Make sure to always walk with the Lord as I've shown you; there isn't anything that he doesn't see or know. Follow his ways and walk his path. When you do these things, he will always take care of you and provide for you and your family.' But Ishmael was not the son that the Lord had chosen. This is the backdrop of our sixth choice, the promised, only son, Isaac.

6th Choice

Isaac will always remember his father Abraham relating the above story to him when he was a young boy. Isaac knew his *chosenness* had nothing to do with his being better than Ishmael. He definitely wasn't the firstborn son and wasn't even his father, Abraham's first choice. But, God himself had chosen him to be the one descendant who would eventually bless every ethnicity in an amazing and miraculous way.

As Isaac began to walk up the mountain with his father, while carrying the wood on his shoulders, he thought about these things and what life's latest adventure would produce. He had been on many adventures with his dad, but none were like this. Abraham wasn't just quiet. It was like he was in another world altogether, being totally consumed by his thoughts. Isaac looked forward to this sacrifice; he knew how special God was to his dad and to him, even as a young man.

Well, now they were at the summit. Isaac wondered what type of sacrifice this would be and where the animal was to be sacrificed. 'Dad,' Isaac asked, 'Why don't we have an animal to sacrifice?' 'You will see,' Abraham said, 'God himself will provide the lamb,' his Dad told him. With that, Isaac was satisfied and yet wondered, even though he gave no resistance while his father bound and placed him on the altar he built. 'Just exactly what would this all mean?' he wondered.

Isaac was strangely calm. He knew this calm didn't originate inside him because, at this point, his father raised his knife and was about to slit his throat. At this exact moment, Isaac heard the angel of the Lord speak from heaven. He told Abraham not to kill his son because his obedience had proved Abraham's trust in the Lord.

The next thing Isaac remembers is his dad quickly cutting him loose, taking him off the altar and catching the ram that was caught by his horns. Isaac's life was spared that day but he always wondered exactly what type of sacrifice the Lord would provide at a later time on this same mountain. Would that sacrifice have the same miraculous aspects that his almost-sacrifice had? Isaac could only wonder.

The answer to the Why of this 6th choice is found in Genesis 22. In this narrative we see Isaac walking in complete submission to his father Abraham and to the Lord. Our sixth lesson on choice speaks of our _submission_ to the Lord's will, which also includes our submitting to the one He chooses. Submission to the Lord or lack thereof, is also a continual theme throughout the Scriptures.

7th Choice

Rebekah, Isaac's wife and Jacob's mother, hadn't been able to conceive a child. At least, she hadn't conceived until Isaac pled with the Lord for his wife and asked that he allow her to conceive. And what a conception it was! She didn't conceive just one child; she produced two twin sons. This pregnancy was one that Rebekah would never forget. Her heaving abdomen didn't rise and fall due to morning sickness, though morning sickness would have been welcomed over the rolling, falling and pitching of her stomach.

As if this pregnancy was peculiar enough, when these two boys were born their wrestling matches didn't end. Esau, born first, was birthed with his brother's hand clamped firmly around his ankle. Jacob had tried unsuccessfully to jerk his hairy brother back inside the womb so Jacob could be the firstborn. But alas, it wasn't to be. He finished second. It was history's first photo-finish but the photo proved he was still second.

Although Jacob may not have been Charles Atlas, he wasn't about to be outdone by his powerful brother. He would bide his time and spring the trap when his brother least expected it. 'The right of firstborn, along with the blessing would be his,' he thought, 'even if it killed him.'

Jacob, along with his mother, concocted a plan to wrest the blessing away from Esau. And this happened after Jacob had earlier wrested the birthright away from his famished brother. Rebekah prepared a goat and then attached the hair of the animal to Jacob's arms. Wow! How extremely hairy Esau must have been! Anyway, this mother-son ruse worked. Isaac blessed Jacob with the firstborn blessing.

But all this deceitfulness came at an extremely high price. Esau was so mad when he found out Jacob deceived him twice. He would have squished Jacob like a bug if he'd been given a chance.

As a result, Rebekah got Isaac to hurriedly send their son Jacob off to her brother Laban's place, far away from the current pressure-cooker-of-a-family. Now, Jacob would run head-on into his Uncle. Laban, one so much like himself, was the conniver of connivers. Jacob almost met his match!

Poor Jacob, so unprepared for this bold-faced lie, woke up to discover he'd been duped, no less than by his own father-in-law. The woman, more beautiful than any other on the face of the whole earth, the one whom he would've willingly died for, hadn't become his wife after all. Nope! Jacob woke up to find he was still very much in his nightmare because the smiling face of his wife was the non-stunning Leah, not the gorgeous Rachel. But this was only the beginning of his torture. His father-in-law would go on to cheat him at least ten more times. Finally, even God had enough but He would teach him too!

The Lord told Jacob to gather up his family, servants and flocks, and go back home. Jacob, however, would encounter another wrestling match. This one would permanently cost him his health. He would fall so hard on the mat that afterwards, Jacob always walked with a limp – a sign of submission.

As Jacob is on his way home, he sends one servant off to find his brother Esau and tell him that his brother Jacob is returning home with his wives, children and livestock. Already intrepid at having to send his brother news of his coming arrival, what Jacob is about to hear will send shivers up his spine and make him wish he never harmed his brother Esau in any way. Jacob's servant arrives, and arriving with him is terrible news. This servant tells Jacob his brother Esau is on his way to meet him and is bringing 400 of his men with him.

Jacob knows his neck, and all his family's necks, is in the proverbial noose. When he hastily left home, it was to save his own hide. His brother Esau swore he would remove Jacob's head from his shoulders. Jacob knew Esau meant exactly what he had said back then. He was panicked at the thought of his brother's intent. 'Oh Lord,' Jacob cried out, 'Esau is coming to wipe me and my family out, and I have no means to stop him from his desire.' But once more, instead of relying on the Lord and his promise, Jacob has at least one trick left up his sleeve.

Jacob puts his plan into play. Jacob divided his family into two groups. He placed his beloved Rachel and Joseph at the very end of the parade, hoping beyond hope that they will somehow escape Esau's wrath and vengeance. After helping his family cross the Jabbok, he goes back across and prepares to face the night alone, in fear and dread. But aloneness won't be the companion of this man on this evening. His night will be an encounter of another kind, one that will forever alter this man's life, perspective and worship.

A wrestling match is about to ensue. But this match will be nothing like any Jacob ever participated in. You see, this one includes an angel, even though he is called a "man" in the text. No matter how hard Jacob works and no matter what hold he uses, his grip is never enough to hold, let alone pin this man. Be that as it may, Jacob will not give up or surrender. He says, *'I'll never quit, not until you bless me.'* And that's exactly what Jacob receives – the best eternal blessing of his life!

The angel of the Lord asks Jacob a very simple question, *"What is your name?"** This question requires only an honest reply. Yet this question is loaded as well. This is nothing you may be thinking. Remember, the last time this man was asked his name was by his father Isaac, and Jacob lied. Remember also, a name in those days represented the person's character. With his father, Jacob not only denies his name but reputation and character – his character of deceit and lying.* I heard this analogy many years ago from a speaker named Ravi Zacharias

Here Jacob responds truthfully by saying, in essence; 'Okay, you got me; I'm a conniving, lying person – one always grabbing someone else's heel.' Upon this answer of truth, the angel gives Abraham's grandson a new name and a new character. Now, this man will be known as a prince; he will forever have a new perspective as we will later find out during our narrative with Joseph's sons.

Our seventh encounter of the Lord's choosing comes in Genesis 25. Above, we've seen that he chooses one of Isaac's twin boys, Jacob, over the other twin Esau. Once again the Lord's choice is made before the child is born. His choice deals with two distinct communities of people. Eventually these two groups are called people of Edom and people of Israel. The Lord again chooses the younger over the older to accomplish His will.

The Why-answer to this choice is found in Genesis 32 when Jacob's name is changed by the Lord to Israel. When we first encounter Jacob in our narrative, at first blush, Jacob is anything but righteous. But within the narrative of Genesis 32, Jacob is noticeably changed – indeed **he becomes Israel!** This change alters his approach to God and life, as we see below.

At this point, it's important to understand that a person's name in Scripture is equated to their character. Jacob was always a conniving, deceiving person but when he encounters the angel of the Lord, his character of deception is changed, proved by his change of name. Till now, Jacob's life was one of personal strife and intrigue in a battle to rise above and overcome. Now, the Lord Himself will overcome Jacob's enemies. Our seventh lesson on choice teaches the importance of God's *choosing* and our choice of Him. Choosing the Lord is another theme throughout the Scriptures, just as Joshua told the Israelites of his day and time, 'Choose today to follow the Lord.'

8th Choice

Joseph, what a man! This is one person whom the Scriptures themselves do not portray as having sinned. I'm certainly not saying Joseph was a perfect man; he was not! But this was certainly one righteous man! This man's life was one of trial, not ease and pleasure – and he shows himself righteous.

The Lord showed this man, even as a boy, what he would endure in life – a man who reveals dreams. But this dreamer, as his brothers called him, experienced a nightmare for over a decade in Egypt, while terribly missing the father who loved him dearly.

But the Lord was not about to let this young Hebrew man continue in his daily nightmare, even as the kings' dungeon so quickly approached. Joseph was purchased by an Egyptian, Potiphar, with a wife who only had eyes for her husband's slave – this handsome Hebrew whom she desired. Joseph refused to sin against his self, his master, and his Lord. He knew the agony one sexual episode would bring. No, Joseph would not give in to such things! But his righteous refusal would cost him dearly.

Potiphar was an extremely jealous husband, and rightly so, since his wife had wandering eyes. After being charged, though innocent, Joseph was thrown into the king's dungeon. Even here, the Lord's hand was upon him. Joseph was placed in charge of the prisoners. As a result of correctly interpreting two of Pharaoh's servants' dreams, two years later he was freed and brought into Pharaoh's presence for a hasty meeting.

This meeting came after back-to-back dreams Pharaoh had that no one could interpret. Joseph, the Hebrew man sold by his brothers and left to rot in the dungeon by accusations of a jealous husband was seemingly in a helpless and hopeless predicament by humanities' standards. But he was rescued by his Lord and God. When Pharaoh told Joseph he heard that he interpreted dreams, he responded by saying, '*No, I cannot interpret your dreams, but my God can, and will give me the interpretation of your dreams.*'

Joseph proceeds to tell this king of Egypt what his dreams meant and give advice as to what plan he needs to implement to keep his people fed. Seeing Joseph's wisdom and knowledge, this Pharaoh placed him in charge of gathering, keeping and distributing all of Egypt's food. Joseph, the Hebrew who was once rotting in Pharaoh's dungeon, eventually became the one to save the people of Egypt, as well as his own family from starvation and extinction. It was this man's righteous determination and trust in God that produced the amazing life that we read about in the Scriptural narrative.

In our ninth encounter, the Lord chooses one of Israel's younger sons, Joseph, for a special purpose. In Genesis 37, He sends Joseph as a slave into Egypt to save the entire family of Israel. In the process, he also saves the known world.

Our answer to the Why of this choice is found in Genesis 39. Here we see this handsome young man rejecting the advances of his owner's wife in order to follow the Lord's commands. Once again, we encounter someone with _righteous integrity_ towards God and his fellow man. This life of Joseph, in our eighth lesson on choice, speaks of the importance of being righteous and living with integrity. These two subjects are also very important themes found within the fabric of the Scriptures.

9th Choice

What a life Judah had! This man lived to see two sons die, his daughter-in-law act as a prostitute, and his father weep inconsolably over the apparent loss of his greatly loved son, Joseph. This son, Joseph, was the very brother Judah hated, the one who was given a one-way ticket to the outback. Not the outback of Australia but the outback of Egypt. Jacob and his brothers sell their own flesh-and-blood as a slave, below the slave price! At least, this was far better than their initial plan to kill him. Judah's life was one of sheep and sleepless nights. But some sleepless nights were brought on by his choices, hatred, and selfishness. And this is the man God chooses, you ask? Yes, this is the man, but Judah's change is in the wind.

Judah, this great-grandson of Abraham, had a heart that was a million miles away from his grandfather's heart. After distressing news arrived, he planned to have his daughter-in-law, Tamar, burned alive. This is quite an inauspicious way to start a life of righteousness! When Tamar showed her about- to-be-killers Judah's property that he had earlier given to her in pledge; Judah announced his guilt and sin. He went as far as to admit Tamar's righteousness compared to his unrighteousness as he lied to her, committed immorality with her, and, to top it off, wanted to have her killed. Confession begins the changes in Judah's life. This is his first step on the "Way of righteousness."

With the rest of his brothers except for the youngest, Benjamin, Judah went to get food in Egypt during a terrible famine in Canaan and the known world. Upon their arrival, they encounter a man they all knew well but didn't recognize – their younger brother Joseph, now Egypt's second in command. And Joseph is the man in charge of food distribution.

After telling this Egyptian they have a younger brother and their father is still alive, they receive the grain they desire. However, there was a problem. The brothers were all accused of being spies and told their truthfulness would only be proved by bringing their younger brother back when they return for food. Joseph knew they would have no choice but to return. This was only the beginning of the famine and its length would be seven long years, so they would return! The Egyptian ruler kept one brother captive until they returned with Benjamin.

Judah and his brother's – minus Simeon – returned home. Once they arrived, they told their Dad everything that happened in Egypt. They told how their brother Simeon had been taken, bound and placed in prison, and they were told not to return unless their youngest brother Benjamin was in tow. Since Jacob had already lost his highly treasured son, Joseph, he was not about to let Joseph's brother Benjamin go to Egypt and possibly lose him too. But the famine drags on, and departure was in the wind. After all, everyone needed food.

Eventually, with a dwindling food supply, they must think about returning to Egypt. Knowing their dire situation, Judah goes to his father and asks him to allow him to take Benjamin with him to

Egypt, so they could get more food. He said he himself would guarantee Benjamin's safety. Finally, Judah convinced his father, so the sons gather what they need for the trip and quickly leave, with their father's blessing.

Once again these brothers arrive in Egypt. They are led into the presence of this mean, gruff, Egyptian. Joseph asks his brothers, "Is your father still alive, and is this your brother you told me about?" "Yes," they reply, "our father is still alive and well, and this is our youngest brother whom our father loves." These brothers get to dine on Egypt's choicest food. Amazingly all the brothers are placed at their table in their birth order. But this trip isn't going any better than the initial trip, as we will see.

Through Joseph's intervention, his servant placed his special cup in Benjamin's sack. Because his cup is missing, all brothers are commanded to return, just after they began their long trip home. Joseph accuses Benjamin, his own brother, of stealing his magic divination-cup. Benjamin's goose is cooked. There's no way out for him; after all, the cup is in his sack. One changed brother is about to save the day, as we see below.

Right now, in the middle of what seems to be another catastrophe for these brothers is where the change in Judah is readily seen, heard and felt. There will be no ignoring their younger brother's plight this time! They are not about to let another brother disappear, at least not on Judah's watch. With his heart in his throat, Judah steps forward.

Judah carefully approaches this ruler of Egypt and asks for permission to plead for mercy on his brother's behalf. Judah explains that if they return to Canaan without Benjamin, this will kill their father. He pleads with Joseph and tells him that he, Judah, assured his father of Benjamin's safety. He could not bear to again see grief on his father's face, nor bear to watch his dad live life in the knowledge of another son's demise. He begs Joseph for mercy with every ounce of his being. Even Joseph is moved by his brother's display of change and true love for his brother, Benjamin, and father Jacob. Judah definitely had a major change towards righteousness, seen by substitutionary actions towards his brother and loving respect for his father.

Jacob has 12 sons; and the Lord chooses again. Our eighth encounter with the Lord's choices once again has Him selecting a younger son over the oldest son. Judah is chosen instead of Ruben. Just as above, again it appears that maybe the Lord made the wrong choice. But similar to Jacob, Judah makes a noticeable change in his life toward the Lord, his father, and two specific brothers, Joseph and Benjamin.

As a result, the Why-answers are found in Genesis 43 and 44. A transformation has taken place in Judah's life as he takes sole responsibility for Benjamin in two references above. This is something he didn't do with his younger brother Joseph, earlier in his life. Our ninth lesson on choice speaks of the importance of *taking responsibility* for ones' actions. Taking responsibility for ones' actions or choices is also a theme found within the Scriptural framework.

10th Choice

Moses is a man of contrasts; he was never supposed to see his second birthday, let alone become a prince of Egypt. A papyrus boat is his cradle as an infant, but royalty and all its pleasures are his norm for the next 40 years. Yet again his life turns and now he's a shepherd until he's 80, on the backside of the desert, no less. Finally, he becomes the under-shepherd of the Hebrews for his final 40 years. This man goes from a slave to a prince to a nomad to a god in a showdown with Pharaoh, and finally to a prophet, priest and shepherd to the people of Israel. His final years especially foreshadow Messiah's life and ministry.

Scripture doesn't tell us how he knew his nationality, let alone how he knew God hand-picked him to lead his people out of their Egyptian bondage, but somehow he knew. Do you think his mother being his nanny explains how he knew? Moses was not a person to sit by and wait for something to happen. Moses was a shaker and mover, unfortunately for him, his moving and shaking was a bit premature for the Lord's mission.

Moses knows his rescue as an infant among the Nile reeds was for a purpose. God made him with a destiny and he can't shake the feeling he must do something to show the people of Israel he is their rescuer. He won't wait for the perfect time; too much time has already passed. Too many Hebrew lives were already cut short. God promised to deliver his people and return them to the land of promise, Canaan. 'I've had enough of my privileged existence and I'm tired of watching my people fall down under their weight of bondage. The time for me to spring into action is at hand,' he told himself.

As Moses was speaking to himself, he saw an Egyptian beat one of his fellow Hebrews. Quickly looking around to make sure no one saw, he overpowered the Egyptian and broke his neck in one move. Immediately he buried the man in the sand. 'Now,' Moses told himself, 'my people will finally see that the time of their release from slavery has come. I will be able to lead them out of this land and back into the land of Canaan.'

But no such understanding of deliverance came upon the people of Israel; however, a different understanding quickly took place. Pharaoh found out about what Moses had done. Now Moses had to quickly "get out of Dodge." And with his exit, all hope of delivering his people came crashing down.

Moses may have "jumped the gun" but he tried to do the right thing. He wanted to obey God and fulfill the purpose and destiny to which he had been born. He wanted to deliver his people from Egyptian oppression and bondage; more than many, he was willing to "step to the plate." Moses did nothing in a grandiose way. He did not dare broadcast his killing of an Egyptian while rescuing a Hebrew from death. It was important that he be obedient to his God and his God-ordained purpose.

Forty years later, while Moses tends his father-in-law's sheep, he encounters the Lord through a strange sight. A bush is totally engulfed in flame yet doesn't burn out, so Moses goes to check it out. When Moses gets to the bush, the Lord speaks to him from within the bush. He wants Moses to perform an assignment, something like he tried to do 40 years ago while he was living in Egypt. The Lord wants Moses to go and bring his people Israel out of Egypt. After a very lengthy dialogue, Moses finally agrees to God's plan and travels on his way to Egypt.

Moses and Aaron finally meet up, just as the Lord had said while Moses makes the last trek of his journey back into the land of Egypt. What a reunion it is! Moses shares with his brother Aaron all his experiences he had with the bush that just wouldn't burn up. He shows his brother the signs that the Lord has given him; then they continue on toward Egypt.

When Moses and Aaron get to Egypt, they show the Lord's signs to the elders of Israel and Pharaoh. Eventually, through ten plagues, Pharaoh lets the people of Israel leave. They then begin their journey back to the Land of Promise.

Not long after The Exodus, and right after they tell God they will obey everything he told them, they decide to abort their trek towards The Promised Land and travel back to The Land of Bondage, with their new golden god in tow. All of this transpires while Moses is on the mountain receiving The Ten Words from the Lord. The Lord tells Moses, 'Go back down to the people; they've made idols to worship.' '*I know these rebellious, stiff necked people,*' the Lord tells Moses, '*now let me wipe them off of the face of the earth. Then I'll make you into a great nation, Moses.*'

'*No Lord,*' Moses replies, '*Remember these are your people. Don't destroy them; please don't let the Egyptians say the Lord only brought the people of Israel out of Egypt in order to destroy them. Turn away from your anger. Remember the covenant you made with Abraham, Isaac and Jacob. Remember you promised them, on a strict oath, that you would give their descendants the Land of Canaan.*' At this, the Lord relented.

'Joshua,' Moses says, 'let's hurry and go down; we have a problem back in the camp.' Hurriedly, they make their way down the mountain as Moses tightly grasps The Tablets. When Joshua hears the noise of the camp, he tells Moses, 'The camp is making the sound of war.' Moses said, 'No, what I hear is singing.' As they approach the camp and Moses sees the Gold Calf, he throws down the Tablets in anger. Because of the people's sin, 3,000 of them die.

The following day Moses goes back up to the Lord but, before he leaves, he tells the people, '*All of you have done something horrendous by making and worshipping the Gold Calf. Now, I'm going back up to face the Lord and see if I can make intercession for your sin, so that he will forgive you.*' When Moses arrives before the Lord, he says, '*Lord, your people have committed a horrendous sin. Now please forgive their sin or blot my name out of your book.*'

Afterwards the Lord tells Moses, '*Take this people and go to the land I promised to Abraham. But I'm not going with you. You are all stiff necked. If I were to go with you, I'd end up destroying you in the process. Well, if your Presence doesn't go with us, we won't go,*' Moses responds, '*since no other nation will know any difference between us without your presence.*' '*Okay,*' the Lord finally says, '*My Presence will go with you.*'

When Moses' days on earth are finished, the book of Deuteronomy tells us something very important. We learn the chief difference between Moses and later prophets is that the Lord spoke with and to later prophets in dreams and visions whereas with Moses He spoke face to face.

As we moved through Genesis, we discovered our tenth encounter. In these chapters, the Lord chooses a man named Moses, the one who will deliver Israel from Egypt. This is a man most would not choose, seeing he had already been rejected by his people while still living in Egypt. In fact, Moses goes so far as to kill an Egyptian in order to spare an Israelite. Despite these facts, the Lord chose him to lead and teach his people.

The Why-answer concerning the Lord's choice of Moses is found in the pages of the Moses-narrative. Two words best summarize Moses' life-response to the Lord – *Obedience* and *Humility* – in answer to our Why-question. The Lord even calls Moses his servant. Later the Scriptures tell us this man was the most humble of all people in his generation. Choice-lesson #10 shows us the great importance of obedience and humility as two major themes within the Scriptures.

11th Choice

Aaron is our 11th choice by the Lord. In this narrative, Korah and 250 other Levite leaders of Israel have had enough. They've decided among themselves they will no longer follow Moses' and Aaron's leadership. In fact, they tell Aaron and Moses face-to-face that they're tired of following them. They say, 'Look, we're all holy, not just you two. You guys think way too highly of yourselves. From now on we're going to lead.'

Moses tells them, *'Wait until the morning and the Lord Himself will show all of Israel who he has appointed as His High Priest'* – the position Aaron currently holds. He continues and says, *'Isn't it enough that the Lord chose you through Levi to serve Him in the tabernacle and before the congregation? Do you now demand the priesthood for yourselves as well?'*

Morning dawns and the fireworks are about to begin. Aaron, Korah, Dathan, Abiram and the 250 men allied with them all come out of their tents with incense in their censers. The Lord says to Moses, *'Get all of the people away from Korah, Dathan, Abiram and the other 250 men, and don't touch anything that belongs to these evil men.'* The Lord speaks through Moses to say, *'If the ground opens up and swallows these men alive, then you will know that it is the Lord who has chosen Aaron.'* With that short speech, the ground opens up to swallow Korah, Dathan and Abiram, and the Lord sends fire to kill the 250 men who conspired against Moses and Aaron.

One might think that what just transpired would be enough to show the truth of God's choice of Aaron, but it wasn't. The next day the congregation accused Moses and Aaron of killing all of the men. They did not understand or see that it was the Lord who performed this miraculous feat, and not Moses or Aaron. So, God provided another sign to prove to the people that He had chosen Moses and Aaron.

Because of this misunderstanding, each tribe of Israel was required to bring a rod with their tribal name on it. Aaron also brought a rod with the name Levi on his rod. All these rods were then placed in the tent of meeting where the Lord's choice appears. *'The man I choose as my priest will be shown by the next morning,'* the Lord says. *'When these rods are inspected in the morning you will know the man of my choosing.'* Sure enough, when Moses goes into the tent of meeting the next day, Aaron's rod had budded and blossomed to produce ripe almonds. The Lord unmistakably confirmed His choice of Aaron.

In Numbers 16, the Lord proves his choice of Aaron over Korah. This is our eleventh encounter of the Lord choosing. Like Moses above, our answer to the Why of choice has to do with Aaron's <u>obedience to the Lord's commands</u>, but there's more to it.

The Lord proves his choice of Aaron as High Priest over Korah and 250 other Israelites with a miraculous sign. Korah and the rest of the men, in rebellion against Moses and Aaron, held censers filled with incense. Aaron also held a censer with incense. As these men gather around, the ground opens up and they all fall into the pit, except for Aaron. As a result of this sign, only Aaron is left standing, proving he and his family alone are chosen as God's High Priests.

The beginning of the Why of the Lord's choice is found in Exodus 4. Here, we see Aaron go into the desert to find his brother Moses. This may seem insignificant in our day, but it was a tremendous act of faith in Aaron's day. Aaron proves his obedience to the Lord and his calling. Many times throughout the Torah, Aaron was the one who brought Moses to see the elders of Israel and spoke to Pharaoh as Moses' prophet.

Again, in lesson-choice #11, we encounter the extreme importance of obedience and having proper humility towards the

Lord's anointed. _Obedience_ and having _humility_ toward the Lord's anointed are themes within the framework of Scripture. Later, King David is seen as our prototypical example of humility towards the Lord's anointed.

12th Choice

Moses numbers the firstborn sons of Israel as the Lord told him, all 22,000. In lieu of these firstborn sons, the Lord tells Moses to substitute the Levites. As a result of this substitution, the Levites are now the Lord's, in place of Israel's firstborn sons.

This choice is found in Numbers 3. The term for this choice is _taken_, which can mean to buy or purchase. We also see here another example of _substitution_. The Why of this choice is found in Numbers 3:12-13. In essence the Lord says He purchased the firstborn sons of Israel when he killed all the firstborn sons of Egypt. These firstborn owe their existence to the Lord Himself! He alone bought and paid for them. We now see the importance of Substitution, another integral theme.

13th Choice

David is another amazing Israelite with an amazing life; it definitely was not dull. Early on, as a very young man, David shows his heart for God, God's Word, and Israel. While the Philistines and Israel go through their yearly battle, Jesse, David's father, sends him to see how the battle is going, and how his brothers are doing. Once he has done this, he is to bring his report back to Jesse. The Lord, however, had David at the battlefront for an entirely different reason.

Right after David arrives, the troops assemble for battle; however, no battle is imminent. The reason for this is that the Philistines have a warrior giant who dwarfs every Israelite soldier, even King Saul. Goliath, the Philistine champion steps forward to "throw down the gauntlet." He's been throwing down this same gauntlet for the past 40 days, both day and night, but there were no takers on Israel's side.

'Come on, you punks,' Goliath shouts from his side of the line, 'Pick your best warrior and let's get it on,' he rants. As soon as Goliath's taunts begin, the entire Israelite army begins to shake in their boots, along with King Saul. You see, Goliath has been a champion warrior since his youth. Not a single man from Israel is willing to take him on in combat. But David chomps at the bit; he can't believe there's a man on earth who has the audacity to demean Israel and their God.

Suddenly a report reaches the men. King Saul agrees to give his oldest daughter to marry the man who fights and kills Goliath. But that's not all, that man and his family will no longer owe any taxes. Again, David can't believe what he heard! He quickly runs up to a group of soldiers to ask them if what he just heard is true. They assure him it is; 'the one who kills Goliath will become the Kings' son-in-law and his family will no longer owe taxes,' they tell him. That's all David needs to hear! He's all in! The battle for God and Israel's honor is about to begin, and David is chomping at the bit to silence this loud mouth.

After dressing in and testing Saul's armor, David realizes he cannot fight with this armor. So, he tells King Saul, 'I'm sorry I can't use your armor but I'm still going to wipe Goliath off the face of the earth. You know, King, any man who blasphemes the God of Israel doesn't deserve to live, much less this loud-mouthed Philistine! I will stand up for God's honor!'

David quickly scoops up 5 smooth stones from a brook as he charges off to kill Goliath. When Goliath sees David coming and realizes he's only a young, inexperienced man, he curses David. 'Come on over here kid and let me show you how to fight. I'll throw your innards to the birds.' His words don't scare or deter David. He yells back while continuing to run forward, placing one stone in his sling, *'I'm going to kill you in the name of the Lord, the same name you've defied. In just a few minutes your head will be food for the birds and the army of the Philistines will know that the God of Israel is Almighty.'*

With that, David lets loose with his sling. The stone hits the bull's eye – Goliath's forehead between his eyes. With a loud grunt, Goliath falls to the ground. David, wasting no time, quickly runs over, removes Goliath's sword and cuts off the giants' head. That day, through David, the Lord brought relief for Israel and triumph over their enemies, and the people of Israel knew their God was alive and strong.

As we move ahead in the Scriptures, we encounter our Lord's 13th choice. During the monarchial period, the Lord makes another choice. Against the people's choice, He rejects King Saul and chooses the shepherd boy, David, as king over Israel. Saul, the people's choice, was not the Lord's choice.

We learn the Why of this choice in I Samuel 13. Here Samuel tells Saul the Lord has rejected him as king in favor of a man after His own heart. Remember, David is the one God called, *"The man after God's heart"* in the Scriptures. Is there anything else that needs to be said concerning the Lord's choice of this shepherd? Now our lesson-choice #13 shows us the great importance, once again, of having a *heart* after the Lord.

14th Choice

Solomon, certainly not one of David's oldest sons, is now the king of Israel. When the Lord appears to him to give him a choice, he asks for wisdom to rule the people of Israel. The Lord gives Solomon exactly what he asks for but far beyond his expectations. His reign is one of peace and prosperity, and he becomes the wisest and richest man alive.

One early ruling has to do with a case between two mothers and their children. One baby is dead and both women claim the living son as their own. Both women present their case to Solomon – an unsolvable one in those days. How can one know for certain the mother of the living child? Finally, Solomon has the answer, "Bring me a sword."

After a sword is brought, he says, '*Cut the baby in two and give each mother a half.*' The mother of the dead son heartily agrees. But the mom of the living son wants her boy to live. So, she says, '*Give the other woman the son, but please, let him live.*' With that, Solomon gives his verdict; '*The living boy belongs to the true mother, the compassionate woman. Give the son to her.*'

Solomon, one of King David's younger sons is our 14th encounter with the Lord's choosing. He is chosen by the Lord to be the next ruler. One Why for this choice is found in I Kings 3. We find Solomon loving the Lord and also having an encounter with the Lord. In his encounter, he asks the Lord for wisdom to lead the people of Israel. This narrative, which is lesson-choice #14, shows us that love for the Lord and wisdom are desired by the Lord. *Love for the Lord* and *wisdom* are two more critical themes within the pages of Scripture.

We could continue to discover the Lord's choosing throughout the Tanakh. This is enough for now but we will continue later. Let me say three more things here before going back to father Abraham. In these Scriptural characters we've encountered, something unfolds that is of utmost importance throughout the Scriptures. This unfolding has to do with the chosen person's love for God. God does not choose human robots to blindly follow every command he gives. The men and women of Scripture are genuine people who make mistakes, even as they can commit grave sins. Yet, despite all these things, what matters most to the Lord is the individual's obedience to him, coming from their heart.

Deuteronomy 7:6 probably typifies **The Chosen People** expression the best. This verse tells us the people of Israel are a holy people to the Lord. It also says Israel was chosen out of all peoples of the world and chosen uniquely for the Lord and by the Lord Himself. Another part of Israel being **The Chosen People** has to do with their influence on the nations or goyim. One place where we see this is in Deuteronomy 4:6-9[5-8]. Here, Moses, in verse 6[5] tells the people of Israel that he has taught them Torah. Now listen to the next three verses below:

Observe them carefully, for this will show your wisdom and understanding to the nations, who will hear about all these decrees and say, "Surely this great nation is a wise and understanding people. What other nation is so great as to have their gods near them the way the LORD our God is near us whenever we pray to him? And what other nation is so great as to have such righteous decrees and laws as this body of laws I am setting before you today?" Only be careful, and watch yourselves closely so that you do not forget the things your eyes have seen or let them slip from your heart as long as you live. Teach them to your children and to their children after them.

Did you notice that it's the nations who take notice of both the people of Israel and their God? This is something I'll also touch on below. You can see this very thing portrayed in the lives of Joseph, King David, Daniel and the Gentile king of Babylon, Nebuchadnezzar.

Let me ask you the following question before continuing our journey: "How many times, when discussing a topic or asking a question, have you heard the following response that says something to the effect of, 'Well, we have to go back to the beginning to properly discuss that?'" Well, that's exactly my point when dealing with the above topic of **The Chosen People**.

Some aspects of this term are overemphasized, others are deemphasized, and others are almost totally ignored. It is because of these very issues that I want to reexamine the topic and issues included in being **The Chosen People** when taken from the perspective of the Hebrew Scriptures.

I want us to see, when we look through the lens of the Hebrew Scriptures as if they are genuine and reliable historical manuscripts, if we can glean anything when we look back at what has unfolded since the first century CE. Do events that happened in the 20th Century and events that unfold in the 21st Century have anything to say concerning the reliability of the Tanakh, including some prophecies that are not yet fulfilled or were seemingly not completely fulfilled in history past? Can we hold judgment until we look at these same Scriptures in light of past, present and what may be future events?

As we look at both of the above issues of **The Chosen People** and **The Historical Pointing of the Hebrew Scriptures** through the lenses of our current historical knowledge, let's see if we can see these two references of the Hebrew Scriptures in a new and different light.

Back to B'resheet

Okay, let's go to Genesis 12 where the LORD calls Abram and tells him to leave his family and ancestral home to begin a trek to a land the LORD will reveal to him. I want us to focus on verses 2 and 3. Look at what the Lord tells this man in verse 2, "*I will make you into a great nation.*"

We all know Abraham produced more than one nation of people; his sons produced many nations of peoples. Yet the LORD says "I will make you *a great nation.*" How do we reconcile this statement? Maybe we should ask at this point, "Exactly how does the Lord of the Tanakh make his choice of destiny?"

Is the LORD really a loving father as the Scriptures claim or does he arbitrarily choose one son over another and delight in that son and family exclusively as he gives no thought toward the other son or family? Well, if I answered that question in its entirety we would get ahead of ourselves and we would skip important parts of our discovery-journey with many important puzzle pieces needed to put our picture into focus.

We can definitely see this much from the Lord's statement: one nation that Abraham produces will be special and specially used. But as we continue to read the rest of this verse, we discover that doesn't mean the Lord will reject Abraham's other sons, throwing them away as rubbish on the ground. Rather, the LORD has a special purpose for an unnamed son, Isaac. In this chapter the Lord tells Abram that this son, Isaac, '*Will be a blessing.*' God's choices bring a double-edged blessing or curse, depending on what we do in response.

Genesis 12:3 brings us to another choice of the LORD where he makes another distinction. He says '*I will bless those nations who bless Abram and curse those nations who curse Abram.*' Blessings are allowable in today's politically correct day but cursing is another thing entirely. The last part of this verse, however, puts everything in a very different perspective. It says these very important and crucial words, *"And all peoples on earth will be blessed through you"* – specifically Isaac!

So these words demonstrate the Lord has not arbitrarily chosen one son or nation over another as a bad unloving father. Instead he has a good and special reason for his decisions of choice and choosing. The LORD has a plan in mind and his plan includes every people group on the planet. His plan is one of blessing for all humanity rather than one of cursing even though the choice is left up to each specific nation and people.

As our subject of *Choice* is considered against the illuminating lighting of Scripture, we are provided with a whole different perspective than we previously pictured. The LORD did not choose to do wrong to people who are not a part of Israel. Nor does he reject people because they're inferior to his "superior" Israelites. No, his purpose in choosing one group, the nation of Israel, is so that the rest of humanity can also experience a blessing.

This blessing is one the nation of Israel experiences first. This is good news, even by today's standards. It means Gentiles are not delegated to the status of second class citizens by the LORD. It also means the nation of Israel is not a chosen people in exclusion to the rest of the world. Rather, they are chosen in an inclusive sense and purpose. Put another way we could say the LORD excluded the rest, the Gentiles, in his choice of one, Israel, to offer the gift of inclusion to the rest of humanity, even as this is brought about through Israel itself.

I think one of the best stories in the Hebrew Scriptures to make my point is the story of Joseph. This inclusive sense and purpose is seen within the Joseph-narrative. Joseph's life takes place mostly in the land of Egypt but inclusively includes his brothers and family who live in the land of Canaan.

From our limited human perspective, we think that as Joseph is sold as a slave and removed from his family and the father he loved, that this is a bad and irreconcilable event. How could the loving Father of the Hebrew Scriptures allow such evil to happen to an innocent boy? Does He have no regard for this son, his plans and future? Quite the contrary, the LORD not only has this boy's best interest at heart, but also those of his jealous brothers who sold him as a slave. This beautiful story helps us look to a higher vision as we consider difficult details of life.

But we don't see all these good things; instead, as we turn around the only sight we see are the backs of the camels as this camel train departs, walks off into the distance, and carries away this captive Hebrew. This horrific journey will eventually plunge this boy into captivity within the land of Egypt but bring him great suffering, beginning with what we see next.

One may ask, exactly what is this innocent boy's crime? He was sold by his brothers, an act that seems to be overlooked by his God. In what seems worse, Joseph will shortly be thrown into prison in Egypt. What was his crime this time? He simply obeyed his Lord and protected his master's honor; and for this, he gets the dungeon? Often, it just doesn't seem fair!

But one may say this is the problem we encounter over and over when we see things from our human perspective and vantage point. We never see the whole picture! We don't know all the details, let alone the end of the story. The climax and ending often occurs after our short human life has ended. We do not have the Scriptural vantage point of extended time; we must keep this in mind as we evaluate our life.

Who would think this boy, now a man, would provide salvation to the very brothers who sold him? Not only does he feed his entire family during a devastating famine but also provides food for a world that may have starved without him. This Hebrew boys' terrible predicament turns out to be his families' and world's salvation, along with his own exaltation. In this story we find many parallels to some events we discover in the pages of the Tanakh. When we see Scriptural narratives through a proper lens of

Scriptural balance and accuracy we gain a more complete understanding, even in our time.

We just saw in Joseph's story the Lord's choice of this young man to endure many terrible and troublesome events to produce a good ending not just for his family of Hebrews but for Gentiles alike. It was the LORD through his choice of this Hebrew son who brought salvation to Egypt and the family of Israel. My hope is that within this backdrop, we will see and understand the term *The Chosen People* as God intends us to realize.

The LORD definitely chose Abram! This choosing works its way down to Jacob and to Israelites as a people. In this, the LORD had a specific purpose in mind to work through the people of Israel to eventually provide something good and necessary for the rest of humanity.

The LORD's plan was meant to be inclusive not exclusive. Not all nations, people-groups or individuals will buy into the LORD's plan, yet refusal to do so falls on sinful humanity rather than on the LORD. This blessing spoken of in Genesis 12:3 is foreshadowed in Abraham, Joseph and Moses and is found interwoven throughout the Tanakh. Yet the great fulfillment is revealed and explained in the Messiah.

One may ask why this blessing was needed and what it is all about. The need for this blessing goes way back before Abram's life; in fact, it goes all the way back to the beginning before the LORD's choice between the two brothers, Cain and Abel. Humanity has a problem, and it started in Genesis.

This problem has been called the *evil inclination*. When Adam sinned, something radically changed in humanity. This, in turn, fundamentally changed their relationship with the LORD. This issue plagued humanity from the first sin and continues through into our present time. It affects all people, Israelites and Gentiles alike. No one is exempt from this sinful inclination. We can see this change in humanity, when the effects are full-blown in Genesis 6:5 that says:

The LORD saw how great man's wickedness on the earth had become, and that every inclination of the thoughts of his heart was only evil all the time.

David and Isaiah talk about this issue in Psalm 51:7[5] and Isaiah 53:6. David's response to this issue comes from a very personal story. Still he relates this to us in verse 7[5] as he speaks of himself personally:

Surely I was sinful at birth, sinful from the time my mother conceived me.

Isaiah uses the LORD's viewpoint of humanity. In Isaiah 53:6 he says, *"We all, like sheep have gone astray, each of us has turned to his own way."* The LORD's blessing that's promised through Abraham has far reaching benefits for all people – the chosen and un-chosen of humanity – indeed all ethnicities.

Can we forget for a short time what has transpired in world history within the past 2000 years and go back to a first Century mindset? Can we look into what was known and understood in the Hebrew Scriptures **B**efore the **C**ommon **E**ra (BCE) and within the first centuries of the **C**ommon **E**ra (CE)?

As we begin this trip of exploration and discovery, will you allow me to open the Tanakh to see if we can possibly find answers to some of our own tough questions concerning the LORD and the Hebrew Scriptures? Let's see if we can find some answers.

I don't understand why the atrocities in our BCE and CE history (B.C and A.D. for Gentiles) had to be the way it's been nor do I think anyone else can explain it to us. We simply don't know everything and definitely can't see things like history as the LORD sees. From the backdrop of his plans and choosing, he works toward a goal.

If this blessing to all humanity is ever to be realized, only chosen individuals who join his plan at the essential levels of the soul will make a difference. We all have a choice to be proactively engaged in the drama of humanity. This is the way that we too find we are the very people through whom he chooses to work his plan. Random choices just wouldn't do in the Scripture, and won't work now in our day.

First Puzzle Pieces of Messiah

Getting back to Abraham, let's once again take a look at things that transpire in his life and lives of his sons. How would the LORD bless all people through Abraham? Well the beginning of that answer can be found in Genesis 15:1-20.

The LORD comes to Abram in a vision and tells him the following, recorded in Genesis 15:1, "*I am your shield, your very great reward.*" In response to this greeting Abram asks a question and then makes a statement:

> *Abram said... what can you give me since I remain childless and the one who will inherit my estate is Eliezer of Damascus....You have given me no children.*

To show Himself as The Source, the LORD tells Abram, "*Your servant won't be your heir; your heir will be a son you will father yourself.*" Abraham and Sarah will have a son, and only through Abraham's coming son will his inheritance be counted.

In Genesis 16, Sarai, after putting up with so many childless years decides to help the Lord out and provide her husband with this promised heir. So Sarai gives Abram her Egyptian maidservant Hagar to be his wife. This arrangement, though not politically correct today, was perfectly permissible in Abram's day. In fairness to Sarai, we must remember she isn't a young woman at this point in her life. She is already what we would call a senior citizen.

Abram listens to Sarai and takes Hagar as his wife. When he sleeps with her, she becomes pregnant. Instead of providing peace and comfort to both Abram and Sarai, this pregnancy ends up being a cause of grief and trouble. Sarai ends up mistreating Hagar, and Hagar runs away.

As Hagar sits by a desert spring, the angel of the Lord finds her and gives a promise related to her yet-to-be-birthed son, "*I will so increase your descendants that they will be too numerous to* count." This angel gives a second declaration, *"You are now with child and you will have a son. You shall name him Ishmael."* Did you notice the LORD in this narrative? The Lord hears of Hagar's misery and does something about it. When Hagar agrees to submit to Sarai because of the angelic directive, she returns to Abram and Sarai, and remains with them.

The LORD confirms his covenant with Abram in our next narrative in Genesis 17. Here the LORD tells Abram he will father many nations. The LORD continues, saying He will be the LORD of Abram's descendants and will give his **chosen** descendants the entire land of Canaan where Abram is currently sojourning.

Here, the LORD changes the names of Abram and Sarai to Abraham and Sarah. God tells Abram, 'Walk before me, and be blameless, that I may make my covenant with you....' Abram bows before God in humble submission and God says, '. . . you shall be the father of a multitude of nations . . . your name shall be Abraham, for I have made you the father of a multitude of nations.' This covenant-confirmation requires all of Abraham's descendants and Abraham, himself, to be circumcised.

The LORD reveals even more information to Abraham. Listen carefully to what's said next. This is important especially to our discussion of being **chosen**. We see a specific distinction being made by the LORD, showing just who has a part within this covenant. Here the LORD continues the conversation with Abraham in Genesis 17:15-17,

> *As for Sarai your wife, you are no longer to call her Sarai; her name will be Sarah. I will bless her so that she will be the mother of nations; kings of peoples will come from her. Abraham fell facedown; he laughed and said to himself, Will a son be born to a man a hundred years old? Will Sarah bear a child at the age of ninety?*

At this point in the conversation, Abraham, a man who likes a good joke, basically tells God tongue-in-cheek, 'Right! That's a good one. Why not just let Ishmael be the one to carry this blessing?'

But God reinforces the truthful magnitude of his declaration to conclude this conversation in Genesis 17:19-21,

> *Yes, but your wife Sarah will bear you a son, and you will call him Isaac. I will establish my covenant with him as an everlasting covenant for his descendants after him. And as for Ishmael, I have heard you: I will surely bless him; I will make him fruitful and will greatly increase his numbers... But my covenant I will establish with Isaac, whom Sarah will bear to you by this time next year.*

While every male, including Ishmael, is circumcised the LORD establishes this covenant with Abraham through only one son, the one not-yet-even-conceived whose name will be Isaac.

Let me ask an important question here. Does the LORD reject and discard Ishmael by his declaration that Isaac will be the heir of the covenant? No, He hasn't! In fact, the LORD tells Abraham he will bless Ishmael to make him into a great nation. Regarding the LORD's purpose in being *The Chosen*, he picks or chooses Isaac specifically. As Scriptures declare, the LORD will bless *both* of Abraham's sons; however, the specific promise to bless all ethnicities, including Ishmael's descendants, finds its fulfillment through Isaac's descendants, rather than Ishmael's.

As the Genesis 18 narrative unfolds, we again walk into a scene that contains something that seems out of place. What we see is extremely peculiar yet very interesting. Verse one tells us the LORD appears to Abraham while he sits at the entrance of his tent. Even though it's late afternoon, in the heat of the day, Abraham is not hallucinating. The three "men" who appear in this scene are not a mirage.

When Abraham sees these men, he immediately goes over to where they're standing and bows, then offers to meet their needs and washes their feet. He offers them rest from their journey and some fresh water to refresh themselves.

Nothing that just transpired is strange or out of the ordinary. In fact what Abraham has just done is to offer the hospitality that is customary in his day and time. What is peculiar, though, will show up quickly.

Once Abraham gets these strangers' permission, he quickly leaves them, goes into his tent and tells Sarah to make some bread. He then hurries to his herd, picks out a choice calf and tells a servant to prepare it for the guests. Once the meal is prepared, he places it before them. Abraham stands nearby under the great trees of Mamre as his guests enjoy their meal.

Here's the beginning of the peculiar yet interesting part. One of the men asks Abraham a question, which seems strange. He asks, "*Where is your wife Sarah?*" What we've read of this narrative to this point contains nothing to make us believe that Abraham knows these men. "Just how does this stranger know the name of Abraham's wife?" But that's not the only thing this man knows, which we might think he has no way of knowing. He knows something else besides Sarah's name, as we find out.

This man tells Abraham in Genesis 18:10, "*I will surely return to you about this time next year, and Sarah your wife will have a son.*" It's doubtful these visitors are just normal men who wander into Mamre. It seems they're on a special mission, and their mission involves both Abraham and Sarah. This "man" knows Sarah's name; that she is barren, and the LORD promised to give her a son. But that's not all that's peculiar.

After hearing this man's announcement of her giving birth to a son, Sarah laughs at the thought. 'Sure,' she thinks, 'At the end of this bad dream, after all these barren, frustrating, disappointing, and humiliating years, now as an old woman I'm going to give birth to a son for my husband?' Yet this peculiar man, after hearing Sarah's laughter and asking Abraham why his wife laughs at this good news, reiterates the same birth-promise-covenant message to them again.

Again, Abraham hears a declaration that seems to him, at

this point in his life so unbelievable, especially the magnitude of this truth-declaration. This man reiterates his proclamation in Genesis 18:10, "*I will return to you, at the appointed time next year, and Sarah will have a son.*" There's no doubt about it, this stranger is *stranger* than any stranger can be! Or is he?

After the birth announcement is firmly pronounced, the three men get up to leave. This strange stranger who happens to be called the Lord in this narrative asks in Genesis 18:17, "*Shall I hide from Abraham what I am about to do?*"

The LORD surely knows this old man, Abraham 'will become a great and powerful nation, and all earth's ethnicities will be blessed through this one man and his special family.'

Again let me ask, "How can this strange stranger know all these things about Abraham and Sarah?" Think about it, in Abraham's day there are no newspapers, magazines or TV cable news networks. So, how did this man know all these things? He certainly hadn't just talked to Abraham's neighbors to gain all of his information. Without Scripture's telling, this seems strange!

In the next chapter, we discover two of these men are angels. This partially explains how this third "man" gains his information. But this still doesn't tell us the identity of this third peculiar man. Just who is this third man who knows so much? And how does he know so much about the promise to this old barren couple – that will fulfill their lifelong dream through the birth of their own son, from their blessed union?

Genesis 18:19 gives a tremendous hint toward this third man's identity. It says; "*For I have chosen him….*" Notice the "I." What does this man mean by saying "*I have chosen him?*" Is he saying that he himself personally knows or chose Abraham? If so, this should change our understanding. We know it was the LORD who chose Abraham so what is this man declaring? Already we should know he's more than he appears.

At this point, our scene is closing – almost! Our strange man doesn't yet go to Sodom but says, "*I will go down and see if what they have done is as bad as the outcry that has reached me. If not, I will know*" (18:21). Who is this man who stands as a territorial judge making rulings and decisions against peoples and communities?

The two angels depart to travel towards Sodom and Gomorrah. They have an appointment to speak with Abraham's nephew, Lot, but he doesn't know it yet. Once again, this "man" is called LORD in verses Genesis 18:19, 20 & 22.

This stranger holds his ground and remains standing – exactly in front of Abraham. It's not like a Western showdown per se but it looks like it. Neither man backs down through the coming, might we say, emotional negotiation. Abraham is boldly willing to put his emotions front-and-center.

Abraham bargains for his nephew Lot's life. Abraham negotiates desperately with this man, and calls him "*the Judge of all the earth*" (18:25). That statement alone is amazing! We all know who the Judge of the earth is! God alone is given that title! So when the Scriptures refer to God himself as *the Judge of all the earth*, how can Abraham give this title to this stranger unless he is the LORD and Judge? Abraham's downsized request for 10 was rejected because Sodom had less than ten righteous people. In the end, Lot and his family were blessed with mercy from the LORD. Abraham negotiates mercy but destruction is on its way! Yes, this is one peculiar, strange, and yet extremely fascinating Scriptural narrative! However, mercy is still extended to Lot.

Genesis 21 reveals Isaac's birth; however, within this scene we once again encounter animosity and suspicion within a family unit. After Isaac is weaned, Abraham holds a great feast to celebrate his world-shattering occasion. Also, Sarah notices Ishmael in a different way, in a way that is not good for a family. As this scene comes into focus, Ishmael is shamelessly having a grand time mocking Isaac on this festive occasion.

We can tell what's coming next – never rob a mother bear of her cub. When a mother bear is protecting her cub, fur will fly and the fight might be to the death. Making a mockery of the cub she loves and protects with her life will cause a reciprocal-amount of Mom's wrath to flow towards you.

And Mom's wrath is on its way! Sarah doesn't take this sitting down, she quickly strides over to Abraham and tells him; 'Get rid of Ishmael and his mother now! I won't put up with this mockery any longer. This must stop! Send them away!'

This demand from Sarah doesn't sit well with Abraham. After all, Ishmael is his son and responsibility, and he dearly loves Ishmael as a father should. Ishmael is also Sarah's son through legal adoption but she doesn't see it this way when Ishmael spews his mockery. Right at this point is where the LORD enters the picture again.

The LORD tells Abraham not to be too distressed over Sarah's request. Just why does the LORD say this to Abraham? The end of Genesis 21:12 gives a partial answer, *"It is through Isaac that your offspring will be reckoned."* The rest of the answer is stated by the LORD as He reiterates his promise to bless Ishmael, *"I will make the son of the maidservant into a nation also, because he is your offspring"* (21:13). Separation is in order but not forgetfulness in the casting away.

We encounter a similar choice and separation later on in Abraham's life. This occurs after Sarah dies and Abraham remarries. Genesis 25:1-4 tell us his new wife, Keturah, births him more sons but all sons receive some inheritance before they are sent away to the East to avoid conflict (5-6), even though history reveals this seems to never work for peace.

Abraham left everything he owned to Isaac. But while he was still living, he gave gifts to the sons of his concubines and sent them away from his son Isaac to the land of the east.

Once again, we have choice and separation. Here, it's not because there's something wrong with Keturah's sons. The choice and separation here has more to do with the LORD's plan for both Israel and Gentile nations, and how his plan will unfold. This choosing was on the LORD's side rather than on Abraham's side. Abraham was only being obedient to do what the LORD directed him to do.

The binding of Isaac or Akedah is another somewhat peculiar yet important narrative. In Genesis 22, the LORD tests Abraham. He commands him to take his son Isaac to the region of Moriah and sacrifice him as a burnt offering on one mountain there (v.2). We need to think about this request for a minute. After all the years Abraham waited for this promised son to be born, roughly 25, and now the LORD wants him to take his promised son and sacrifice him. How could Abraham think straight? How many thoughts were going through his mind?

Some very interesting terminology is used in Genesis 22:2. The first is, "your *only son, Isaac*." How can the LORD call Isaac Abraham's "only son?" Had the LORD forgotten Abraham had more than one wife and each woman had provided him with a son? No, the LORD wasn't suffering from dementia, he knew what he was saying and requesting.

The second terms used are *the region of Moriah* and the *mountains*. The third terms are *Sacrifice* and *burnt offering*. The fourth terms are concepts of *father* and *son*. This story of the birth of a son, the location of Mount Moriah, and a sacrifice involving a father and son prefigures historical events that will take place within Israel to another Israelite family many generations later, as the Hebrew Scriptures proclaim.

The term *"only son"* is interesting indeed. The emphasis on *only* isn't about the son's soleness as it is about the uniqueness of the one son over all of the rest. You may ask, "Okay, so what makes Isaac so unique?" What a great question. Isaac's uniqueness has to do with the fact of his conception and his being chosen. His birth is unique from the rest of Abraham's sons. The unique conception of this son came as the result of a miracle from the LORD.

Isaac's mother Sarah, unlike Hagar and Keturah, was barren. As a result of Sarah's barrenness and her being past childbearing age, it took a miraculous act of the LORD for Sarah to conceive at all. In this way, Isaac's birth was the result of a "wonderful" miracle, thus his uniqueness or *"onlyness."*

The region of *Mount Moriah*, while not specifically mentioned in the above narrative, is specifically designated in a later Scriptural reference. II Chronicles 3:1 says this of Moriah, the place where the temple of the LORD would be built, *"Then Solomon began to build the temple of the Lord in Jerusalem on Mount Moriah."* Very interesting, the same mountain where Abraham brought his son to sacrifice him to the LORD is the same place where the LORD's temple is eventually built!

From Scripture, we know *sacrifice* and *burnt offering* occurs within the temple on a continual basis. But just what does our above quote from Genesis 22:14 mean? This verse says, "On the mountain of the LORD, it will be provided." The context in this narrative deals with sacrifice and burnt offering and the two players are a *father* and *son*. Could it be that the future event referred to in this narrative is speaking of an event also featuring a Father and His Son? Let's look at this possibility.

Abraham obeys the LORD and takes a three-day trip to Moriah with his son Isaac and servants. From this narrative we find so many interesting things. Verse 6 tells us that *"Abraham took the wood for the burnt offering and placed it on his son Isaac, while, he himself carried the fire and the knife."*

Isaac asks a great question in verse Genesis 22:7, *"The fire and wood are here,"* Isaac said, *"but where is the lamb for the burnt offering?"* Abraham answers his son, *"God himself will provide the lamb for the burnt offering, my son."*

We could say of Abraham's response to Isaac, "Well, there you have it!" But that's a premature conclusion. When the Lord provides on the mountain, he provides the ram caught by its horns, and this ram does end up taking the place of Isaac. The ram loses its life and is sacrificed in Isaac's place. But if we speak too fast concerning the meaning of the statement, "*On the mountain of the LORD it will be provided*," we will miss something magnificent.

What we would have missed is that Genesis 22:14 predicts a future event, not just the specific event we just witnessed in this narrative. The verse says, "And to this day it is said, 'On the mountain of the LORD it will be provided.'" This speaks of a future event where the LORD provides something in the context of Mount Moriah – a sacrifice and "offering of substitution" that specifically deals with a Father and a Son that is yet future.

Is it only me or does the LORD seem to have a plan for the future – what with all of the choosing He's done since the beginning of Genesis? Does his All-Wise plan seem evident?

We're coming to the end of the narrative of Abraham, the LORD's friend. Genesis 25 gives us the last chapter of this great man's life. This chapter introduces us to Abraham's third wife and their children. But there's more to see. We discover Abraham is faithful to the LORD's call and choice even to the end. Abraham particularly sets aside or chooses Isaac (5-6),

> Abraham left everything he owned to Isaac. But while he was still living, he gave gifts to the sons of his concubines and sent them away from his son Isaac.

So Abraham took care of all his children at the same time as he was obedient to what the LORD told him in Genesis 21. Remember, Sarah told Abraham to send away both Hagar and Ishmael. This is almost too much for Abraham to bear but the LORD tells him to listen to Sarah and tells his friend the choice-reason in 21:12, "*Because it is through Isaac that your offspring will be reckoned.*" Sometimes we just need assurance and Abraham gets comfort. Yes, the LORD will take care of Ishmael and Keturah's sons but his special plan for Isaac will be a blessing to the nation of Israel and the rest of the world.

Just as the nation of Israel will experience multitudes of turmoil, pain, death and problematic existence, Abraham also experiences many of these same things himself. Here was a man who was promised a son in his old age and yet that son didn't materialize until he is 100 years old. He had to deal with his wife's barrenness and having to send away his oldest son Ishmael, whom Abraham loved dearly.

The LORD then required Abraham to sacrifice his *only son* on an altar. And yet Abraham really believed that even if he followed through with this required sacrifice the LORD would somehow restore Isaac to life. You may ask, "Just what did this great man base his tremendous trust on?" He based his trust on the truthfulness of the LORD's promise which was to bless his descendants and all ethnicities through his son Isaac.

Abraham lived as a wandering nomad. He never had a place he continually called home. He was in danger for his life on many occasions and yet proved to be a valiant warrior. He even rescued his nephew Lot who was taken captive.

Truly Abraham was a man of integrity and faith! He was one amazing man! He was a man whom the LORD called his friend. What more needs to be said? Well, there's more.

Isaac the Son of Promise

We now find ourselves at Genesis 25:21. Once again a wife is barren and unable to produce children, let alone a son. As a result of Rebekah's barrenness, Isaac prays to the LORD for his wife and her status or condition.

The LORD answers him; Rebekah gets a two-for-one blessing. She is pregnant with twins. This narrative gets better; the two boys are sparring partners in Rebekah's womb. These "boxing matches" go on so long that Rebekah eventually asks the LORD,

'What exactly is taking place in my womb?' This is what the LORD tells her:

Two nations are in your womb, and two peoples from within you will be separated; one people will be stronger than the other, and the older will serve the younger.

Well, here we go again. The LORD once again chooses one son over the other. Once again, it's not the firstborn son who wins the day. This sibling rivalry continues throughout this pregnancy and even during the birth. These two boys are very determined competitors. Esau, the first one to be born, makes his appearance but there's something attached to his heel. You guessed it: his brother's hand is firmly affixed to Esau's heel. Jacob was not about to be outdone by his older sibling.

Let me tell you more things about the uniquely-born son, Isaac. What amazing stories he must have heard from his father Abraham. And what marvelous stories he could tell, even today. This patriarch knew of his miraculous birth, miraculous intervention of the LORD on Mount Moriah, and substitutionary sacrifice that occurred. He can explain the LORD's intervention with his wife and how she birthed twin sons as a result. Isaac could offer stories telling how his two sons' personalities were uniquely different. He could unpack how the LORD took care of Jacob and brings him back after 20 years in a foreign land. Yes, this son of Abraham had seen and experienced much but it was enough for Isaac to know the LORD's truthfulness in his word.

In trying to limit the size of this book I won't go into the entire story of this special man named Isaac. Instead, I will just touch on the highlights of this great man's life.

In Chapter 26, once again a famine has come upon the land. Isaac travels to Gerar where the Lord speaks to him and tells him to remain in the land and not to go to Egypt. The Lord reiterates to Isaac what he promised to his father Abraham. He tells Isaac in verses 3-4:

...to you and your descendants I will give all these lands ....and through your offspring all nations on earth will be blessed.

Isaac, the child who survived being "sacrificed" did not live a life without adversity. Exactly how does one survive being sacrificed? This man of trust willingly placed his life in his father Abraham's hands. His father was promised a nation through Isaac yet his wife, Rebekah, was barren. When the LORD finally answers his prayer and blesses him and Rebekah with a child, he receives two-for-one. But the sibling rivalry and struggle for the blessing nearly cost him one of his sons' lives.

Isaac seemingly encounters conflict wherever he goes. When arriving in a new location he would dig a well, only to have it plugged up by neighboring, hostile shepherds. Just as his father did, Isaac continually traveled from place to place. He had no permanent place to call his own. But just as his father, Isaac worshipped the LORD, followed his word, and did what the LORD directed him to do.

Jacob, a Man Who Has an Amazing Encounter

Jacob is a scheming individual while he grows up. Eventually, he ends up bartering himself into the birthright. And Jacob is not about to let this birthright-exchange take place with only a handshake. No, he makes Esau swear an oath as he sells him the birthright.

To add to family tension, in Genesis 25:28 we see Esau is Isaac's favorite son, and Jacob is Rebekah's favorite son. Later in chapter 27, Rebekah tries to push her favorite son up the succession ladder. Rebekah's shrewd plan unfolds and Jacob ends up deceiving his father to get the blessing. Taking the birthright is one thing but stealing the blessing is more than Esau can take. Because Esau is fed up he decides to kill his conniving brother, Jacob. Esau's plan to kill Jacob becomes known to Rebekah so she comes up with another plan to save her sons' life. Rebekah pleads with Isaac to send Jacob, who is still unmarried, away to her family in order to get him a wife.

Even though it's easy to see how the characters in the Scriptural narratives work and plan to save their own lives and those of their family, sometimes we "lose sight" of the fact that the LORD works behind the scenes to protect the ones he chooses. The LORD does this so his plans will not be stopped. I believe the LORD does this not only throughout the Scriptural narratives but even in our current time in the 21st century CE.

This protection of providence is the reason for Joseph's life being spared and his being sold into slavery in Egypt. The LORD protects David and his descendants by protecting His name and the covenant He promised. We see him protect the southern kingdom of Judah in the backdrop of their Babylonian captivity. He brings them back to their land just as he promised. He worked out history in order for Israel to once again live back in the land today, just as He promised they would do. But we're getting ahead of ourselves in the story.

We left off in Genesis 28 with Jacob about to be sent to Paddan Aram by his father, Isaac, to get a wife. As Jacob travels on his way to Haran, he arrives at a certain place called Luz to spend the night. While he sleeps, he has a dream and sees the angels of the LORD walk a stairway both up to heaven and down to earth. What a dream! Above this stairway stands the LORD, and he repeats the very same promise he previously gave to both Abraham and Isaac. He says in verses 13-15:

> I am the LORD, the God of your father Abraham and the God of Isaac. I will give you and your descendants the land on which you are lying.

But there's more; the Lord continues:

> All peoples on earth will be blessed through you and your offspring. I am with you and will watch over you wherever you go, and I will bring you back to this land. I will not leave you until I have done what I have promised you.

Now that's what I call a promise! Notice the last line again; the LORD promises not to leave Jacob until he had done the very things he just promised to him.

I believe these promises live on within the Jewish people today. Even as the Lord was with Jacob through every trial and abuse he suffered, even to possible extermination by his brother, the Lord was with him as he is with Israel today.

Because of the above encounter with the LORD and his angels on the Ladder, Jacob names this place Bethel. He makes a vow to the LORD to give him a tenth or tithe if he will be good to Jacob and eventually bring him back to his father's house.

Jacob finally arrives at his mother's country in Genesis 29 and comes upon shepherds and their flocks. As he talks with the shepherds to inquire about Laban, his mother's brother, his cousin Rachel comes toward him with her sheep. Jacob tells her he is her father's relative and Rebekah's son. When she hears this news, Rachel runs to tell her father, Laban, about her cousin Jacob who just arrived. As Laban hears Rachel's announcement, he goes to meet Jacob and bring him to his home.

Laban puts Jacob to work right away to shepherd his flocks. After Jacob worked for his Uncle Laban for a month, he tells Jacob, 'Name your wages!' Jacob, who had already fallen hopelessly in love with Rachel, was waiting for this day. He lays out his wage demands to his uncle in verse 18, "*I'll work for you seven years in return for your younger daughter Rachel.*" Laban agrees to Jacob's terms so Jacob will work for Uncle Laban for seven years for Rachel. Genesis 29:20 gives Jacob's perspective on these seven years, "*they seemed like only a few days to him because of his love for her.*" Love sure sees things differently!

When the seven years were completed, Jacob goes to Laban and tells him the time has come to give him his wife, Rachel. Laban agrees, prepares a great feast, and invites all the local people. Instead of giving Rachel to Jacob as promised, Laban slips in Leah, Rachel's older sister, to wed Jacob.

In the morning light Jacob realizes he's been deceived when he sees his wife is Leah rather than Rachel. Jacob is not happy to find he consummated a marriage with a woman he did not want. He goes to find his father-in-law for a talk. When he finds Laban he asks, 'Why did you deceive me by giving me Leah, another woman for my wife?' Jacob's new father-in-law assures him it's their custom to marry the oldest sister first.

To soften the hostility and gain some valuable labor, Laban promises to give Rachel to Jacob on one condition — he will work another seven years. So Jacob agrees to this contract. Since he's hopelessly in love with Rachel, what else can he do? Due to this new arrangement, Jacob finishes his marriage week with Leah. Only then does Laban give Rachel to Jacob as his second wife.

Does anyone else see this arrangement as a set-up for disaster? Yet this family and its makeup is exactly what the LORD uses to advance his plan to bless Abraham's descendants and the nations. Leah, the wife Jacob didn't want and doesn't love, gives birth to four sons, Reuben, Simeon, Levi and Judah. In contrast, Rachel, the wife Jacob dearly loves and works 14 years to obtain is barren and can't produce children at all.

As a result of her barrenness and sibling jealousy over her sister having four sons, Rachel gives her maidservant Bilhah to Jacob as his wife so perhaps she can birth a child for Rachel. Sure enough, Bilhah bears two sons for Rachel by Jacob, and their names are Dan and Naphtali. Since Leah knows that Jacob doesn't love her, she isn't about to admit defeat without a fight, maybe thinking to herself, 'Two can play this game.' Just like her sister Rachel, Leah gives her maidservant Zilpah to Jacob as his wife to produce more children for Leah. Her plan works too! Zilpah bears two sons by the names of Gad and Asher. What a brewing sibling rivalry; and they're just getting started.

Again Leah wins her way back into Jacob's life; this time to purchase Jacob's time and affection by giving Rachel some mandrakes. The only condition to this deal is that Jacob must spend the night with Leah. I'm sure Rachel unwillingly agrees. As a result of this bartering agreement Leah gets pregnant twice and bears Jacob two more sons, their names are Issachar and Zebulun. She also bears a daughter by the name of Dinah.

Can you imagine what Jacob was going through? He is caught in the middle of two sisters, his wives no less, concubine wives, and all their sibling rivalries. In the midst of tensions and frustrations the LORD finally responds to Rachel's prayers. She conceives and gives birth to a son named Joseph.

By now, Jacob had enough of being taken advantage of by his father-in-law. So he went and talks with Laban. He asks to be allowed to return to his father's home. That "escape" will not be as easy as he once thought as Jacob is caught in a pressure cooker!

Besides all the escapades of his wives, he has to deal with the used-car-salesman dealings of his father-in-law.

Laban doesn't want Jacob to leave; he knows he has been blessed as a result of Jacob and Jacob's work ethic. So, Laban comes up with a plan. Jacob will continue shepherding Laban's flocks but something happens that Laban didn't foresee. Through all the years, Jacob's flocks continue to increase and he ends up with the strong, healthy, and fertile sheep and goats. Laban, on the other hand, ends up with smaller, inferior flocks. This doesn't settle too well with either Laban or Laban's sons. They believe Jacob gained all his success and wealth by cheating or stealing their father's livestock. About this time one wonders whether this man, Jacob, will ever get to return home.

Whether it's seen in Hebrew Scriptural narratives, in extra-Scriptural accounts, or just in world-histories up to and including this present time, animosity and tension exists. It seems continual tension exists between *Chosen Ones* or *The Chosen People* and those who are not the *Chosen Ones*.

This hostility and hatred towards the Patriarchs, the Nation of Israel, and eventually Jewish people in general continues to increase through time. Whether you are Jacob, David or Elisha, the fact that the LORD is with you doesn't make life easy or pain-free. This fact is only too evident in Jacob's story.

Getting back to our story, once again the LORD enters into the narrative and takes things into His own hands. In Genesis 31 the LORD tells Jacob to return to his home, and that He will be with him in his continuing life-journey.

Jacob discusses this declaration and the mistreatment he has suffered working for Laban with Rachel and Leah. Rachel and Leah respond to Jacob with support in Genesis 31:14-16,

Do we still have any share in the inheritance of our father's estate? Does he not regard us as foreigners? Not only has he sold us, but he has used up what was paid for us. Surely all the wealth that God

took away from our father belongs to us and our children. So do whatever God has told you.

At this response, Jacob gets everything he owns and all of his family together and begins the journey back to his father, Isaac. Of course, nothing is easy for Jacob. Three days after his departure, Laban hears that Jacob left without notice.

Laban takes off in hot pursuit. After seven days, he finally catches up with Jacob in the hill country of Gilead. Again the LORD intervenes. He comes to Laban at night in a dream and gives Laban some sobering advice (Genesis 31:24), He says, *"Be careful not to say anything to Jacob, either good or bad."*

Although Laban has great ability to harm Jacob, when he awakes, the words of the LORD's warning still ring in his ears so he decides to step carefully and allow Jacob to leave. After over 20 years of service, animosity still exists in this relationship. Despite this, these two men make a covenant. They agree not to harm each other. Jacob agrees not to mistreat Rachel or Leah, or marry other wives. After spending the night, Jacob and his family depart for Canaan after Laban blesses his daughters and grandchildren. For this chapter, things end well.

More trouble is brewing just over the horizon. Chapter 32 begins with Jacob again encountering the LORD's angels; this can bring assurance, but clouds of trouble are coming.

As Jacob approaches the land of Seir he sends some messengers to his brother Esau to let him know he is returning home after 20 years. I'm sure Jacob experienced great anxiety as he thought of encountering his brother, even after 20 years of being apart. Jacob's trepidation came from the fact these two brothers didn't leave each other on great terms. In fact, Esau made a commitment to himself to kill his brother Jacob. Even with all this in mind, I don't believe Jacob was prepared to hear the story of his returning messengers.

The messengers say, 'Yep, we found your brother all right. He's coming to see you. And, oh yeah, he's bringing 400 men with him.' At this point, Jacob's trepidation turns to panic mode. Jacob begins to prepare for Esau's impending attack. He divides his family and all he has into two different groups. His hopeful plan is that if Esau attacks one group, maybe the other group will get away and survive. Jacob's momentous turmoil is readily evident in the words of his prayer in Genesis 32. His inner turmoil is expressed in verses 9[10] to 12[13]:

> O God of my father Abraham, God of my father Isaac, O LORD, who said to me, Go back to your country and your relatives, and I will make you prosper. I am unworthy of all the kindness and faithfulness you have shown your servant. I had only my staff when I crossed this Jordan, but now I have become two groups. Save me, I pray, from the hand of my brother Esau, for I am afraid he will come and attack me, and also the mothers with their children. But you said, I will surely make you prosper and will make your descendants like the sand of the sea, which cannot be counted.

What outright honesty and unflinching appeal to the LORD! Jacob knew he had nothing in his power to stop Esau from harming him or his entire family. But he did know it was the LORD who kept Laban from harming him while he worked for him and when he left Laban to return home. He had to learn more about how the LORD works in His chosen one's lives.

Jacob spent the night where he was while he waited on the storm clouds of his brother's approach. I'm sure Jacob did not have a peaceful night's sleep. In the morning, he prepares a gift for his brother, Esau. And what a gift it is! Jacob puts aside 220 goats, 220 sheep, 60 camels, 50 cows and 30 donkeys; this is no small herd! He places these animals in the hands of his servants. He tells them to put quite a bit of space between the two herds. In Genesis 32:18 Jacob tells his lead servant what to tell Esau when he meets him.

Esau is curious about this herd, so he asks the servant about them. Here is the servants' response in verse 18, "*They belong to your servant Jacob. They are a gift sent to my lord Esau; and he is coming behind us."* This is the same thing Jacob instructs all his servants to say to Esau if they meet him. Notice, the one who always tried to wrest family-control away from his older twin Esau, is not so bold. Here, as his brother's approach is near, he tells his servants to refer to Jacob as Esau's servant and to call Esau lord. At this Jacob sends his servants on toward his brother Esau, hopeful of mercy that he never gave before.

Later that night, before Esau's arrival, Jacob gathers up the rest of his possessions, his wives, servants and children, and crosses the Jabbok River. Jacob then goes back across to the other side of the Jabbok to spend the night alone with his troubling thoughts. What a night it was; we can only imagine!

From my own perspective that has come from many sleepless fretful nights, when foreboding disaster seems to loom large, I never experienced a good night's sleep, or any peace. However, that's not the case with Jacob; he doesn't even get time for sleep due to his encounter once again with an angel, or is this angel more than angelic substance?

Jacob left to be alone but he is alone no longer. In fact he endures a workout, but not like any workout we would think. This wrestling match between him and this angel interrupts his aloneness. This human/angelic match continues until dawn when the "angel," unable to break Jacob's grasp, touches his hip causing it to wrench as they continue to wrestle. Similar to his womb-struggle with Esau, Jacob will not let this man go! The "angel" tells Jacob to let him go but Jacob responds in verse 26[27], *"I will not let you go unless you bless me."*

I think Jacob realized or learned something here. We know a true blessing can only be given by a greater person to a person of lower standing. Jacob asks one who is greater than himself to bless him. But this isn't all the difference between these two individuals, as we will see shortly.

The angel asks Jacob his name. By telling him his name, Jacob must admit to who he's been; he's been a heel grabber! This is someone who, though on a lower rung of the "corporate ladder," attempts to displace someone higher up by grabbing their leg and throwing them from the ladder. Is it any wonder Jacob had a ladder-dream in Genesis 28:10-22 with the LORD standing at the top. Apparently Jacob still needs to learn.

Because of the Lord's work in his soul and his humble confession related to his given name, the "angel" gives Jacob a different name. From the angel, he is given the name Israel that can mean he struggles with the LORD himself. In the Scriptures, when the LORD changes someone's name this typically indicates a covenant relationship was mutually applied and accepted. Just as his grandfather Abraham and his father Isaac did, Jacob has now placed his trust in the God of Abraham and Isaac.

While Jacob might not have felt like it, he moves up the ladder by the LORD's doing, not by his own *grabbing*. Jacob, who struggled with people his entire life, now struggles with the LORD and "overcame." One who struggles with the LORD in this way only overcomes in the scriptural sense: they win through the LORD becoming ruler of their heart. This move up-the-ladder speaks of Jacob gaining a new heart-status, this is what the LORD does to those whom he chooses. Jacob is *graced* by the LORD, went through a heart change, and gains a new name, Israel (Genesis 32:28).

Some might think, "Wait a minute, how can you say Jacob wrestled with the LORD? Hadn't he just wrestled with an angel?" Yes, you're right, he wrestled with an angel, but notice what Jacob says about this encounter in verse 30[31]. Here, in Genesis 32:30[31] Jacob names this location, Peniel. Why did he give it this name? He named it Peniel because Jacob said, "*It is because I saw God face to face, and yet my life was spared.*" Do these words tell us he knew the angel was the LORD, even though he still lived?

These amazing words parallel words his grandfather Abraham said as he encountered the LORD and angels. We will continue to see this throughout the Hebrew Scriptures – people who encounter a mysterious angel of the LORD and the amazing responses to these encounters. Jacob's name was not all that was changed. A result of this encounter is that he now limps as he walks because of his wrenched hip.

Jacob crosses back over the Jabbok – the side with his family – and when he looks up, he sees Esau bearing down on him with his 400 men. He quickly arranges his family. He places the servants first in line, followed by Leah and her children, with Rachel and Joseph bringing up the rear. As a true leader, Jacob goes on ahead of this group. When Jacob meets Esau, he bows down seven times as to a lord as he approaches Esau.

Jacob's panic attack is over when Esau runs to meet him, hugs him, grabs him by the neck, and kisses him. At this, they both weep. What else would long-time-estranged twins do? Now listen to some words of these two brothers' happy reunion found in Genesis 33:5-10:

> Then Esau looked up and saw the women and children. Who are these with you? he asked. Jacob answered, They are the children God has graciously given your servant. Then the maidservants and their children approached and bowed down. Next, Leah and her children came and bowed down. Last of all came Joseph and Rachel, and they too bowed down. Esau asked, What do you mean by all these droves I met? To find favor in your eyes, my lord, he said. But Esau said, I already have plenty, my brother. Keep what you have for yourself. No, please! said Jacob. If I have found favor in your eyes, accept this gift from me. For to see your face is like seeing the face of God, now that you have received me favorably.

After spending catch-up time and accepting Jacob's gifts, Esau departs and goes back to Seir, while Jacob goes to Succoth. Upon arriving safely back in Canaan, Jacob purchases some land from Hamor. On this land – as a result of what he's been through – he makes an altar which he calls El Elohe Israel.

Once again a blow of adversity strikes Jacob and his family, recorded in Genesis 34. While living in Shechem, Dinah, Jacob's only daughter by Leah, goes out to visit the women of the area. As she visits these women, she is noticed by a man, Shechem, who is the ruler's son. Shechem notices Dinah, is instantly infatuated, and desires to have her as his wife. His infatuation goes overboard to the point that he grabs and rapes her. Now Jacob's daughter is violated and this doesn't set too well with her brothers. They want to meet out justice and they want blood – of the man who raped their sister Dinah.

Shechem tells his father Hamor, a Hivite (Genesis 34:4), *"Get me this girl as my wife."* As a result of his son's desire for Dinah, Hamor goes out to meet with Jacob. In the meantime, Jacob hears about his daughter Dinah's defilement but doesn't say anything or do anything about this matter until his sons come back in from the fields. When they return and discover what happened to their sister Dinah, we see exactly how her brothers felt about this rape, *"they were filled with grief and fury"* Genesis 34:7). Now, low and Behold, who shows up for a conference? None other than the perpetrator of this evil, Shechem and his father, Hamor, show up to discuss marriage.

Hamor requests that Jacob and his sons give Dinah to Shechem as his wife. He appeals to their sense of community. He tells them to become part of his society, acquire land, and intermarry with them. Shechem chimes in and tells Jacob and his sons, 'Make the price for Dinah whatever you want and I will pay it. No price is too large.' On the surface, this seems fair.

Well Jacob's sons have a plan of their own, an unspoken one at that. They answer the two men cunningly because their sister has been raped. They hear no remorse and this doesn't sit too well. Jacob's sons tell Hamor and Shechem the only way they can intermarry and be a part of their society is if all their men are circumcised. Hiding their true motivation, they tell these men, 'This is our condition; take it or leave it.'

Shechem, who desperately wants Dinah for his wife agrees to the brother's condition. Right away, he goes to the gate of his city to speak with all the townspeople. He tells them of this great opportunity with many reasons to do what these men require.

'After all,' he says, 'when we intermarry with them, all the flocks and herds of theirs will become ours too. So, let's accept their condition of circumcision.' In this way, Hamor's community had a devious basis for agreement. One might wonder if Dinah's brothers had already figured this out.

Shechem must be a very convincing man because they all agree to be circumcised. Every male of their city will endure this procedure. This is where the cunning of Jacob's sons comes into the picture. Three days after these males are circumcised Dinah's brother's Simeon and Levi walk into the unsuspecting town and kill every male, including Hamor and Shechem.

Levi and Simeon take their sister from Shechem's house and leave. All Jacob's sons take every item of value from this town including animals, livestock, women and children. Did you notice above that Levi was one of the brothers who kill the men of this town? Levi would one day become one tribe of Israel; and not just a tribe but *the* tribe the LORD chooses to become the priests of the country. With what he does, "How can Levi be one of God's Chosen ones?" you might think.

Jacob is none too happy about what his sons Simeon and Levi did. He knows only too well he cannot stand against the strength and power of the Canaanites and Perizzites who live nearby. A single united attack by these two groups would destroy Jacob, his sons, and all of Israel.

The LORD intervenes once again. In Genesis 35:1, He tells Jacob, "Go up to Bethel and settle there, and build an altar there to God, who appeared to you when you were fleeing from your brother Esau." When Jacob pulls up his tent stakes and moves out on his way to Bethel, the fear of the LORD falls on surrounding towns so that no one pursues Jacob and his family. The LORD once again stepped in to protect his plan and choice. Chapter 35:9-12 tells how the LORD directs this untried group,

God appeared to him again and blessed him. God said to him, Your name is Jacob, but you will no longer be called Jacob; your name will be Israel....And God said to him: I am God Almighty; be fruitful and increase in number. A nation and a community of nations will come from you, and kings will come from your body. The land I gave to Abraham and Isaac I also give to you, and I will give this land to your descendants after you.

Just as the Lord said to Abraham and Sarah, he again reiterates to Jacob that part of the reason for the LORD's choice of this family line is that they will produce kings. But they will not produce just any kings. This is another piece of the puzzle on the way to complete the *chosen* picture.

What a life Jacob, now called Israel lived! He created or endured hostility from the womb. His life was one of endless struggle – with his brother, his father-in-law, his sons, and even with an angel. Yet this man overcame in all his struggles. He saw the LORD's hand deliver him from harm many times over. Israel, just as his grandfather Abraham did, spoke prophetically of his family and what the LORD would do through them. The Scriptures show a tremendous change of character within this man Israel and at least two of his sons.

Joseph – Israel's Lifeline

Joseph's life comes onto the scene front and center in this narrative. When Joseph's story begins in Genesis 37, he is 17 years of age. We're introduced to Joseph as he shepherds his father's flocks with brothers Asher, Dan, Gad and Naphtali. Evidently these men did something that didn't set right with Joseph because he tells his father about it when he sees him.

Talk about sibling rivalry! This family had sibling rivalry multiplied four ways because Jacob had 12 sons with four wives. Now it's about to get worse. The choice we're about to hear about can produce dire consequences in a family with only a single mother, let alone one with four mother's.

Jacob should have known better but he does the very thing that both his parents did. Isaac and Rebekah both chose a favorite son. Esau was Isaac's favorite and Jacob was Rebekah's favorite. Parental choices can produce great hostility; however, Jacob has a favorite son too. Here we go again! Joseph is Rachel's first son. That's not a good reason but Jacob loves Joseph more than any son, and makes him a special robe.

I can hear it now, 'Why can't you be like Joseph? He always does what's right. Why aren't your grades as good as Joseph's? Can't you shepherd as Joseph correctly does?' Joseph was probably a great son but he was younger, maybe sharper, maybe a harder worker, more than likely very naïve, and definitely a threat to the family status quo.

The tension is already thick enough to cut with a knife. Yes, that special coat did the trick. They were jealous before; now they see red. The coat of many colors doesn't help family unity or comradery among the brothers. Maybe it was only youthful ignorance but, to his brothers, he was nauseating at times. Maybe Joseph felt left-out and hurt. Before, his brothers only dislike him as a nuisance but now they can't stand to see him, let alone be around him. Oh yes, they hate him alright!

Immature, naïve Joseph only makes matters worse by sharing a recent dream with his brothers. Two dreams become the icing on his cake and seal his doom. Tongue-in-cheek, I don't know why Joseph's dream would make his brothers hate him all the more; after all, his dreams were only about work.

The dream was about work alright. After the rest of the brothers bind their sheaves of grain, Joseph's stands up. Well Joseph's didn't only stand; in fact, the rest of his brothers' stood up as well. But then – as he tells the dream – they gather round his sheave and bow to it. Oh, their "love" for Joseph just oozes out everywhere after he shares this dream. In Genesis 37:8 they respond, *"Will you actually rule us?"* If only they knew!

As if this wasn't bad enough, Joseph has another dream with the audacity to tell it to his entire family. Ignorance really is not bliss! In this dream, the sun, moon and eleven stars bow to Joseph. Jacob rebukes Joseph for his latest dream; in Genesis 37:10 he asks, *"Will your mother and I and your brothers actually come and bow down to the ground before you?"*

We read something interesting in verse 11. It says after Jacob had rebuked Joseph, he kept Joseph's dream in the back of his mind. We'll see if this boy is just a cocky jerk or if in fact there's more to his dreams and more to this boy than meets the eyes of his brothers, parents, and family. Time will tell!

Sometime later Jacob sends Joseph to the place where his brothers are grazing the flocks. Jacob wants Joseph to see how they're doing and bring word back. Now, I don't know if Jacob wants Joseph to spy on his brothers or if he simply wants to know how they're doing with the flocks. This much is sure: after the special coat and two dreams incidents, choosing to send a relative or servant would've been a much better choice but as the saying goes, "Hindsight is always 20/20 vision!"

Joseph arrives on the sheep-scene in Shechem. But there's only one problem; his brothers are nowhere to be found. He could return home but, always one to do his duty, he continues to look. A man finds him wandering from field to field, and tells him that his brothers moved on to Dothan.

Being an obedient son, Joseph sets off in pursuit of his brothers and flocks. Joseph finds his brother's just outside of Dothan, and they spot him as well. But they aren't too excited about their most recent Joseph-sighting. As Joseph is coming closer they already plot their next move and keep it all in the family. It's the same move Esau decided to make against his brother – murder. These guys were fed up with this *special* son and his superiority and domination dreams. Oh do they have a plan for him! What they say is recorded in Genesis 37:19-20,

> Here comes that dreamer! They said to each other. Come now, let's kill him and throw him into one of these cisterns and say that a ferocious animal devoured him. Then we'll see what comes of his dreams.

But Reuben doesn't want to kill his brother. Instead he tells his brothers, 'Let's just throw him into this dry cistern that is next to us, and not kill him.' Reuben's advice seems to work, at least for the time being. So when Joseph arrives and greets his brothers, the "welcoming committee" springs into action. They take him, strip him of his coat, and throw him into the cistern. Then they sit down to casually eat their meal.

About this time a caravan comes by. It is on its way to Egypt, loaded down with spices. Evidently Reuben moved away from the rest of his brothers at this point, and they decide to do one better than Reuben. They manufacture a plan to sell their brother as a slave to these traders instead of kill him; after all, they might as well make some money on this deal.

And that's exactly what these brothers do; they remove their brother Joseph from the dry cistern and hand him over to these merchants. What's the going slave-price? We might say it's the price they were paid – 20 pieces of silver – but the slave price was 30 pieces of silver. This indicates how much they hate him; and this may prophetically point to money in a sack.

Joseph, the favorite son, with a special gift of dreams enters a nightmare. His nightmarish existence is only beginning. The brothers now must come up with a ruse to fool their father. They concoct a plan, take Joseph's special coat, kill a goat, make plenty of rips and tears in the coat, and put the goat's blood all over it. Now they're ready to take their next step and present this special coat to their father for identification purposes.

After Jacob hears the story of what happened to his favorite son and sees the coat, Jacob is overcome with grief. He knows his son met his doom by the jaws of a wild animal. The rest of his family does their best to "comfort" their father, but he refuses their comfort and declares he will die in his grief and join his son, Joseph. How could they rip the heart out of their father's chest with this lie? How could they all live with this bold-faced lie and go on with life as if nothing happened?

After the caravan arrives in Egypt, its *special* cargo with the name of Joseph is unloaded to a man named Potiphar. He is sold to Potiphar, the captain of Pharaoh's guard. Although he is still in a state of shock, he hopes for better treatment; however, better treatment is not what he will endure!

Judah and Tamar

Around the time of Jacob's grief over Joseph's "death," another son leaves the family. In Genesis 38, we learn Judah goes to Adullam and stays with a man by the name of Hirah. After marriage and sons, tragedy and sin smacks Judah in the face. Is this what the LORD uses to bring Judah to repentance?

While Judah is in Adullam, he marries a Canaanite woman, and they have three sons. When Judah's firstborn, Er, grows up, Judah gets a wife for him named Tamar. But there's one problem; Er is WICKED! As a result of his wickedness, the LORD kills him. When Er dies, Judah tells his second-oldest son, Onan to marry Tamar in order to have a son for his brother. This arrangement doesn't sit well with Onan. He has his own plans, and this one doesn't fit his plans at all because he doesn't want to share his wealth with his dead brothers' "offspring."

As a result of his WICKED attitude, Onan refuses to get Tamar pregnant. Onan's refusal to honor his brothers' name to produce a son for his posterity doesn't sit well with the LORD; so he kills Onan as well. Judah already lost two of three sons and isn't about to lose his third son. So he tells Tamar to go back and live in her father's house as a widow because his third son is too young. Judah tells her he will give her Shelah for her husband when he grows up.

After Shelah is fully grown, Tamar notices that Judah has no intention of giving him to her as her husband. Maybe Tamar appealed this decision and was turned down, anyway she creates her own plan. If she can, she will remove her reproach of widowhood and childlessness. After all, this is only right!

Tamar discovers that Judah goes to Timnah when his sheep are being sheared. So Tamar enacts her plan. She takes off her widow's clothes, puts on a veil, disguises herself, and goes to the gate of Enaim, before Timnah. Judah must pass this way, so she sits and waits for her father-in-law to arrive.

Now, Judah's wife had only recently passed away, so when he sees Tamar sitting down he assumes she is a prostitute and bargains with her so he can sleep with her. As a pledge of payment, Judah gives Tamar his seal, cord and staff – quite a payment. Judah sleeps with Tamar and her plan literally "hatches;" she is now pregnant with Judah's child.

By now Tamar takes off her prostitutes' wardrobe and once again dons her widows' garb. However, her continually expanding abdomen can't remain hidden forever. At this point Judah is told his daughter-in-law is pregnant by prostitution. When Judah discovers his daughter-in-law's condition, he tells the messenger to have Tamar brought out and burned to death.

Judah is such a "compassionate, understanding" man; he wants justice. At this point, Tamar produces her trump card. As she is brought out, she sends Judah a message. The message contains the following words from Genesis 37:25, a man's seal, cord and staff. She says, *"I am pregnant by the man who owns these. See if you recognize whose seal, cord and staff these are."* When Judah sees his own property, he tells those around him, *"She is more righteous than I, since I wouldn't give her to my son Shelah."* And he did not sleep with her again.

Tamar gives birth to twin boys named Perez and Zerah. Judah has more than we've seen; the story ends better than the beginning. Perez is the forefather of Boaz who marries Ruth; both of these men are in King David's lineage. It is amazing how the LORD works through sin-history to expose his redemptive plan through the very ones who are chosen. As we learn from Judah's sin, we now go back to Joseph's story.

Joseph's Trial, Dungeon and Exaltation

Let's go back to the LORD's story of Joseph. Things look up for Joseph at the beginning of this narrative. While he lives with Potiphar, the Lord blesses Joseph's work. Potiphar notices that everything Joseph does prospers. With Joseph's success, Potiphar places him in charge of his entire household. The Lord blesses his work; with Joseph in charge everything Potiphar has – what he owns, household affairs and all his crops and lands –"produces success." Potiphar's only issue for each day is deciding what food he will eat as he works for Pharaoh.

A twist in the Joseph saga begins as Potiphar has a wife who notices this handsome, strong Hebrew slave. She does more than notice; she begins to ask Joseph to sleep with her. Joseph lets her know she is out of bounds; he will not touch her improperly! His response to her is found in Genesis 39:8-9,

> With me in charge, he told her, my master does not concern himself with anything in the house; everything he owns he has entrusted to my care. No one is greater in this house than I am. My master has withheld nothing from me except you, because you are his wife. How then could I do such a wicked thing and sin against God?

Joseph doesn't just refuse Potiphar's wife's sexual advances, he refuses to go anywhere near her. But this woman is cunning and slick; she knows the duties Joseph must perform each day and puts a planned meeting in the works. Here's how it unfolds: one day as Joseph goes into the house to perform his duties, no other servant is in the house with Potiphar's wife. She takes the initiative (v.12), grabs Joseph's cloak and tries to entice Joseph, saying, *"Come to bed with me!"* Joseph refuses her advance, slips out of her grasp, leaves his cloak in her hand, and exits the house. In other words, Joseph runs from evil.

Not to be outwitted by a slave, this seductive woman awaits her husband's return, already having all the evidence she needs to seal Joseph's doom. Not to be thwarted by any lack of real evidence, immediately after Joseph exits, she summons her household servants and tells them in Genesis 39:14-15,

She said to them, this Hebrew has been brought to us to make sport of us! He came in here to sleep with me, but I screamed. When he heard me scream for help, he left his cloak beside me and ran out of the house.

When Potiphar returns home, his wife immediately tells him about the rape incident with his Hebrew slave. Cunningly she shows "proof" of his attack, Joseph's cloak. Potiphar is enraged and, without an ear for an honest defense, Joseph is hauled off to jail. Joseph isn't taken to just any jail; instead, he throws him into prison where Pharaoh's prisoners are kept.

Again, another man is in charge of Joseph yet the prison warden notices something strange about this Hebrew slave. Whenever Joseph is put in charge, everything always ends in success. Imagine that! With this success, the warden places Joseph in charge of all prisoners and workings of the prison. Again, Joseph is successful and rises to the top – like cream. Eventually two of Pharaoh's attendants, his chief cupbearer and chief baker become new prisoners. He is specifically assigned to these two men and Joseph is responsible for their care.

One night both men have dreams; however, they don't know what their dreams mean and need someone to interpret them. It's amazing how God works to orchestrate details. He placed Joseph, His "Dream Revealer" in this same prison. When Joseph sees them in the morning, they seem downhearted so he asks them, 'Why are you so down today?' They admit they each had a dream but have no understanding of their meanings. They say, 'There's no one here to interpret our dreams.'

Joseph responds to their dismay in Genesis 40:8, *"Do not interpretations belong to God? Tell me your dreams."* So they both tell Joseph their dreams. Both dreams relate to their individual professions, involving grapes and baked goods. The cupbearer goes first and receives an interpretation. Joseph tells him in Genesis 40:13, "*Within three days Pharaoh will lift up your head and restore you to your position.*" Joseph asks a request of the cupbearer and tells his story in verses 14-15,

> *But when all goes well with you, remember me and show me kindness; mention me to Pharaoh and get me out of this prison. For I was forcibly carried off from the land of the Hebrews, and even here I have done nothing to deserve being put in a dungeon.*

Hearing the good report for the cupbearer, the chief baker tells Joseph his dream about three cake baskets and waits for its interpretation. Joseph tells the chief baker in Genesis 40:19, "*Within three days Pharaoh will lift off your head and hang you on a tree. And the birds will eat away your flesh.*" This is not the interpretation the chief baker wanted to hear.

Sure enough, three days later both men are removed from prison for Pharaoh's birthday. During his birthday feast he restores his chief cupbearer to his former position but the chief baker is impaled as Joseph told him. The chief cupbearer totally forgets about Joseph and his request for freedom and justice goes unheard. Never fear, the LORD's "Chosen" plan is still working.

Do you ever ask yourself what would have happened if the chief baker told Joseph his dream first? How was it that the chief cupbearer was first to tell his dream? What "dumb luck" some might say; well, maybe not. Maybe, just as there is so much more going on behind a movie set than what meets the eye, there is much more going on behind the curtain of this narrative than meets our eyes. Let's see how it unfolds.

Two years later, Joseph is still unnoticed, unreleased and unrepresented in prison. But his long wait is almost over, as more dreams continue. Pharaoh has not one but two dreams. In the morning, his thoughts trouble him and he needs to find out what his dreams mean. Since he feels the need to have his dreams explained, he summons all the wise men and magicians in Egypt. He tells his dreams but not one of them can tell him their meanings. What does he do now?

Finally, the chief cupbearer's memory is jogged and he remembers his promise to Joseph while he was in prison two years earlier. He tells Pharaoh, 'There's someone in Egypt with the ability to interpret dreams; he's a Hebrew and his name is Joseph. But, there's only one problem,' Pharaoh hears, 'Joseph is locked up in prison.' One of the most hurried prison releases has now commenced. Joseph is quickly dressed in new clothes and hurriedly brought in to see Pharaoh. When Pharaoh sees Joseph he briefly tells him his story in chapter 41:15:

> I had a dream, and no one can interpret it. But I have heard it said of you that when you hear a dream you can interpret it.

Joseph replies, 'Well that's not totally accurate. I can't give you the interpretation since it's only the LORD who knows the meaning of a dream; but the LORD can." Then Pharaoh tells his dreams of cattle and grain; each dream has two groups of seven. In one dream seven well fed, strong cows are eaten by seven sickly, scrawny cows. In the other, seven abundant heads of grain are swallowed up by seven dry, burnt heads of grain. Joseph tells Pharaoh his dreams are one-and-the-same.

"God has revealed to Pharaoh what he is about to do" Joseph says in Genesis 41:25. He goes on to tell Pharaoh the seven plump cows and seven beautiful heads of grain represent seven years of abundance for Egypt. But that after these seven extremely bountiful years a seven year drought – pictured in the sickly scrawny cows and dry burnt heads of grain – will make everyone forget all the years of plenty. Famine will ravage the land. Overall, the interpretation is both dreary and hopeful.

Joseph doesn't even wait to be asked; he proceeds to tell Pharaoh what he should do to prepare himself and nation for the seven years of devastation that will come. Pharaoh listens well to every word Joseph speaks. Because of Joseph's wisdom and knowledge, Pharaoh puts him in charge to ensure Egypt's survival during this upcoming extreme famine.

Joseph is now the number two man in all of Egypt. He wastes no time in travelling throughout Egypt in order to set up grain storage for the seven years of abundance. Joseph, being a number cruncher at heart, keeps track of the total amount of grain that's in storage throughout Egypt. But, eventually the number is too great to track, so Joseph quits keeping records.

When seven years of famine come, Egypt is adversely affected. The entire region, including Canaan, suffers too. The countries surrounding Egypt quickly run out of food and turn to Egypt for help; in God's providence, they can. By this time Joseph is already distributing grain to people in Egypt.

As the famine continues to drag on, Jacob hears some exciting news that comes out of Egypt. He hears 'Egypt has grain; and it's for sale.' Great! Anyone can travel to Egypt and buy it. After this great news, Jacob sends ten sons to Egypt to purchase food. Only Benjamin remains with Jacob in Canaan. There's no way Jacob will let anything happen to his youngest son like what happened to Joseph. He is on-guard this time.

After a long trip Joseph's brother's finally arrive in Egypt to find themselves in the presence of someone they know but don't recognize. He's second in command – in charge of Egypt's worldwide grain distribution. He's none other than their long-lost – but alive – brother Joseph, their little "braggart". Joseph immediately recognizes his brothers but their insight isn't quite as advanced, so his identify goes unnoticed to them.

For Joseph, there's no better opportunity to test his brothers' character. He doesn't treat them with kid gloves; in fact, he treats them a bit roughly. Yet they bow to the ground before him. Wait a minute; I thought these men would never bow down to

Joseph. That's the very thing they stated when he shared his dream with them in Genesis 37 when they asked:

Do you intend to reign over us?....Will your mother and I and your brothers actually come and bow down to the ground before you?

Here they are – bowing down to the very brother they despised and totally disregarded. His brothers had seen nothing in Joseph that would cause them to think well of him; of course, they did not see him without jaded eyes and godly appreciation. Maybe that's typical brotherly conduct to not appreciate one in your own home, but he deserved better. Now, he is well aware of them and able to inflict damage upon them to gain revenge but that's not in Joseph's thoughts or plan.

As these brothers stand before the governor of Egypt he speaks to them rather roughly and accuses them of coming to Egypt in order to spy on the land. Of course his brothers deny this charge and respond that they've only come to Egypt to buy food for their family. Joseph continues on with his accusation of their being spies but his brothers respond they are all from one family from the land of Canaan.

They tell Joseph there were originally twelve brothers but one died (Really?) and the youngest is with his father back in Canaan. Joseph acts as if he is unconvinced and tells them how they can prove their truthfulness. His plan for either their acquittal or conviction is this: nine brothers will remain in prison while the other one returns to Canaan to retrieve his youngest brother. Then he must return to Egypt with him and present him to the governor, Joseph, to earn the release of the other nine. His plan is quite ingenious as he certainly grabs their full attention. He puts them all behind bars to ponder their choice.

After his diatribe, he locks all his brothers up for three days. But on the third day he brings them out and tells them he fears the Lord. As a result of his fear of the Lord he will let them go and return to Canaan on only one condition – that one of them will remain behind in Egypt, in prison, while the other nine return to Canaan to get their youngest brother and bring him before Joseph. 'Do this,' Joseph says, 'And it will prove your innocence.' The decision is in the brother's court now.

This sets off a firestorm of regret and finger-pointing among the brothers where, at least privately, they admit their guilt and the wrong they did to their brother Joseph – all the while without knowing they were dealing with Joseph in this whole situation. Reuben tells them, 'I told you not to harm our brother; now, as a result of not listening to me, we must endure all this trouble. I wish you had listened.' Maybe their sins are finding them out.

All of this goes on without them realizing that Joseph understands every word they speak. The reason they thought he didn't understand was because he always spoke to them through an interpreter. At this point, Joseph can't bear the familial memories this conversation brings so he turns away from his brothers and begins to cry. After he recovers his composure he once again faces his brothers and takes Simeon, binds him while they watch, and has him taken away.

Joseph adds to the suspense when he commands those who fill his brother's bags of grain to place their payment of silver back in their bags and also give each brother provisions for their long trip home. Once they are given the bags of grain, the brothers load up their donkeys and begin their trip.

When they stop for the night, one brother opens his sack to feed his donkey to make an amazing fearful discovery. There, in top of his sack is the money he gave to buy the grain. When he tells the rest of his brothers, all shake with fear because they perceive the LORD's hand is raised against them. At least the LORD's grabbed their attention. With trepidation, they continue on their way home.

Their hard journey is over as they arrive once again in

Canaan with their father Jacob – with great fear and without Simeon. They immediately tell him the whole story, not leaving out one minute detail. Total honesty is almost unheard of in manly conversation. Men only want the facts; they believe the minor details are unimportant. Well, these brothers tell every single eerie detail to their father and their trauma is evident.

They tell Jacob of how, upon their arrival in Egypt, they appear before the lord of the land. And he immediately accuses them of being spies. But they told him, 'No, we're honest men, twelve brothers of one man from Canaan. One of our brothers died; the other is with our father at home.' After rehearsing the entire story to their father, they all empty their bags' contents and their silver falls out. This is too much for any of them to handle, including Jacob. They are scared stiff after seeing this.

Jacob is out of sorts and tells his sons, 'It's your fault that two of my sons are no longer with me. To make matters worse, now you want to take Benjamin away too?' Jacob says, 'There's no way I will allow Benjamin to go to Egypt, forget it!' Reuben pleads with his father and promises to take care of Benjamin himself. He puts up his two sons as security, but to no avail. Jacob will have none of it, and refuses to let Benjamin go. Jacob's extreme love for Rachel is still evident in this scene where he continues to protect her youngest son, Benjamin.

After all their grain is nearly consumed Jacob tells his sons to return to Egypt and once again buy some grain. But Judah says, 'Father, there's no way we can return to Egypt and buy grain. The governor of Egypt warned us severely.' He said, 'You'll not see me unless you return with the youngest brother.'

Judah tells Jacob, 'We will return to Egypt and buy more grain if you allow Benjamin to go with us. But if you don't send him with us, we won't make the trip.' We gain more insight into the brothers' conversation with Joseph at this point. We learn that

Joseph inquired about Benjamin and their father, Israel. Basically Joseph asked if Jacob was still alive without giving his intentions away. He so much wanted to see his father!

Now we easily see a character change took place in Judah. Remember he was the one who got his daughter-in-law pregnant. All the brothers had plotted Joseph's demise; now he takes responsibility for Benjamin's safety and return. We will see more of his character change later. Judah's explanation and offer of personal responsibility for his youngest brothers' safety finally convinces his father to let Benjamin go along.

Jacob tells his sons, 'Take twice the money you did before and take some of the lands' best products to give to the governor.' He says, 'Hopefully someone made a mistake; now go at once and return to the man.' In Genesis 43:14, "*And may God Almighty grant you mercy before the man so that he will let your other brother and Benjamin come back with you.*" With his blessing, the brothers once again depart for Egypt.

When they arrive in Joseph's presence, he notices they brought his blood-brother Benjamin. He tells his steward to take his brothers to his house and prepare a dinner. Joseph plans to have dinner with his brothers.

When the brothers arrive at the house, they're afraid for their lives as they believe they've been brought to Joseph's home because the silver was returned in their grain sacks. This is exactly what they tell Joseph's steward but he tells them he received their silver the last time and the Lord gave them a gift in their sacks. At this, he returns their brother Simeon to them.

Upon Joseph's arrival, the brothers again bow before him. They present their gifts and Joseph asks how they've been and about their father's welfare. They reply, "Your servant, our father, is alive and well." Once again they bow before him. He looks around, spies Benjamin, and asks, "Is this your youngest brother?" He utters a blessing to Benjamin, and is overcome by seeing his own mother's son. He leaves his brothers' presence to regain his composure. For all concerned, this is difficult.

When he reaches his room, Joseph allows himself to unload all the emotions bound up within him; he cries deeply. After composing himself, he returns and tells his servants to serve his brothers. Joseph is served by himself, his brother's by themselves, and the Egyptians present by themselves. Joseph made the seating arrangements and the brothers look around in amazement when they realize that they are all seated based on their age, from oldest to youngest. When each receives their heaping portion of food, they notice that Benjamin is given five times as much as any of them.

Joseph has another surprise for his brothers. If they thought their first trip was painful and difficult, wait until they leave this second time. The suspense builds. Joseph gives his steward these instructions in Genesis 44:1-2,

> Fill the men's sacks with as much food as they can carry, and put each man's silver in the mouth of his sack. Then put my cup, the silver one, in the mouth of the youngest one's sack, along with the silver for his grain.

Early in the morning Joseph's brothers are sent on their way so they can return home to Canaan. However, when the brothers have barely left the city, Joseph tells his steward to go after them. He tells him to ask his brothers, 'Why have you repaid good with evil by stealing Joseph's silver cup?'

When Joseph's steward catches up to them and repeats Joseph's words, they're once again shocked and ask, 'How can you say such a thing about us?' They remind him they returned their silver to him; in fact, they tried to pay him twice as much for their grain as the first time. They know their innocence and state, 'We're not thieves!' Their actual reply is in Genesis 44:9, "If any of your servants is found to have it, he will die; and the rest of us will become my lord's slaves." They were certain of their innocence and would prove it, they thought. But the "joke" is upon them this time. Will they be able to endure?

Now I don't know about you, but I don't think I would have made a statement like that especially after how everything was going for them lately. The steward responds, 'Okay, I'll do it your way, but whoever has the cup will become my slave. The rest of you can go free.' The steward begins to go through each bag, beginning with Reuben's and finally checking Benjamin's. Behold, in Benjamin's bag the steward finds Joseph's silver cup. What else is there to do? Each brother tears his clothes, gets back on their donkey, and returns to Joseph's house.

When the brothers return and appear before Joseph, they throw themselves at his feet (Again?). Joseph asks, 'What did you mean to prove by taking my cup? Don't you know I have ways of finding out things you have done?' Notice Judah speaks for the group. He answers Joseph in Genesis 44:16, 'There's nothing we can say to you about this, nothing at all. Is there any way for us to prove our innocence to you? Okay, the LORD uncovered our guilt. We are now all your slaves.' Joseph says, 'No way! Only the one who took my cup will be my slave. The rest of you are free to return to your father and families.'

Listen to Judah's reply to Joseph in verse 18, 'Please don't be angry with me. Allow me to speak freely. You're the one who inquired about our father and asked if we had other brothers. We told you our father is very old and our youngest brother who was born to him in old age is with him. We told you his brother is dead; he is the last of his mother's sons left, and his father adores him.'

But you said, 'Bring your youngest brother so I can see him myself.' We said, 'He can't leave his father; if he leaves, our father will die.' Your reply was, "Unless you bring your brother, you will never see my face again." 'When we returned home, the first thing we told our father was every word you said.'

'Later our father told us to go back and get some more grain. We told him we couldn't return to buy more grain unless our youngest brother accompanied us. Our father reminded us of how our other brother was torn to pieces by a wild animal.' He said, 'If you take my son and something happens to him, I won't be able to continue to live.'

'So now, if I return home to my father without my brother, this will be the cause of his death. Besides, I am the one who guaranteed our youngest brother's safety. I told my father if anything happened to his son, I would bear the blame the rest of my life. Please let me stay as your slave. Allow our youngest brother to return home to his father. Don't make me return to our father. I do not want to see the pain and grief on his face because my youngest brother hasn't returned with us.'

Judah has indeed changed! He's not the same man who left his father to marry a Canaanite woman. He's not the same man who ordered his daughter-in-law to be burned to death after his adultery with her. He's not the same brother who carelessly ate while Joseph pled for his safety and life. He's not the same man who sat on a huge lie about the death of Joseph. Indeed, He is a changed man.

Judah's plea on Benjamin's behalf is too much to take. Joseph can no longer control his emotions. Joseph tells all his attendants, "*Leave the room!*" He then says something the brothers can't believe. He says, "*I'm Joseph, your brother.*"

As if everything that happened over the last months wasn't enough! Now this Egyptian ruler tells them, in Hebrew no less, he's their long lost brother. Joseph encourages his shocked brothers with these words from Genesis 45:5-8

Do not be distressed and do not be angry with yourselves for selling me here because it was to save lives that God sent me ahead of you . . . But God sent me ahead of you to preserve for you a remnant on earth and to save your lives by a great deliverance. So then, it was not you who sent me here, but God.

Joseph explains more to his brothers, 'There's more to the story; the famine, which has only lasted for two years, has five more years to go. No crops will be planted nor harvested during these remaining years. Because of all of these things I need you to return quickly to Canaan. Gather up everything you own and our father Jacob and return to me. I will make sure you are allowed to live in the land of Goshen when you return.'

As his brothers turn to leave, Joseph adds one little comment found in Genesis 45:24, *"Don't quarrel on the way!"* Do you think Joseph knew his brothers' tendencies? Yep I think he did and wanted his family brought from Canaan to Egypt as quickly as possible – without delay and without argument.

When Joseph's brothers see their father they tell him the good news. They tell Israel (Jacob), 'Your son Joseph is still alive in Egypt. He's second in command under Pharaoh, the man we've been dealing with.' With this news, it's a wonder their father doesn't have a heart attack. After his shock wears off, Jacob prepares for the long, hard trip to Egypt that will now seem like a romp in the park since his heart is so light. A sparkle returns to Jacob's eyes as he cherishes the idea of reunion with his beloved son Joseph. He can hardly wait!

Israel sets out for Egypt with his entire family and every-thing they own. Upon arriving in Beersheba he offers sacrifices to the LORD of his father, Isaac. Later that night the LORD speaks to Israel in a vision, telling him he is God, the God of his father, and then continues in Genesis 46:3-4,

> Do not be afraid to go down to Egypt, for I will make you into a great nation there. I will go down to Egypt with you, and I will surely bring you back again. And Joseph's own hand will close your eyes.

This vision certainly brought great comfort to Jacob as he had endured so many struggles in his life to this point. The LORD was still with him to guide his soon-to-be complete family.

When Israel and his family arrive in Egypt, he sends one son ahead to Joseph to get directions to Goshen. Which son do you think he sends? The son he chooses for this task is Judah. Immediately upon hearing of his families' arrival, Joseph gets in his chariot and goes to Goshen to greet his father. And what a reunion these two men have; tears of joy flow long and hard as they celebrate their joyful reunion. Certainly the whole family joins in the festivities of this long-awaited needed reunion.

After telling Pharaoh of his family's arrival and bringing a few brothers to give credibility, Joseph brings in his father. Jacob blesses Pharaoh. As these two get acquainted, Pharaoh inquires as to the age of this patriarch. Jacob tells him, 'I am 130 years of age but my life's been one of long hard years and they don't equal those of my fathers.' As their conversation ends, Jacob once again blesses Pharaoh, and then leaves.

Joseph makes sure his family is well taken care of. He makes sure they live in the best land as Pharaoh had directed him. Joseph locates his family in the district of Rameses.

After 17 years of living in Egypt, Jacob's family has grown tremendously. Now 147 years old, this Patriarch is about to rest with his father Isaac and grandfather, Abraham. Joseph goes to see his father when Jacob summons. Jacob tells him to make sure after his death that he isn't buried in Egypt but he is taken back to Canaan and buried with his fathers. Joseph swears to his father that he will carry out his wishes.

Later Joseph is told his father is ill (Genesis 48). So Joseph takes both his sons, Manasseh and Ephraim, and goes to see his father. Upon notice of Joseph's arrival Jacob musters his remaining strength to sit up in bed. When Joseph comes into the room, Jacob reiterates to his son the blessing he received from the LORD while he was in Canaan. Jacob, in Genesis 48:4, says what the Lord told him at that time:

I am going to make you fruitful, and will increase your numbers. I will make you a community of peoples, and I will give this land as an everlasting possession to your descendants after you.

Because of this promise that Jacob tells Joseph, 'The two sons who were born to you here in Egypt, Manasseh and Ephraim, will be counted as my sons, as Reuben and Simeon.' When Jacob blesses Joseph, again we find a peculiar utterance in a Scriptural narrative; these words are in Genesis 48:15-16,

May the God before whom my fathers Abraham and Isaac walked, the God who has been my shepherd all my life to this day, the Angel who has delivered me from all harm may he bless these boys.

Did you notice the peculiarity in these verses? It's found in verse 16. Jacob, while he refers to the LORD, he uses the term *Angel*. Just who blesses "these boys" in this narrative? Is it the LORD or an angel? We saw earlier in Jacob's encounter with the angel — before meeting his brother Esau – that Jacob referred to this man in a unique way. Is there something more to this angel than what meets the eye?

Jacob sees Joseph's two sons Ephraim and Manasseh standing there and tells Joseph, "*Bring the boys to me so I can bless them.*" Jacob, an old man, has failing eyesight by this time so Joseph brings his sons as close to their grandfather as he can.

Joseph places his oldest son Manasseh in front of his father's right hand and puts Ephraim next to Jacob's left hand. Despite Joseph's well-meaning maneuvering of his sons, Jacob crosses his hands. In so doing, he crosses up Joseph as well. This patriarch places his left hand on Manasseh's head and his right hand on Ephraim's head. Knowing his father is nearly blind and believing his father isn't aware Manasseh is his oldest son, Joseph begins to take his father's right hand off Ephraim's head. He's about to place it on Manasseh's head when Jacob let's Joseph know, 'I know exactly what I'm doing even though my eyesight is bad.' Maybe his "eyesight" is perfect as far as the future goes. Jacob tells Joseph in Genesis 49:19, "*I know, my son, I know. He too will become a people, and he too will become great. Nevertheless, his younger brother will be greater than he."* With this, Jacob blesses Joseph's sons.

Do you really believe Jacob's choice of Ephraim over Manasseh was just dumb luck? Or, maybe this old man was just embarrassed by his mistake and refused to change what he did? Just maybe, this nearly blind man saw things even clearer than his son and grandsons saw. Maybe this patriarch saw things as clearly as his later descendants would in the land of Israel, those men the Hebrew Scriptures call seers and prophets. I think that, just as his grandfather Abraham saw, Jacob was seeing through prophetic eyes to give Ephraim the blessing of the firstborn.

Have you noticed the narrative happenings? A trend developed. That trend is: As the Lord works out the fulfillment of his promise to his friend Abraham often the choices don't include the firstborn as the chosen one. Remember the choices were Isaac over Ishmael, Jacob over Esau, Joseph over all other brothers, and here it's Ephraim over Manasseh. It will be Judah over the rest of Jacob's sons in our next chapter. It is Moses over Aaron, and David over his brothers. Already that's seven times where the LORD chooses the younger over the older.

While the Lord makes these *choosing* choices he also blesses the ones *not chosen*. These *not chosen ones* aren't kicked to the proverbial curb or cast aside and discarded as some think. The LORD "merely" chooses to bless one other than the firstborn as _The Chosen_ in these instances.

This nearly blind, but clearly "seeing" patriarch, Jacob, isn't finished. Jacob tells Joseph he is about to depart this life and reminds Joseph of an extremely important thing. That thing is this, *'One day the Lord will take the people of Israel on a return trip back to the land of Canaan.'* Just as his grandfather Abraham, Israel (Jacob) has tremendous faith. He truly believes the LORD will do exactly what he promised. He will once again return his promised family of Israel back to the land of promise in Canaan. These people will shortly have every ounce of their faith tested but will indeed possess the Land of Promise, just as the LORD himself promised. Exciting times will continue!

After blessing Joseph's sons, Jacob calls for all his sons in chapter 49. When they arrive he tells them to gather around so he can tell them what will occur in the coming days. How can this patriarch tell his sons future things unless he is a prophet or the LORD himself told him these future events? Beginning with Reuben, the firstborn, Jacob speaks to all his sons about past and future things, and gives each their individual blessing.

Please notice something specific in Genesis 49:8-12 when he blesses Judah. He says, *"Your brothers will praise you. Your hand will be on the neck of your enemies; your father's sons will bow down to you."* He continues with these words,

> You are a lion's cub, O Judah...Like a lion he crouches ... The scepter will not depart from Judah, nor the ruler's staff from between his feet, until he comes to whom it belongs and the obedience of the nations is his.

These prophetic words give a peek into what we find later as we continue in our progressing journey of this people by the name of Israel. Many don't realize the Hebrews of the Scriptures are called **Israel** or **Israelites** because their Patriarch Jacob had his name changed to Israel. The tribe of Judah will become King over the other tribes of Israel. Again, this is God's choosing lived out before Scripture's "eyes."

As Jacob reaches the end of his earthly sojourn he declares he will soon be gathered to his people. He makes a request in Genesis 49:29, *"Bury me with my fathers in the cave in the field of Ephron the Hittite."* When his words are finished this great patriarch lies back down on his bed, breathes his last breath, and is "gathered" to his people. What an amazing man and an amazing journey we have been following.

After his father's death, Joseph instructs physicians in his service to embalm his father. They take 40 days to embalm this man and Egypt mourns for Jacob for 70 days. That's quite a tribute to a great man who is a transplant to Egypt. Joseph and his brothers do exactly as they were told and take their father's body back to Canaan to bury him in the cave.

After Jacob's death, Joseph's brothers are consumed with undue alarm as we see in chapter 50. Now that their father is dead they wonder whether Joseph will take vengeance on them because of what they did to him when he was young. Instead Joseph reassures his brothers of the LORD's plan for him and them. Totally against their fears, Joseph assures them in Genesis 50:20, "*You intended to harm me, but God intended it for good to accomplish what is now being done, the saving of many lives.*" Despite their past wrongdoings, Joseph only has mercy and thoughts of the LORD's good in mind.

Just as his father had spoken prophetically to the 12 sons, Joseph speaks to the 11. He tells his brothers in the last chapter of Genesis, chapter 50:24, "*I am about to die.*" But that isn't all; he tells them what to expect in their future,

> But God will surely come to your aid and take you up out of this land to the land he promised on oath to Abraham, Isaac, and Jacob.

Joseph makes his brothers swear that when they leave Egypt they will also take his bones with them to bury them in the land of Canaan. Like his father, he wants to return home! Joseph again (verse 25) reiterates to his brothers that the Lord will do exactly as he promised, "*God will surely come to your aid.*" Joseph dies at the age of 110 and another great man has now been gathered to his fathers.

God never stops working his plan. So after Joseph dies, the LORD continues to fulfill the promises he gave to his friend Abraham to build a great nation through him. The people of Israel experience an explosion of growth to become a large number of people. They become so large, with a new Pharaoh who forgets or disregards their heritage, that they're brutalized for being who they are – Hebrews, the chosen ones of God who are called for a specific purpose.

As the LORD said, the people of Israel find themselves under a new Egyptian ruler, and in dire straits. Even though this period may look like the end of the beginning, it's really the beginning of the end for Israel in Egypt. In fact, the bigger they get, the more trouble they have in Egypt. Only God can work his plan to get them back to Canaan, and it will occur!

While we're about to leave the life of this amazing son of Israel, consider a brief sum of Joseph's life. He was an amazing boy and man who endured great adversity through the LORD's power. As a young lad who was never accepted by his brothers, he was totally loved and accepted by his father. He was sold into slavery by his brothers after they decide not to kill him. When he does what is right by not committing adultery as the LORD commands, he ends up in the dungeon. With no notice, he's thrown into the limelight and brought before Pharaoh, the king of Egypt. He endures over a decade of never seeing or hearing from his family, especially his father and brother Benjamin. Yet, the LORD used this man in a tremendous way. "He" saved his very family – the ones who treated him so poorly and sold him into slavery – from being destitute and obliterated. In all his life Joseph lives a life of praise to the LORD; He is the one who lead his life and would bring him home.

Moses, the Boy from the Ark

Egypt has a new king. We don't know whether he knew how Joseph saved Egypt and the Egyptians during the famine, or if he just chose to forget what Joseph did. Anyway, this king did notice the Israelites' exponential growth. Instead of seeing this as a bonus for Egypt, he's afraid of Israel's numbers and fears, as foreigners, they may help Egypt's enemies in later conflicts.

This new king seems to only think about how he can make the lives of the Israelites miserable. He places harsh task masters over the people; however, a strange thing happens. Instead of making the people of Israel weak and decreasing their numbers, this harsh treatment produces the opposite result and Israel only increases in numbers all the more.

Since forced labor doesn't bring about a decrease in Israelite numbers, this cruel king comes up with another plan to terminate Israelites. Pharaoh summons the Hebrew midwives and gives them the command, 'When you go to the birth of a Hebrew baby and see a boy has been born, kill him, but let all the girls live.' His hope is to significantly reduce male babies.

This plan doesn't work well because Hebrew midwives refuse to kill the boys who are born. So this ruthless king comes up with still another plan. He tells Israelites they must throw every boy that is born into the Nile River but can allow girl babies to live. This is the backdrop for our next narrative – the birth and life of another great Israelite by the name of Moses.

A Levite couple, Amram and Jochebed, have two lovely children, Miriam and Aaron, when they discover Jochebed is pregnant with their third child. She births a son and keeps him hidden for three months. When it's no longer possible to keep this child a secret, the family develops a plan to keep their baby boy alive. This couple decides to make a boat from a papyrus basket. So they coat the basket with tar and pitch, place their baby boy inside, and put their son among the reeds of the Nile River. Thinking well in advance, they also place their daughter nearby to keep watch over her baby brother.

I'm sure the location for their sons' "launching" was not a random choice. Amram and Jochebed probably knew in advance the location of their baby son's boat was the same place where Pharaoh's daughter went for her ritual bath. When Pharaoh's daughter arrives for her usual Nile bath, something unusual is floating among the reeds, and it isn't a crocodile.

Pharaoh's daughter notices this floating papyrus boat and sends a servant to get it. When she opens the basket, she finds a Hebrew baby inside who's not too happy with his new environment, and shows it by loud crying. His sister, Miriam, makes the most of this opportunity. She comes out of hiding and approaches Pharaoh's daughter to suggest she can get a Hebrew women to nurse the baby for her. Pharaoh's daughter agrees to Miriam's advice, so she races off to get her mother.

As Miriam returns with Jochebed, Pharaoh's daughter tells her to take the boy home to nurse him for her. She agrees to pay Jochebed for her help. This mother-and-son reunion probably seemed too good to be true as Jochebed was filled with joy and relief at her son's rescue and return. This family saves their baby son's life and receives him back into their lives to raise him a little longer. When Moses is weaned, Jochebed returns him to Pharaoh's daughter to raise him as her own son.

The first mention of the adult Moses in the Hebrew Scriptures is found in Exodus 2. Soon after Moses grows into a man, he desires to go and be among his own true people, the Israelites. One day as he observes their forced labor he notices an Egyptian beating a Hebrew. Moses looks around quickly, and goes to the aid of the Israelite. He kills the Egyptian and then buries him in the sand. But someone saw the dead Egyptian disappear under the sand at Moses' hand.

The following day, Moses shows up as if nothing has happened. Two Israelites get into an argument and a fight ensues. Moses confronts the one in the wrong and asks, 'Why are you hitting your fellow Hebrew?' Well, Moses' interference doesn't sit well with the Israelite in the wrong, so he asks Moses an eye opening question of rejection found in Exodus 2:14, "*Who made you ruler and judge over us? Are you thinking of killing me as you killed the Egyptian?*" It seems the jig's up!

Moses now knows what he did the day before is well known. When Pharaoh finds out about what Moses did, he tries to kill Moses but he escapes his grasp and flees for his life. Moses' refuge-choice is the land of Midian over 200 miles away. When Moses arrives in Midian, he goes and sits down by a well. This move leads to a new life-choice that changes his direction.

The Mysterious Bush that's Never Consumed

In Exodus 3, we once again encounter this mysterious figure called the Angel of the LORD. In this narrative Moses led his father-in-law's flock to the back side of the desert – all the way to the Mountain of the LORD, at Horeb.

Here, in the outback of Midian, the Angel of the LORD appears to Moses but his appearance is no normal appearance. In fact, the Angel of the LORD is "inside" a bush that is aflame but isn't consumed by the fire. As he watches this bush burn, he notices the fire continues and yet does not consume the bush. A curious Moses goes over for a closer look.

As Moses nears the burning bush in Exodus 3:4-5, the LORD calls out from the bush, *"Moses! Moses....Do not come any closer....Take off your sandals, for the place where you are standing is holy ground."* The LORD tells Moses he is the LORD of his father Amram and Abraham, Isaac and Jacob. At this, Moses hides his face because he's afraid to look at the LORD.

The LORD again speaks to Moses. He says 'I am well aware of the Israelites' suffering and their miserable lives as slaves in Egypt.' He tells Moses 'I have come down to rescue my people from the Egyptians. This rescue will eventually bring the Israelites back to the land of Canaan, the land I promised to Abraham, Isaac and Jacob.' He also tells Moses, 'Since I heard my people's cries and pleas for help in release, I will send you Moses back to Egypt – to Pharaoh himself.'

One may think Moses would be delighted to hear this news. After all, this was Moses' goal for his fellow Hebrews 40 years earlier when, as a much younger man, he came to the aid of a fellow Hebrew to deliver him from an Egyptian whom he killed. As we remember, Moses' attempted rescue provoked curt words, *"Who made you a ruler and judge over us?"* In fact, that rescue mission was the "cause" of him having to flee Egypt in the first place. Actually he is not too happy about this offer.

Because of all that, Moses wanted nothing to do with the LORD's plan. Moses hid in the desert for 40 years to save his life. He wasn't about to return to the pressure cooker of Egypt, let alone return to confront Pharaoh himself. No one needed to remind Moses of how life worked in Pharaoh's Egypt.

Moses knew if one was concerned to keep oneself alive, one must not enter Pharaoh's presence and bring news to make him livid. This was not how one stayed alive. This insanity was how someone died. Moses wasn't about to embark on a suicide mission! Even though Moses had no great love for livestock, he would just as soon stay in the desert and raise sheep and goats than lose his life by returning to Egypt. No, no, Moses would not take this mission! The Lord needed to find someone else.

Conversation between the LORD and Moses continues in Exodus 3:11 when Moses asks the LORD, *"Who am I that I should go to Pharaoh and bring the Israelites out of Egypt?"* The LORD tells Moses he will be with him and give him a sign to prove the LORD sent him back to his people. The LORD will give Moses a sign that all Israel will worship the LORD on Mt. Horeb after their release from Egypt. The LORD says, 'Tell the Israelite elders that "I Am" sent me.' He says the Israelite elders will listen to him but he's not yet convinced to accept the mission.

Exodus 4:1 continues this dialogue between Moses and the LORD. Moses, still hesitant to take this leadership position, asks the LORD a pertinent question, *"What if they don't believe me or listen to me and say, The LORD didn't appear to you?"* The LORD gives Moses three signs to prove the authenticity of his word to the elders of Israel. These signs are: a staff that can become a snake, a normal hand that turns leprous when placed inside his cloak, and water that turns to blood when poured on the ground. These three miracles are crucial signs to prove the authenticity of the LORD's word and direction through his signs.

After the Lord becomes angry with Moses for his stubborn

refusal to listen to Him, the LORD says his brother Aaron is on his way to find Moses. In Exodus 4:14 the LORD, in reference to his excuse about a lack of his speaking ability says, *"I know he can speak well,"* as he speaks of Aaron. He tells him that Aaron will speak for Moses, the LORD will help both of them speak, and he will put his words in both of their mouths.

Finally Moses is convinced. He returns to his father-in-law to tell him he must leave and return to Egypt. It's doubtful this discussion went this quickly but Moses puts his wife and two sons on donkeys and begins the long trip back to Egypt. When Moses arrives at Mount Sinai, he finds Aaron and tells him everything the LORD told him to say. Moses also shows him the signs the LORD told him to perform.

When Moses and Aaron arrive in Egypt the first thing they do is assemble the elders together. Aaron tells these men everything the LORD told Moses, who performs the LORD's signs before them. Their next step is to gain an audience with the king, Pharaoh. Remember that when Moses goes before Pharaoh, he doesn't go to represent himself. He is the LORD's spokesman who represents the LORD and Israel to Pharaoh.

When Moses and Aaron go to Pharaoh to tell him the LORD of Israel has a message for him in Exodus 5:1. Their message is, *"Let My people go, so that they may hold a festival to me in the desert."* Pharaoh, the abusive ruler of Egypt, isn't the least bit moved by this request. He asks them this question, *"Who is the Lord that I should obey him and let Israel go?"* This Egyptian King refuses to allow the Israelites to leave, just as the LORD told Moses he would do. He is not about to bow before the LORD of Israel!

This conversation only makes things harder on the Israelites. Pharaoh refuses to provide them with any straw to make bricks. He tells his slave drivers and Israelite foreman to tell the people, 'Go and find straw wherever you can; however, your brick production must not diminish in the least.' What does this cruel leader expect?

The gauntlet was thrown down by Pharaoh, and now the showdown commences. After Moses' three signs fail to move Pharaoh's hardened heart to allow Israel to leave, the LORD initiates the beginning of 10 plagues that will fall on Egypt and its people. Hang on, because the battle will be fierce.

During these plagues, Pharaoh barters with Moses over who will leave to go worship the LORD in the desert. Inch by stubborn inch Pharaoh gives concessions to Moses, but he still refuses to allow all Israel to leave. Just as the LORD knew and told Moses, it would come down to one last encounter and then Pharaoh would be only too happy to let Israel leave Egypt.

After this last plague – the death of the firstborn – the LORD provides deliverance for the people of Israel. Why does he do this? Does the LORD once again show indiscriminate favor to one group of people over another? Not according to what the Scriptures tell us. The LORD gave Pharaoh plenty of time with opportunity to do the right thing and let the Israelites leave and worship the LORD in the desert. In fact, the LORD had not asked Pharaoh to allow Israel to leave Egypt, return to the land of Canaan, and never to return to Egypt again.

Despite how little the LORD asks, however, Pharaoh stubbornly refuses to listen or give in to the LORD's demands. His stubborn refusal brought all ten plagues and this final showdown. Now this epic struggle is strength versus strength, and name versus name. The burning question is: Who will come out as the victor of this epic battle? Who will be shown as almighty; will it be the house of bondage or the LORD? Who will receive fame for their name; will it be Pharaoh and Egypt or the LORD and Israel? This last night in Egypt will decide these questions.

This night, called Passover, is a very special night. The LORD gave Moses specific instructions on how to handle this night of blood, death and substitution. We discover this in Exodus 12 when the LORD instructed Moses to have the Israelites take a year-old lamb for each family. This lamb or kid must be without defect, and is to be held until the 14th day.

At the right time, this lamb will be slaughtered. After this lamb is killed, they must take some blood and place it on the sides and tops of the doorframes of their dwellings. They must eat this lamb within this same locale; they must not go out of the house. The lamb must be roasted and eaten along with bitter herbs and unleavened bread.

None of this lamb may remain until morning. If any remains, it must be burned. The Israelites must eat this meal in haste, with their cloak tucked into their belts, with sandals on their feet and ready to leave, and with their staff in their hand. According to Exodus 12:11, *"It is the LORD's Passover."*

The blood on the doorframe of their homes will be a sign. When the angel of death sees the blood, he will <u>pass over</u> the home – thus the name of this night where life is the exchange for imminent death. Notice the part that substitution plays in this drama. The Passover lamb dies in the place or stead of the firstborn son of each family. Death will come to all firstborn males – animal and human alike – if they don't have lamb's blood on their doorframes. Verse 12 says,

> *I will pass through Egypt and strike down every firstborn — both men and animals — and I will bring judgment on all the gods of Egypt.*

The LORD continues in Exodus 12:13, *"When I see the blood, I will pass over you."* After all the years of slavery in a foreign land, the LORD brings his people out of Egypt, just as he had promised to his friend Abraham so many years before.

The LORD gave further Passover regulations in Exodus 12:43-49. Some regulations follow:

> *No foreigner is to eat of it. Any slave you have bought may eat of it after you have circumcised him, but a temporary resident and a hired worker may not eat of it. It must be eaten inside one house; take none of the meat outside the house. Do not break any of the bones. The*

whole community of Israel must celebrate it. An alien living among you who wants to celebrate the LORD's Passover must have all the males in his household circumcised; then he may take part like one born in the land. No uncircumcised male may eat of it. The same law applies to the native-born and to the alien living among you.

This is this beginning of Israel's Exodus from Egypt, the House of Bondage. What a beginning it is! These people of Israel will see the LORD defeat the Egyptians in battle. When Pharaoh hears that Israel indeed left Egypt, this very stubborn man once again hardens his heart and sets off in pursuit of Israel with his Army. However, Pharaoh and his Army are defeated by the LORD, and his Army drowns in the sea.

As Israel leaves Egypt and begins their journey towards Canaan the LORD speaks to Moses about his Torah. In Exodus 23:20, the LORD tells Moses he is sending a being – one who is surrounded by mystery – with the people of Israel during their journey. This "person" will be an angel. You may ask, "What's so mysterious about an angel going on this journey?" After all, angels are mentioned many times in the Hebrew Scriptures.

This angel's mystery is seen in verse 21 as the LORD's advice to Moses and Israel; he says, "*Pay attention to him and listen to what he says. Do not rebel against him; he will not forgive your rebellion since my Name is in him.*" The LORD goes on to tell the people He will be an enemy to their enemies and will oppose any who oppose them.

The LORD confirms his covenant with the people of Israel in Exodus 24:9. He tells Moses to come up to see him and bring Aaron, Nadab, Abihu and Israel's seventy elders. We read that, "*Moses and Aaron, Nadab, and Abihu, and the seventy elders of Israel went up and saw the God of Israel.*" But Exodus 24:11 says God, "*did not raise his hand against these leaders of the Israelites; they saw God, and they ate and drank.*"

The next seven chapters tell us about the Tabernacle that

Israel is commanded to make with the different furnishings, clothing for priests, altars, oil, incense, etc. The LORD tells Moses to make the Tabernacle according to the pattern. What is the pattern to which the LORD refers? The pattern is the heavenly tabernacle.

These commands bring us to the point in the narrative that addresses the great sin of Israel with the golden calf in Exodus 32. It also shows more of Moses' greatness. After this terrible sin by the Israelites in Exodus 32:30 Moses tells the people, *"You have committed a great sin. But now I will go up to the Lord; perhaps I can make atonement for your sin."* Moses continues to tell the Lord in verses 31-32,

> ...*what a great sin these people have committed! They have made themselves gods of gold. But now, please forgive their sin — but if not, then blot me out of the book you have written.*

Moses is willing for the LORD to blot out his name in order to save his people Israel. Was Moses attempting to atone for Israel's sin with his own life or prophetically pointing towards a better plan?

We learn about the Tent of Meeting in Exodus 33 as Moses directs the people to set up this tent outside the camp of Israel. Anyone who desired to inquire of the LORD could go out to this tent. When Moses enters the tent, we learn in verse 9, the pillar of cloud would come down and, *"stay at the entrance, while the Lord spoke with Moses."*

We find an interesting bit of information in Exodus 33:11, *"The LORD would speak to Moses face to face, as a man speaks with his friend."* The last part of verse 11 tells another point of interest in this story, *"Then Moses would return to the camp, but his young aide Joshua, son of Nun, did not leave the tent."* The LORD tells us Joshua, who will be Israel's next leader, often remains in the Tent of Meeting after Moses leaves. Have you ever wondered why he stayed behind and what he did?

Moses and the LORD speak again in Exodus 33:12. Moses tells the Lord, 'You've been telling me, *"Lead these people,"* but you haven't let me know whom you will send with me.' The LORD's reply is in verse 14, *"My Presence will go with you."* Just exactly how will the LORD's presence go with Moses and Israel on their journey? As this conversation continues in verse 18, Moses asks the LORD to show him his glory. To this request the LORD replies in Exodus 33:19,

> *I will cause all my goodness to pass in front of you, and I will proclaim my name, the LORD, in your presence.... you cannot see my face, for no one may see me and live.*

According to the Scripture Moses has been speaking to the LORD face-to-face for some time. Knowing this, how can the Scripture turn around and say Moses can't see the LORD's face? Just whose face has Moses been seeing and speaking to? This is where the LORD places Moses in the cleft of the rock nearby. The LORD instructs Moses in Exodus 33:22 and says,

> *When my glory passes by, I will put you in a cleft in the rock and cover you with my hand until I have passed by. Then I will remove my hand and you will see my back; but my face must not be seen.*

This is very interesting indeed because Moses, a man, will see the LORD's back but can't see his face. Is this God Almighty or someone else?

How do we reconcile Exodus 33:22 with an earlier verse in Exodus 24:9 where the LORD tells Moses to bring Aaron, Nadab, Abihu and the 70 elders of Israel up – and we're told all these men saw the LORD? This theme of Moses seeing the LORD face-to-face recurs throughout Moses' life. Remember, Exodus 33:11 just told us the LORD spoke to Moses *"face-to-face, as a man speaks with his friend."* So, what's going on here? How do we reconcile this seeming dilemma?

Normally one doesn't speak to a friend only when their back is turned. Deuteronomy 34:10 also says the LORD speaks with Moses *face to face*. How can we reconcile these apparent contradictions? Did the LORD speak to Moses *face to face* or not? If not, who is it? We'll get back to this dilemma.

Exodus 34:5-7 tells us about the new Stone Tablets that will replace the two originals Moses broke. We read about what happens when Moses goes back up on the mountain:

Then the LORD came down in the cloud and stood there with him and proclaimed his name: the LORD. And he passed in front of Moses proclaiming, 'The LORD, the LORD, the compassionate and gracious God, slow to anger, abounding in love and faithfulness, maintaining love to thousands, and forgiving wickedness, rebellion and sin. Yet he does not leave the guilty unpunished.

During Moses' intercession for the people in Exodus 34:9, he pleads with the LORD, *"Forgive our wickedness and our sin, and take us as your inheritance."* As the LORD continues to speak with Moses, we encounter another interesting aspect of the LORD. He says in Exodus 34:14, *"For the LORD, whose name is Jealous, is a jealous God."* Jealousy is another part of the LORD's essence? Is this a good thing? We will see.

The LORD also speaks to Moses of keeping the festivals and of another important recurring theme in Scripture. This theme is called redemption. The LORD tells Moses that all of Israel's firstborn sons must be redeemed.

As we continue on our journey with the people of Israel we encounter another interesting narrative in Numbers 21:4-9. In this narrative the people of Israel make their way around the land of Edom. As they travel, they grow impatient and begin to speak against the LORD and Moses.

Because they complain, the LORD sends venomous snakes among them. These snakes bite many people, and many Israelites die. As this plague continues, the people come to Moses and ask him to pray to the LORD on their behalf so the LORD will take the snakes away from them.

Moses prays for the people and the LORD provides a way of salvation. The LORD tells him how to cure the people of their snake bites and how to keep them from dying. 'Moses,' the LORD tells him, 'build a bronze replica,' "*Make a snake and put it up on a pole, just like the venomous snakes that have bitten the people.*"

The LORD also tells Moses to take this bronze replica on the pole and hold it up in the middle of the people. Any person who is bitten *and* looks on this snake will be spared, and they live. That's how this outbreak of death is stopped in the camp of Israel. Death is averted by a snake on a pole. When people in the throes of death look on this snake-on-a-pole, their lives are spared even though they were bitten by venomous snakes and sure death is minutes and for some, seconds away.

Now, let me ask another question here. Is it just the fact that these people *look* at the snake that makes them well? Or is something more involved? Is their trust involved at a deeper level than a mere glance? Later we will explore some of these questions.

Judah, a Star and a King

As we saw in Genesis when Jacob speaks concerning Judah and the fact that he would rule over his brothers, we see here in our next narrative more revelation concerning a King who will someday reign in Israel.

As Israel is camped near the plains of Moab, King Balak, who knows what Israel already did to the Amorites, is terrified. He wants to solve the problem of Israel being camped nearby. His solution requires him to send for a sorcerer named Balaam. He wants Balaam to come and place a curse on Israel so he will be able to defeat them in battle. However, when Balaam finally arrives, he does the exact opposite of what he was hired to do. Balaam blesses Israel, and not just once.

Balaam says of Israel, *"No misfortune is seen in Jacob, no misery observed in Israel. The Lord their God is with them; the shout of the King is among them"* in Numbers 23:21. We know from the Scriptures that the LORD is the King of Israel.

In Numbers 24:7 we again find Balaam speaking about Israel; he says, *"Their king will be greater than Agag."* We know the LORD has always been greater than Agag, so just who is this King who is being referenced? In verse 17, Balaam continues to speak of this coming King, *"I see him, but not now; I behold him, but not near. A star will come out of Jacob; a scepter will rise out of Israel."* Just who does this refer to? We'll get into this in detail later; please be patient in our dig for truth. Balaam continues his declarations of Israel's future in Numbers 24:9,

> Like a lion they crouch and lie down, like a lioness – who dares to rouse them? May those who bless you be blessed and those who curse you be cursed!

Once again the LORD continues to add to this mystery of Abraham's later descendant who will come onto the scene. Yet, as Balaam says above, he sees him! But at this point in Israel's history, he's not near nor ready to burst on the scene at any moment. Israel will definitely have a King. Although there will be many kings over the centuries, one King in particular will be chosen and identified in a special and particular way.

Moses the man we've been following through all the above verses, chapters and books was an amazing man. He stood before Egypt's king. He performed amazing miraculous wonders in Egypt and also during the Wilderness wanderings. He led Israel out of the House of Bondage, received the LORD's 10 Words, and even prophesied Israel's eventual rebellion.

Now we come to a song called the Song of Moses. After speaking of what will happen, due to Israel's rebellion against the Lord, we find these words in Deuteronomy 32:43,

> Rejoice, O nations, with his people, for he will avenge the blood of his servants; he will take vengeance on his enemies and make atonement for his land and people.

Three more themes are found in these verses. The *First theme* is rejoicing; the Gentiles rejoice together with Israel. This theme is also found many times in the books of the prophets.

The *Second theme* is about vengeance; the LORD takes vengeance on his enemies. Just who are the LORD's enemies? I know one thing certainly; I don't want to fit into that category! The LORD's enemies are those who inflict great harm on his people Israel. Remember the LORD told Abraham: "*I will bless those who bless you and curse those who curse you.*" Just as the LORD took vengeance on Assyria and Babylon, the LORD will once again take vengeance in the last days on His enemies. This vengeance of the LORD is His jealousy. His stated enemies happen to be the enemies of Israel.

The *third theme* is one of atonement; the LORD will make atonement for his land and people. All three themes are found in Israel's prophets who speak the LORD's words. We must ask another question: "Do these themes have anything to do with Messiah?" That's a question we're about to dig into.

We wrap up the story of Moses, the prophet/shepherd of Israel in Deuteronomy 34. Moses climbs up Mount Nebo to Pisgah, and the LORD shows him the entire land of Israel. He is told he will not go into this promised rest, the Land of Canaan. Years later, as we will see below, we read about Moses in a Jewish writing from the 1st Century CE. In this book, written long after Moses' death, we encounter Moses in the Promised Land with another prophet, the chariot rider Elijah no less. In this life, he cannot go in; however, in the Land of the Living, with life in the LORD's presence, Moses does go in.

Moses, the LORD's servant dies in Moab and is buried in the valley across from Beth Peor. Even today, no one knows where he is buried. Verse 7 tells us more about this amazing man; *"Moses was a hundred and twenty years old when he died, yet his eyes were not weak, nor his strength gone."* Deuteronomy 34:10 gives his fitting epitaph,

> *Since then, no prophet has risen in Israel like Moses, whom the LORD knew face to face, who did all those miraculous signs and wonders the LORD sent him to do in Egypt – to Pharaoh and to all his officials and to his whole land. For no one has ever shown the mighty power or performed the awesome deeds that Moses did in the sight of all Israel.*

Yes indeed, Moses' exploits in themselves would take a book to cover. It has been very interesting to read and study Moses' exploits as they relate to the man whom the LORD spoke with face-to-face.

The Commander of Israel's Army Meets the Commander of the Lord's Army

Joshua is another great man of the people of Israel. He was one of the original 12 men to spy out the land of Canaan before the people of Israel took possession of it. He was also Moses' right hand man and Israel's military commander.

We encounter another interesting man in the Joshua 5 narratives. In the ramp-up to Israel's first Canaanite battle at Jericho, Joshua 5:13 says that when he took an early morning reconnaissance walk near Jericho he looked up to see a man standing in front of him with a drawn sword in his hand.

Joshua, in charge of the nation and Army of Israel, goes to the man to ask his intentions. Joshua asks, "*Are you for us or for our enemies?*" I don't think the answer he receives is what he expects but the man replies, "*Neither, but as commander of the army of the LORD, I have now come.*" Joshua just had an encounter similar to Moses with the burning bush. This "man" tells Joshua, "*Take off your sandals, for the place where you are standing is holy.*" Who is this Commander of the LORD's Army?

Through Joshua, Israel finally arrives in their promised country, finally realizing the fulfillment of the promise that the LORD had given to Abraham. Just as Moses had done, Joshua leads Israel. He always encourages them to remain faithful to the LORD and believe his promises. In Joshua 24, he renews the LORD's covenant with the people of Israel at Shechem. Listen to his words in verses 14, 15 and 23,

> Now fear the LORD and serve him will all faithfulness. Throw away the gods your forefathers worshipped beyond the River and in Egypt, and serve the LORD. But if serving the LORD seems undesirable to you, then choose for yourselves this day whom you will serve, whether the gods your forefathers served beyond the River, or the gods of the Amorites, in whose land you are living. But as for me and my household, we will serve the LORD....throw away the foreign gods that are among you and yield your hearts to the LORD, the God of Israel.

Once again we encounter another important theme in the Hebrew Scriptures – the <u>heart</u>. Let's finish this section with the fulfilled promise that Joseph's brothers vow to him while they are still in Egypt. Remember, like his father, he told them to take his bones with them when they leave and to bury them in Canaan. This is what we find in Numbers 24:32,

> And Joseph's bones, which the Israelites had brought up from Egypt, were buried at Shechem in the tract of land that Jacob bought.

Joshua is another amazing character in the Scriptural narratives. He also faced tremendous adversity and extreme challenges. Remember, Joshua stayed in the presence of the LORD after Moses left the Tent of Meeting to talk longer. He saw the Army of Israel experience both victory and defeat. He was hoodwinked by a cunningly devised ruse performed by a small contingent of Israel's enemies. Whether in victory or defeat, his advice to the people of Israel – to remain faithful to the LORD by continually following him – is well known.

This brings two stories to a close, the promise to Joseph and the life of Joshua. We are now on the threshold of Israel's Judges who lead the people of Israel.

Samuel the One Received from the Lord

Samuel, the last judge of Israel, is another amazing man. His reality or existence is owed to 1) his mother's perseverance in prayer and 2) the choosing of the Lord. Samuel's mother, Hannah, couldn't bear children, let alone a son for her husband, Elkanah. Hannah isn't Elkanah's only wife. His other wife had children, and she abused Hannah by mocking her infertility. In fact, this abuse continued for years until Hannah's heart was broken with sorrow because of her continual barrenness.

One year while at the Tabernacle, Hannah, in bitterness of soul makes a vow to the LORD. This story is found in I Samuel 1. Hannah cries at the altar as she prays silently in her heart to the LORD. Her prayer to the LORD is found in 1 Samuel 1:11,

> ...if you will only look upon your servant's misery and remember me, and not forget your servant but give her a son, then I will give him to the LORD for all the days of his life.

Hannah didn't care if she was ridiculed for her prayers. Eli, the High Priest, thought she was drunk and rebuked her in verse 14, *"How long will you keep on getting drunk? Get rid of your wine."* Eli misunderstood Hannah but the LORD didn't. A short time later this barren woman was barren no longer. The LORD gave her a gift – the birth of a boy she named Samuel.

Hannah has a heart full of joy after the LORD answers her prayer for a child, specifically a son. In I Samuel 2, this grateful woman exalts the LORD as she declares his great deeds. Here's the last part of Hannah's prayer in verse 10; it says, *"The LORD will judge the ends of the earth. He will give strength to his king and exalt the horn of his anointed."* We find another reference to this *anointed one* in 1 Samuel 2:35. The following words were spoken by a prophet of Israel who came to Eli to deliver a word of the LORD. Here's what this prophet says,

> I will raise up for myself a faithful priest, who will do according to what is in my heart and mind. I will firmly establish his house, and he will minister before my anointed one always.

Remember that the above-two *anointed*-references were spoken before Israel even envisioned or asked for a king. Samuel is both a Judge and Prophet of Israel. Samuel begins to hear the LORD's voice at an *early* age as he attends to Eli the High Priest. Very early in his instruction under Eli, God was calling Samuel – to set his choice upon him – and it took three false starts before Eli realized God was calling Samuel. As he tries to sleep one night, he has a vision from the LORD and shares it with Eli in the morning. We hear much of this Judge/Prophet of Israel in 1 Samuel 3:19 in a few words,

> *The LORD was with Samuel as he grew up, and he let none of his words fall to the ground. And all Israel from Dan to Beersheba recognized that Samuel was attested as a prophet of the LORD. The LORD continued to appear at Shiloh, and there he revealed himself to Samuel through his word.*

Notice the important last three words – through His Word. Desiring to follow the LORD requires us to heed his Word. The LORD revealed himself to Samuel through his word.

During Samuel's time, the LORD gives the people of Israel a King as they demanded. But we see the Choice of the LORD again taking place. After rejecting Israel's initial King, Saul, the LORD chooses another King, one after His own heart. The LORD's King is the young man, David. The fact that this king is from the tribe of Judah is no mistake. It's not just the "luck of the draw." Do you remember the prophecy Jacob made over his sons right before his death? Judah would be ruler and King among his brothers. In First Samuel, we discover who the first King from the tribe of Judah will be; it's the shepherd boy David.

Even though the LORD rejects King Saul because of his disobedience, the Prophet/Judge Samuel continues to pray and mourn for King Saul. After all, he invested time in mentoring a man who was a failure as King. The LORD finally tells Samuel in 16:1 to take his horn, fill it with oil, and travel to Bethlehem.

The LORD tells Samuel why he will take this trip, "*I am*

sending you to Jesse of Bethlehem. I have chosen one of his sons to be king." The next action from Samuel is not of himself setting out on a journey to Bethlehem to anoint another king. After all, King Saul is very much alive. Samuel's act of obedience could cost him his life. The LORD tells Samuel how to complete his mission without raising King Saul's suspicions. He will go to Bethlehem to sacrifice to the LORD after inviting Jesse and his sons to attend. In traveling to Bethlehem unannounced, Samuel startles the elders of this little town but not Saul.

When Jesse and his sons arrive, Samuel notices Jesse's oldest son, Eliab (16:6). He must have been tall, dark and handsome. These verses don't tell us what stirred Samuel but upon seeing this son, he truly thought, 'Surely the LORD's anointed stands here before the LORD.' But he was wrong.

Who could blame Samuel for his assumption? After all, Scripture says Saul stood a head taller than any Israelite and was an impressive specimen. When Samuel sees another tall, impressive young man, who can blame him for thinking he just saw the new king of Israel? However, the LORD had other plans for this son of Jesse, and turning the kingdom over to him was not one of his plans. The LORD adjusts Samuel's perspective in verse 7 of chapter 16; as a result, he says,

> *Do not consider his appearance or his height, for I have rejected him. The LORD does not look at things man looks at. Man looks at the outward appearance, but the LORD looks at* <u>*the heart*</u>*.*

Once again we've run into this important theme of Scripture – <u>the heart</u>.

Samuel tells Jesse to present his next son for approval. Jesse sends Abinadab to walk in front of the prophet but Samuel tells Jesse, 'The LORD hasn't chosen this one either.' In all, seven of Jesse's sons parade before the prophet Samuel. Yet the LORD does not choose any of the first seven sons.

A puzzled Samuel asks Jesse in 1 Samuel 16:11, *"Are these all the sons you have?"* Jesse replies, *"There is still the youngest ... but he's tending the sheep."* You may not want to bring your son to meet the Prophet/Judge of Israel if he's hot and sweaty but there seems to be another reason for not calling David. Did Jesse think he wasn't worthy? Samuel tells Jesse, 'What are you waiting for; send someone to get this son and bring him to me.' So, when this cute young kid arrives in verse 12, the LORD tells Samuel, *"Rise and anoint him; he is the one."*

Once again, the leader of Israel will be a shepherd, just as Moses. The Shepherd of Israel just appointed a shepherd of Israel to be king! Another puzzle piece is found and revealed.

The Prophet Samuel definitely has a complete and full life. Yet even this Prophet and Judge is not without adversity. His sons don't follow the LORD as Samuel did; rather than meet the people's needs, they meet their own needs – like Eli's sons.

The first King Samuel appoints over Israel fails to measure up to his or God's expectations. Saul never quite makes up his mind whether he wants to follow the LORD's desires, his desires, or man's desires. He talks and walks out of both sides of his mouth and actions. Saul's failures, rebellion and disobedience troubles Samuel. After he anoints David as King, great trouble still exists in the kingdom.

Yet, this prophet is an amazing man in Israel's history. He followed the LORD from childhood, and the words of Torah were extremely important to this man. While he might not receive many votes, it would be difficult to find a better man than Samuel when it comes to obedience and following God.

David, the Psalter of Israel

Sometime after being anointed by Samuel, David finds himself in the employ of King Saul himself. This boy who would become Israel's Psalter begins playing the harp for this king – to settle King Saul's fragile nerves. And David's playing typically calms the savage beast, otherwise known as King Saul.

Now we embark on the amazing events of this shepherd boy's life. Jesse sends David to a military standoff between the Philistines and Israel in I Samuel 17. David's appearance on this battleground is due to the fact that three of his brothers are in King Saul's Army. Jesse gives David food to take to his brothers with the ulterior motive being that he wants to know how the battle is progressing and bring back word to him. With this, David departs and travels to the Valley of Elah.

When David arrives on the battlefield, he's just in time. Saul's army takes their position for battle; actually it's only saber rattling. David, not one to wait for something to happen, leaves his goodies with the keeper of supplies and runs out to greet his brothers. When he arrives, he greets his brothers and begins to talk with them about the battle. Eliab, remember he's David's oldest brother and maybe a bit jealous, wasn't happy to see him. In fact, he rebukes him and calls David cocky and wicked – two things far from the truth. This might give insight into why God rejected Eliab earlier as His choice for king.

While David catches up on brotherly news, a Philistine champion, Goliath steps forward from the Philistine line. Next this Philistine does what he's been doing every day for the past 40 days. He calls out to the army of Israel in 1 Samuel 17:8-10,

Goliath stood and shouted to the ranks of Israel, "Why do you come out and line up for battle? Am I not a Philistine, and are you not the servants of Saul? Choose a man and have him come down to me. If he is able to fight and kill me, we will become your subjects; but if I overpower him and kill him, you will become our subjects and serve us." Then the Philistine said, "This day I defy the ranks of Israel! Give me a man and let us fight each other."

Listen to Saul's response in 1 Samuel 17:11; *"On hearing the Philistine's words, Saul and all the Israelites were dismayed and terrified."* We all know why both Saul and his entire army are scared to death of this Philistine. This man, Goliath, is the Philistine's champion warrior and held that title since he was a youth. He strikes terror into enemies' hearts.

This guy is also huge. He stands over 9 feet tall. This isn't just an NFL lineman; this is an NFL lineman on steroids times two. This man is undefeated and is the reigning champion of this part of the world. These aren't like boxing matches; no, these are winner-take-all events, and the loser is dead. This is why we see the panic-stricken faces of Saul and his Army. And these men have endured this Philistine champion's words of doom for 40 days – day in and day out, morning and night.

All this and David hasn't even been on the battlefield for one day. He can't believe his ears! David, still a very young man, easily draws his brothers' ire. He asks the soldiers of Israel near him a question, *"What will be done for the man who kills this Philistine and removes this disgrace from Israel?"* Amazingly, this shepherd from Bethlehem doesn't live in fear of this bully champion from Gath. Why, you ask? Let David answer from 1 Samuel 17:45 as he responds to Goliath,

> *You come against me with sword and spear and javelin, but I come against you in the name of the LORD Almighty, the God of the armies of Israel, whom you have defied.*

David knows something that no one on the battlefield seems to know. David knows the LORD watches over his own with jealousy for his name and reputation. David found this out firsthand as a shepherd for his father's sheep. He is willing to step out and jealously defend the LORD's name and reputation.

On at least two occasions a wild animal came into the flock and carried off one of Jesse's plump sheep. When this happened,

David didn't just take his lumps; this shepherd ran after a lion and a bear and struck them. When these wild beasts turned around to devour David, he grabbed them by their hair and killed them. And now, David says that's the very same thing he's going to do to this Philistine champion. Except in this case, he's going to cut off the head of this defiant loud-mouth.

Some might ask, "How is this shepherd boy going to perform this amazing feat?" Well, he's going out after this Philistine with his sling, 5 stones, and the LORD's power. And, just as he promised this champion, he strikes him in the middle of his forehead with his first stone and this humungous man falls down head first. David, losing no time, runs over to him, removes his sword from its scabbard, and kills Goliath.

Do you think all this happened because a young cocky warrior wanted to make a name for himself? No! Remember back to when David was anointed as king. The Scriptures tell us in I Samuel 16:13 the following words, *"From that day on the Spirit of the LORD came upon David in power."* What David just did was not foolish. The one who spent time with the LORD while watching sheep received strength and confidence from the very one who directed his life. He received strength and humble confidence from the LORD.

This above narrative is just the beginning of David and his men's exploits. We see what type of heart this man has as we follow his story from beginning to end.

Against a "movie-story line," David doesn't live happily ever after. No, this man will flee for his life several times. Why, you ask? Simply, King Saul is very self-absorbed, and jealous of David. Even though Samuel anoints David as king, David never takes the initiative to kill King Saul and wrest the kingdom from this man from Benjamin. Instead David allows the LORD to deal with Saul as He chooses. David remains faithful to the LORD as his servant and chosen-King-in-waiting.

After David was King, near the end of his reign, he decides to build a permanent home for the Ark of the Lord. In David's time, the Ark was still kept inside a tent.

After initially telling David to go ahead with his plan to build the Temple, the prophet Nathan receives a word from the LORD. Nathan goes back to David to tell him he is not the one to build the Temple. Instead it will be Solomon, his son, who will build the Temple of the LORD. Speaking through Nathan, the LORD says this to David in 2 Samuel 7:11-12,

> The LORD declares to you that the LORD himself will establish a house for you: When your days are over and you rest with your fathers, I will raise up your offspring to succeed you, who will come from your own body, and I will establish his kingdom.

Here in 2 Samuel, the LORD promises to permanently establish a house for David. This promise says one of David's descendants will continually sit on Judah's throne. Now that's some promise. It's one we need to remember and another puzzle piece – another step towards completing our puzzle. This term *"the House of David"* is often referred to throughout the prophets' writings. Many times these references speak specifically of David's Son, Messiah.

Most stories I shared are positive but I wasn't trying to sugar-coat David's life. His life wasn't easy. He wasn't perfect. But David's life-goal was to obey the LORD. He twice escaped death from being pinned by King Saul's spear. He eventually fled and lived life as a hunted fugitive. Often his hiding places would be revealed to King Saul by David's own countrymen.

David's army wasn't necessarily what one would choose either, yet many of these men became champions in their own right. Let me relate a story from Scripture that speaks of the men David had.

I Samuel 22:2 gives the background on David's fighting men, *"All those who were in distress or in debt or discontented gathered around him, and he became their leader. About four hundred men were with him.*" At a later time some of these same men talked of stoning their leader, David, to death.

No, David didn't live a charmed life. Yes, it's true; he killed the giant Goliath and gained Israel a great victory. He was best friends with Saul's son, Jonathan. He even won the heart of Saul's daughter, Michal, and won her as his wife. However, he also had to survive all of Saul's attempts on his life and two coups by his own sons, among myriad other things.

David took over a divided nation and united them under his leadership. Many other events of near calamity could be added here but the above should suffice. However, in the midst of all David's trials, the LORD brought him through. And David, whose heart was after the LORD's, survived to see the scepter of his kingdom passed on to one son in peace, and see Solomon reign on his throne.

Jedidiah – David's Son – Loved by The LORD

Solomon, one of King David's sons is another specially chosen person of the Hebrew Scriptures. Remember, Solomon is Bathsheba's son. After the son from David's adulterous relationship dies, Solomon is born. God shows his mercy and choosing in Solomon. Second Samuel 12:24-25 says, *"The LORD loved him; and because the LORD loved him, he sent word through Nathan the prophet to name him Jedidiah"* to symbolize God's forgiveness of wayward David.

By the time Solomon sits on the throne of Israel, two of his brothers have already declared themselves to be king ahead of him. His two brothers who declared themselves king are Absalom and Adonijah. Their presumption does not bode well.

Neither of the brothers receive their father's blessing before they declare themselves king. As a result, Absalom's declaration and reign caused a short-lived civil war in which he was a casualty. Adonijah's declaration caused Nathan to send Bathsheba to see King David to protect her and Solomon from death. When David heard Adonijah was declared the new king, he immediately had Solomon declared the new ruler over Israel. When Adonijah heard this, he begged for his life from King Solomon. At least temporarily, Adonijah saved his neck.

David speaks specifically of Solomon as the next king when he speaks about his plans for the temple. He also speaks of the LORD's choosing through his family and of David himself. These references are in I Chronicles 28:4-7.

After telling the summoned officials that the LORD had not allowed him to build the temple, he relays the following:

> Yet the LORD, the God of Israel, chose me from my whole family to be king over Israel forever. He chose Judah as leader, and from the house of Judah he chose my family, and from my father's sons he was pleased to make me king over all Israel. Of all my sons, and the LORD has given me many, he has chosen my son Solomon to sit on the throne

of the kingdom of the LORD over Israel. He said to me: Solomon your son is the one who will build my house and my courts, for I have chosen him to be my son, and I will be his father. I will establish his kingdom forever.

Take notice of four critical things in this passage. **First**, is Solomon's *choice* by the LORD to replace David as King. Also notice Solomon is not the oldest of David's sons. **Second**, the LORD has chosen Solomon to be his *son*. **Third**, the LORD has chosen to be Solomon's *father*. **Fourth**, Solomon's house or dynasty will be like David's; in other words, being established *forever*. As far as Solomon's House is concerned, however, it is conditional on Solomon to be obedient to the LORD's directives.

One designation found in the Hebrew Scriptures often tells us King David was faithful to the LORD. This is partially why we read many references to the *House of David*. In contrast, we don't see a continuation in the House of Solomon.

Sadly, after beginning well and having the LORD appear to him on two occasions, Solomon's heart turns away from the LORD. Partially as a result of this turning away, it is David's House that eternally continues to reign in Judah's Kingdom.

Solomon's narrative is bittersweet. Someone so gifted and given such an amazing opportunity somehow lets the things of the LORD – especially obedience to Him – fall through the cracks. Many others do the same thing but the magnitude of wisdom and opportunity makes Solomon's fall so anticlimactic. He is eventually overcome by his wives' idolatry, exactly as the LORD had earlier warned against. Thankfully, per the end of Ecclesiastes, Solomon shows a repentant heart of sorts. Because of Solomon's divided heart and his rejection of the LORD's commands, the kingdom of Israel is divided into the Northern and Southern Kingdoms.

Scriptural Thematic Imagery

Torah, the Prophets and the Writings

At this point, our focus will change somewhat from the personal narratives to more specific themes. Since we have mentioned the House of David that points to his future Son and King, Messiah, we will look at certain Scriptural themes and concepts within these Scriptures, especially those concerning Messiah and his future mission to Israel.

First, let's look at the priesthood of Israel. We will begin in the Torah, go onto the prophets of Israel, and then to the Writings. The prophets of Israel were amazing men and women. They were continually used of the LORD to speak His words. Their primary themes were to call Israel back to the LORD.

Exodus 19 is our first narrative. We see in this Scriptural reference that it's the LORD who chooses Israel for himself. But he has a specific mission in mind for his people Israel.

The beginning of this specific distinctive is found in Exodus 19, verse 6, *"You will be for me a kingdom of priests and a holy nation."* This distinctness has two aspects, priesthood and holiness. This is our first reference to Israel being a nation of priests. Later in Exodus 27 we discover that Aaron, his sons and their descendants will be the specific priests of Israel. We also know the tribe of Levi will handle specific priestly duties.

Israel was not the first nation with priests. In fact the first Scriptural reference to a priest is tied to Abraham and is found in Genesis 14. An obscure man, Melchizedek, is called King of Salem and priest of the Creator of Heaven and earth. He blesses Abraham when he returns from decimating several kings and retrieving his nephew Lot. Abraham gives a tenth of the spoils he captured during this battle to this king/priest.

A key reference to Melchizedek in relation to Messiah is found in a Psalm of David – Psalm 110. The imagery found in this narrative of David speaks of Messiah's rule, triumph over his enemies, being arrayed in holy majesty, the judgment of the nations, and his being a priest after the "order" of Melchizedek. All this is interesting indeed, and worthy of serious study.

We will examine the office of the High Priest next. Leviticus 21:10 teaches the strict requirements for the LORD's High Priest. The High Priest, chosen by the LORD, plays an important and significant role in Israel's life. Later, we examine more Scriptural passages that pertain to the High Priest in *The King* and in *The Servant of the LORD* sections.

The Day of Atonement was a special day set apart each year. On this day, the High Priest offered a sacrifice, first for his own sin and then one for the people's sins. These offerings consisted of 2 male goats for a sin offering, one young bull for a sin offering, and a ram for a burnt offering. The High Priest next presented these 2 goats before the LORD and then the lots were cast. This is where we learn of the term *scapegoat*.

When the lot is cast, the goat on which the lot falls is sacrificed as a sin offering for the people. The second goat is kept alive and becomes the way of atonement for the people by being taken into the desert as the scapegoat.

After the High Priest finished offering the bull and goat, and made atonement for the Most Holy Place, the Tent of Meeting and altar, he brings out the live scapegoat. Aaron, the High Priest, lays both hands on the goat's head and confesses all the wickedness and sins of Israel and "puts them" on this goats' head. Once this is done, the scapegoat "carries away" all the sins of Israel into the desert where it's released. In this way all the people's sins are removed and carried away each year.

Only the High Priest is allowed to be inside the Tent of Meeting and Temple while he is inside the Most Holy Place. Leviticus 16:34 says, "*This is to be a lasting ordinance for you: Atonement is to be made once a year for all the sins of the Israelites.*"

Let me ask at this point, "What part of this ordinance made atonement for the High Priest and the people?" Leviticus 17 provides the answer to our question. According to verse 11, it's the blood that makes atonement for sins,

> ...the life of a creature is in the blood, and I have given it to you to make atonement for yourselves on the altar; it is the blood that makes atonement for one's life.

We dealt with Passover earlier but let's go into more detail here. The firstborn of Israel, Passover, and the Passover Lamb are tied together. Remember we already talked about an exchange that took place on the night Passover was instituted.

The cost of Israel's deliverance from the bondage of Egyptian slavery was secured through the Lamb's blood. Each house was required to take a lamb, kill it and sprinkle its blood on the door posts and over the door of each house where the Passover was eaten. This sprinkled blood and eaten lamb is what secures the life of each firstborn son. So, the lamb's blood helps purchase Israel's freedom and dies in the place of each firstborn son, keeping death from each family of Israel.

We see significance to the firstborn in the narrative in Exodus 13:2 where the Lord tells Moses:

> Consecrate to me every firstborn male. The first offspring of every womb among the Israelites belongs to me, whether man or animal.

Exodus 34:19-20 gives us another aspect concerning the firstborn, "The first offspring of every womb belongs to me...Redeem all your firstborn sons." As these verses show, the fact of redemption is seen within the Law's requirements concerning the firstborn of Israel.

This fact of a redemption that takes place within the Passover and Exodus of Israel is stated in Scripture repeatedly. Exodus 6:6 and 13:15 both speak of the LORD's redemption of Israel during the Passover and Exodus. Exodus 6:1-6 says:

Then the LORD said to Moses, "Now you will see what I will do to Pharaoh: Because of my mighty hand he will let them go; because of my mighty hand he will drive them out of his country." God also said to Moses, "I am the LORD. I appeared to Abraham, to Isaac and to Jacob as God Almighty, but by my name the LORD I did not make myself known to them. I also established my covenant with them to give them the land of Canaan, where they lived as aliens. Moreover, I have heard the groanings of the Israelites, whom the Egyptians are enslaving, and I have remembered my covenant. Therefore, say to the Israelites: I am the LORD, and I will bring you out from under the yoke of the Egyptians. I will free you from being slaves to them, and I will redeem you with an outstretched arm and with mighty acts of judgment."

These Hebrew Scriptures below refer to the redemption from Egypt and of the LORD being Israel's Redeemer: Exodus 15:13; Deuteronomy 7:8; 9:26; 13:5; 15:15; 21:8; 24:18; II Samuel 7:23; Is. 49:26; Micah 6:4; Psalm 74:2; 77:15; 78:35; 106:10; 107:2; 111:9; and I Chronicles 17:21.

The fact that the LORD Himself alone is the Redeemer of Israel is seen throughout the Hebrew Scriptures. Aside from Job 19:25 and Genesis 48:16, no Scriptural reference specifically speaks of a redeemer or redemption until the time of Passover and the Exodus from Egypt. Now back to the firstborn.

The LORD adds requirements concerning the firstborn in Numbers 3:12-13. Here the LORD speaks of the Levites:

I've taken the Levites from among the Israelites in place of the first male offspring of every Israelite woman. The Levites are mine, for all the firstborn are mine. When I struck down all the firstborn in Egypt, I set apart for myself every firstborn in Israel, whether man or animal. They are to be mine. I am the LORD.

In Numbers 3:40-50 the LORD continues on with his instructions concerning the firstborn of Israel. These verses say:

Count all the firstborn Israelite males....make a list of their names ....Take the Levites for me in place of all the firstborn....To redeem 273 firstborn....who exceed the number....collect five shekels for each one....Give the money for the redemption of the additional Israelites to Aaron and his sons....the redemption money from those who exceeded the number redeemed by the Levites. From the firstborn of the Israelites.

The LORD speaks of the reason for the Levites helping Aaron and his son with their duties in Numbers 8:16-18. Listen to what the LORD tells Moses in verse 19:

> *I have given the Levites as gifts to Aaron and his sons to do the work at the Tent of Meeting on behalf of the Israelites and to make atonement for them so that no plague will strike the Israelites when they go near the sanctuary.*

The LORD speaks of the firstborn of Israel in Numbers 18:15. Let me ask a question, "If an animal that could be redeemed was not redeemed, what happened to it?" This animal was killed. In the price paid to Aaron, and within the Levite duties, there was an exchange made. As a result of this exchange, atonement was made for the people of Israel so they were not destroyed when they came near the sanctuary. As a result of these things, the lamb of the Passover is seen as both an exchange and a type of redemption. Through these things, atonement was made for the people of Israel.

Redeem

To redeem or "the act of redemption" are important aspects within the Hebrew Scriptures to the people of Israel. Moses was dispatched by the LORD to go to Egypt and redeem the people of Israel from their captivity. Moses provided signs of proof to show the LORD sent him as Israel's redeemer. Yet, Israel still rejected him in the wilderness, choosing to follow a gold calf instead. Moses' own family and some of the leaders of Israel spoke against him, yet Moses was the LORD's spokesman who spoke the words the LORD gave him to speak.

There are primarily two different Hebrew words used for redeem and its derivatives in the Scriptures. These words speak of the kinsman redeemer and of a ransom being paid for their ransom or release. The first word used in the Kinsman Redeemer sense is where someone who is next of kin buys a person back. This exchange can also be when someone marries a widow. A great illustration of this can be found in the book of Ruth, with Boaz, who is her kinsman redeemer.

The second term means to sever, ransom, release and preserve. Isaiah 52:1-12 illustrates the implications of this term:

> *Awake, awake, O Zion, clothe yourself with strength. Put on your garments of splendor, O Jerusalem, the holy city. The uncircumcised and defiled will not enter you again. Shake off your dust; rise up, sit enthroned, O Jerusalem. Free yourself from the chains on your neck, O captive daughter of Zion. For this is what the LORD says: You were sold for nothing, and without money you will be redeemed. For this is what the Sovereign LORD says: At first my people went down to Egypt to live; lately; Assyria has oppressed them. And now what do I have here? declares the LORD. For my people have been taken away for nothing, and those who rule them mock, declares the LORD. And all day long my name is constantly blasphemed. Therefore my people will know my name; therefore in that day they will know that it is I who foretold it. Yes, it is I. How beautiful on the mountains are the feet of those who bring good news, who proclaim peace, who bring good tidings, who proclaim salvation, who say to Zion, Your God reigns! Listen! Your watchmen lift up their voices; together they shout for joy. When the LORD returns to Zion, they*

will see it with their own eyes. Burst into songs of joy together, you ruins of Jerusalem, for the LORD has comforted his people, he has redeemed Jerusalem. The LORD will lay bare his holy arm in the sight of all the nations, and all the ends of the earth will see the salvation of our God. Depart, depart, go out from there! Touch no unclean thing! Come out from it and be pure, you who carry the vessels of the LORD. But you will not leave in haste or go in flight; for the LORD will go before you, the God of Israel will be your rear guard.

Isaiah proclaims that the LORD will _redeem_ his people. He does this in sight of the nations, and all the earth will see the LORD's _salvation_. Both terms are used throughout Scripture as we see the LORD portrayed as the Redeemer of Israel. And both terms are used to describe what the LORD has done for Israel, what he is doing for Israel, and what he will do for future Israel. In the end, we must see it's the LORD who bought Israel through ransom and preservation – by His own strength.

Another term used repeatedly in messianic references is the word save and its derivatives. This term is expressed in four different Hebrew words: yeshuwah, yasha, yesha and teshu'ah. Yeshuwah means "something saved...deliverance...aid, victory, prosperity." Yasha means "to be open, wide or free... to be safe...succor"(rescue). Yesha means "liberty, deliverance, prosperity." Teshu'ah means to "rescue." All four words are used a multitude of times throughout Scripture. Even though the release from captivity, victory over enemies, etc. are used, there's another important aspect that's tied to these terms as well.

The prophet Isaiah uses these terms repeatedly in his writing. Let's take a look at a few of these narratives to see if we can find another term that is seen with the above four terms and linked in many instances. I will use four references: three from Isaiah, and one from Jeremiah. Isaiah 30:15 is our first reference that begins to speak of stillness and rest:

In repentance and rest is your salvation, in quietness and trust is your strength, but you would have none of it....Yet the LORD longs to be gracious to you; he rises to show you compassion. For the LORD is a God of justice. Blessed are all who wait for him! O people of Zion, who live in Jerusalem, you will weep no more….As soon as he hears, he will answer you….your teachers will be hidden no more; with your own eyes you will see them. Whether you turn to the right or to the left, your ears will hear a voice behind you, saying, This is the way; walk in it. Then you will defile your idols overlaid with silver and your images covered with gold; you will throw them away…and say to them, Away with you!

Isaiah 43:1-25, as our next reference, has the LORD speaking of his forming and creating Israel:

But now, this is what the LORD says – he who created you….he who formed thee, O Israel: Fear not, for I have redeemed you …you are mine….Do not be afraid, for I am with you; I will bring your children from the east and gather you from the west. I will say to the north, Give them up! and to the south, Do not hold them back. Bring my sons from afar and my daughters from the ends of the earth – everyone who is called by my name….Lead out those who have eyes but are blind, who have ears but are deaf. All the nations gather together and the peoples assemble. Which of them foretold this and proclaimed to us the former things? Let them bring in their witnesses to prove they were right….You are my witnesses, declares the LORD, and my servant whom I have chosen, so that you may know and believe me and understand that I am he….I, even I, am the LORD, and apart from me there is no savior…. Forget the former things; do not dwell on the past. See, I am doing a new thing! Now it springs up….I am making a way in the desert and streams in the wasteland….to give drink to my people, my chosen, the people I formed for myself that they may proclaim my praise….I have not burdened thee with grain offerings….But you have burdened me with your sins and wearied me with your offenses. I, even I, am he who blots out your transgressions, for my own sake, and remembers your sins no more.

Isaiah 59:1-20 is our third reference but we will only quote the first few verses,

Surely the arm of the LORD is not too short to save, nor his ear too dull to hear. But your iniquities have separated you from your God; your sins have hidden his face from you, so that he will not hear. For your hands are stained with blood…. So justice is far from us, and righteousness does not reach us….The LORD …saw that there was no one, he was appalled that there was no one to intervene; so his own arm worked salvation for him and his own righteousness sustained him...The redeemer will come to Zion, to those in Jacob who repent of their sins.

Our last reference is Jeremiah 30:11 where he speaks of Israel's sin and says,

I am with you and will save you....This is what the LORD says: Your wound is incurable....I have struck you as an enemy would ...because your guilt is so great....This is what the LORD says: I will restore the fortunes of Jacob's tents and have compassion on his dwellings; the city will be rebuilt on her ruins, and the palace will stand it its proper place.... I will punish all that oppress them. Their leader will be one of their own; their ruler will arise from among them. I will bring him near and he will come close to me, for who is he who will devote himself to be close to me....The fierce anger of the LORD will not turn back until he fully accomplishes the purposes of his heart. In days to come you will understand this.

Did you see the term intertwined in many redemption and salvation Scriptural references? The term is *sin*. So, in messianic passages, victory over the LORD's enemies and sin is offered; therefore, Messiah's mission is seen with at least two aspects – victory over Israel's enemies and sin but there's more.

As we continue our Scriptural journey we encounter the book of Daniel where we learn the Messiah has five parts to his mission. Daniel 9:24 says:

Seventy sevens are decreed for your people and your holy city to finish transgression, to put an end to sin, to atone for wickedness, to bring in everlasting righteousness, to seal up vision and prophecy and to anoint the most holy.

To place the emphasis of sin as seen within the Hebrew Scriptures in a new light, let's examine two additional passages. Isaiah 6 is our first reference; this narrative takes place after the death of King Uzziah. In the first verse the prophet Isaiah shares something he saw,

In the year that King Uzziah died, I saw the LORD seated on a throne, high and exalted, and the train of his robe filled the temple. Above him were seraphs, each with six wings:...they were calling to one another: Holy, holy, holy is the LORD Almighty; the whole earth is full of his glory. At the sound of their voices the doorposts and thresholds shook and the temple was filled with smoke. Woe to me! I cried. I am ruined! For I am a man of unclean lips, and I live among a people of unclean lips, and my eyes have seen the King, the LORD Almighty.

If Isaiah pronounces himself as ruined, what does that say about you and me? I can only speak for myself, but I know if a true prophet of the LORD cries, "*Woe to me,*" then I have no hope at all. And yet there's more to this narrative.

In verse 6 one of the two seraphs flies to where Isaiah is with something in his hand. He has something in his hand that he took from the altar with tongs. In his hand is a live coal and, with this live coal, he touches Isaiah's mouth. In verse 7, he says, "*See, this has touched your lips; your guilt is taken away and your sin atoned for.*" If the prophet Isaiah needs to have his sins atoned for, should that say anything to us today?

David, the great king of Israel is involved in our second reference. In this narrative David speaks about his mother and his description may not sound very nice. The reference is found in Psalm 51 and we'll begin in the 5th[7th] verse:

Surely I was sinful at birth, sinful from the time my mother conceived me. Surely you desire truth in the inner parts; you teach me wisdom in the inmost place. Cleanse me with hyssop, and I will be clean; wash me, and I will be whiter than snow. Let me hear joy and gladness; let the bones you have crushed rejoice. Hide your face from my sins and blot out my iniquity. Create in me a pure heart, O God, and renew a steadfast spirit within me. Do not cast me from your presence or take your Holy Spirit from me. Restore to me the joy of your salvation and grant me a willing spirit, to sustain me.

If Isaiah and David, two men of Israel, need the LORD's help to overcome sin, we need his help too!

Gentiles

We can see through the Scriptural narratives how the LORD is at work through Abraham and his lineage to honor his promise to bless all nations through him. Notice again that this blessing is for the nations as well as Abraham's descendants.

Jacob, or Israel, as he was renamed has a son, Joseph. Remember Joseph came to the rescue of Egypt, Canaan and all the surrounding nations. He rescues his part of the world from a seven-year famine and total devastation. One can say that Joseph was definitely a blessing to his part of the world.

One may ask, "I thought there was basically only war and devastation; what was Israel's blessing to the nations after the Canaan conquest?" That's a great question. Surely war and devastation were in play during those years, but surrounding nations could witness the blessing of the LORD through the nation of Israel. Let's examine an example below.

A Gentile woman from Jericho, Rahab, who was a prostitute no less, chose to follow the LORD of Israel because she knew he was the true God. This woman hid the two spies of Israel. In the text of Joshua 2:1, 8-9, and 11 we read her words,

> Then Joshua son of Nun secretly sent two spies from Shittim …. they went and entered the house of a prostitute named Rahab, and stayed there….Before the spies laid down for the night, she went up on the roof and said to them, "I know that the LORD has given this land to you….for the LORD your God is God in heaven above and on the earth below."

These are pretty amazing words, especially coming from a Gentile. This Gentile woman and her family were to be wiped out by the army of Israel. But because of this woman's faith in the LORD – shown because she rescues the two spies, the LORD saved her and her family from destruction. But Rahab isn't the only Gentile who was positively affected by Israel's LORD.

An enemy of Israel and a military commander of Aram is our next Lord-following-Gentile. We find this man's story in 2 Kings 5. What's even more amazing about this story is not the fact that this Gentile has leprosy but that this Gentiles' servant girl, a captive of war, who was taken from Israel, is the one with the desire to help her captor. She is the one who tells her master's wife to send her husband, this enemy military commander, to Israel to see the prophet in Samaria, who, she says will heal him from this disease. How did she know this or how did she reach this conclusion?

This man, Naaman, listens and does just that. He takes a trip to Samaria – to the prophet's house. The prophet of the Lord, Elisha, won't even leave his home to talk with this Gentile. Instead he sends his servant out to say, 'Go to the Jordan River and dip seven times' with a promise his leprosy will disappear.

This powerful proud man doesn't take too kindly to this prophet's welcome. He not only refused to greet him, but sent him to take a dip in a river, a dirty river no less. After all, he thought, 'The rivers of Aram are much better than the Jordan River.' In anger he turns back toward home, humiliated that this prophet had the nerve to ask him to do this thing.

I'm sure this man thought, 'After all the things I've done! I've traveled all the way from Aram, humbled myself by coming to this prophet's home, and now he wants to humiliate me by crawling into this forsaken Jordan River to dip myself. Just who does this man think he is? I'm not going to do this! I'm going back home!'

Somehow this man's servants talk him into giving the Jordan a try. So, reluctantly Naaman goes to the Jordan and dips in its waters seven times. To his utter amazement, he finds his leprosy totally disappeared. In great excitement, he returns to the Prophet Elisha's house to tell him the great news.

It's at this point, we find out that more than just this Gentiles' flesh was changed; his heart was changed as well! After

Elisha refuses Naaman's gifts; this man will not be refused what he requests next of this prophet from Samaria. Naaman requests to be given as much earth from Israel as two mules can carry. This request seems rather strange. Does this warrior just want some memento to remember his trip to Israel?

But Naaman fills in the details in 2 Kings 5:17, *"For your servant will never again make burnt offerings and sacrifices to any other god but the Lord."* In my estimation, the Lord made good on his promise to Abraham and he definitely blessed the nations. But this isn't the end. This blessing to Abraham, Isaac and Jacob has an ultimate fulfillment just as the Hebrew Scriptures tell us.

Ruth is another Gentile who was positively influenced by the Lord of Israel. And this woman became the ancestor of King David himself. The book of Ruth tells her story. She lost her husband and devastation struck her life through famine. Yet she discovered ultimate joy and fulfillment after leaving her native land to become part of the people of Israel.

Ruth 1 tells us that both of Naomi's sons died, leaving two widows. At this point, Naomi tells Ruth, her daughter-in-law, to return to her father's house like her sister-in-law had done. But Ruth is not persuaded to leave Naomi. Read her pledge of faith in Ruth 1:16, *"Don't urge me to leave you... Where you go, I will go...your people will be my people, and your God my God."* Ruth chose to leave her family and country behind to follow her mother-in-law into the great unknown – into a land with the Lord's promise.

A valid argument can be made that the blessing to the Gentiles is already underway – even during the time of the conquest of Canaan. And it is still underway today.

Israel and the Gentiles

Israelites and Gentiles form a topic we've already discussed briefly. But let's look at this in more detail in light of messianic references. Our first reference on this topic is Isaiah 2:2-4 as they speak about the mountain of the LORD:

In the last days the mountain of the LORD will be established as chief among the mountains; it will be raised above the hills, and all nations will stream to it. Many peoples will come and say, Come, let us go up to the mountain of the LORD, to the house of the God of Jacob. He will teach us his ways, so that we may walk in his paths. The law will go out from Zion, the word of the LORD from Jerusalem. He will judge between the nations and will settle disputes for many peoples.

This Root of Jesse is also mentioned in relation to Gentile nations in Isaiah 11:10, *"...In that day the Root of Jesse will stand as a banner for the peoples; the nations will rally to him, and his place of rest will be glorious."*

Gentiles and Israel are mentioned again in Isaiah 51:4, *"Listen to me, my people; hear me, my nation: The law will go out from me; my justice will become a light to the nations."*

In Isaiah 55, this narrative speaks of the covenant and faithful love promised to David. This promise to David was that one of his descendants would always sit on his throne. Here, Messiah, David's descendant is seen as being sent to Israel and the Gentiles. Verse 4 says:

See, I have made him a witness to the peoples.... Surely you will summon nations you know not, and nations that do not know you will hasten to you, because of the LORD your God, the Holy One of Israel, for he has endowed you will splendor.

In Isaiah 60:3 we learn the following concerning the nations, *"...Nations will come to your light, and kings to the brightness of your dawn."* Victory is also seen in Isaiah 61:11, *"So the Sovereign Lord will make righteousness and praise spring up before all nations."* We read of Righteousness and glory in Isaiah 62:2; *"The nations will see your righteousness, and all kings your glory."* Isaiah 66:19 speaks of the LORD's glory in reference to the Gentiles,

> *I will send some....to Tarshish...to the distant islands that have not heard of my fame or seen my glory. They will proclaim my glory among the nations.*

The LORD tells the prophet in Jeremiah 1:5 that he called him as a prophet from his mother's womb. And to whom has this prophet been called? He *"Appointed you as a prophet to the nations."* Why to the nations, one may ask? These nations are also mentioned in Chapter 16:19-21. In this reference these nations are coming to the LORD:

> *O LORD, to you the nations will come from the ends of the earth and say, "Our fathers possessed nothing but false gods ...." Therefore, I will teach them ... then they will know that my name is the LORD.*

Joel 3[4] is another amazing narrative that speaks of the end of days and the Gentiles. Beginning in Joel 3:12-21 [4:12-21], the LORD says,

> *Let the nations be roused; let them advance into the Valley of Jehoshaphat, for there I will sit to judge all the nations on every side. Swing the sickle, for the harvest is ripe. Come, trample the grapes, for the winepress is full and the vats overflow – so great is their wickedness! Multitudes, multitudes in the valley of decision! For the day of the LORD is near in the valley of decision. The sun and moon will be darkened, and the stars no longer shine. The LORD will roar from Zion and thunder from Jerusalem; the earth and the sky will tremble. But the LORD will be a refuge for his people, a stronghold for the people of Israel. Then you will know that I, the LORD your God, dwell in Zion, my holy hill. Jerusalem will be holy; never again will foreigners invade her. In that day the mountains will drip new wine, and the hills will flow with milk; all the ravines of Judah will run with water. A fountain will flow out of the LORD's house and will water the valley of acacias. But Egypt will be desolate, Edom a desert waste, because of violence done to the people of Judah, in whose land they shed innocent blood. Judah will be inhabited forever and Jerusalem through all generations. Their bloodguilt, which I have not pardoned, I will pardon. The LORD dwells in Zion!*

According to these verses, peace will come at last for Jerusalem and the people of Judah. The LORD himself stands against nations who seek Jerusalem's and Israel's demise. As stated elsewhere in Scripture, we see once again the fact that the LORD does not take lightly the shedding of innocent blood.

Another Gentile reference, found in Zephaniah 2:11 speaks of the Lord's awesomeness; it says:

The LORD will be awesome to them when he destroys all the gods of the land. The nations on every shore will worship him, every one in its own land.

The prophet, in Zechariah 2:10-13[14-16], speaks again of Gentile nations and the LORD living among his people. This passage tells us the following:

Shout and be glad, O Daughter of Zion. For I am coming, and I will live among you, declares the LORD. Many nations will be joined with the LORD in that day and will become my people. I will live among you and you will know that the LORD Almighty has sent me to you. The LORD will inherit Judah as his portion in the holy land and will again choose Jerusalem. Be still before the LORD, all mankind, because he has roused himself from his holy dwelling.

The LORD will also be sought by many nations as we hear in Zechariah 8:22-23; this reference says:

many peoples and powerful nations will come to Jerusalem to seek the LORD Almighty and to entreat him. This is what the LORD Almighty says: "In those days ten men from all languages and nations will take firm hold of one Jew by the hem of his robe and say, Let us go with you, because we have heard that God is with you."

Zechariah 9 continues to speak of Messiah and tells us in verse 10, *"...He will proclaim peace to the nations."*

Malachi 3:12 speaks concerning Israel and the Gentiles, and speaks of a delightful land, *"Then all nations will call you blessed, for yours will be a delightful land."*

In Psalm 22:27-28[28-29] David also tells us of the Gentiles who turn to the LORD, *"All the ends of the earth will remember and turn to the LORD, and all the families of the nations will bow down before him, for dominion belongs to the LORD and he rules over the nations."*

In Psalm 67 we read a song that asks the LORD to allow his salvation to come among the nations. Solomon also speaks of the Gentile nations serving the LORD in Psalm 72:11; it says, *"...All kings will bow down to him and all nations will serve him."*

Returning to David in Psalm 86:9, this king of Judah tells us of the time when, *"All the nations you have made will come and worship before you, O LORD; they will bring glory to your name."* Again in Psalm 108:3[4] David says, *"I will praise you, O LORD, among the nations."* Psalm 113:4 tells us, *"The LORD is exalted over all the nations, his glory above the heavens."* Psalm 117:1 speaks of all nations praising the LORD, *"Praise the LORD, all you nations; extol him, all you peoples."*

The below references are slightly different as they do not deal directly with messianic references. Passages from the book of Daniel also speak to the term Gentiles. In Daniel 4:2-3 [3:32-33], Nebuchadnezzar sends a proclamation to the nations,

> *It is my pleasure to tell you about the miraculous signs and wonders that the Most High God has performed for me. How great are his signs, how mighty his wonders! His kingdom is an eternal kingdom; his dominion endures from generation to generation.*

This Gentile king speaks of what he learned as a proud man at the hand of the LORD in Daniel 4:37[34],

> *Now I, Nebuchadnezzar, praise and exalt and glorify the King of heaven, because everything he does is right and all his ways are just. And those who walk in pride he is able to humble.*

Quite a difference exists between two kings when their response to the LORD is compared. Neither king had previously encountered the LORD. The two kings are the Pharaoh of The Exodus and Nebuchadnezzar of Babylon. Both are world rulers with great and powerful kingdoms. In both cases, the people of Israel (Judah) are captive in Egypt and Babylon respectively.

When Pharaoh is confronted with the LORD by His message to him, he stubbornly refuses to listen or do what the LORD tells him. As a result he loses everything, and his nation is devastated and ravished.

Nebuchadnezzar, who is initially disobedient, is amazed by the LORD's power and miraculous signs. This ungodly Gentile king learns a tremendous lesson as he is humbled by the LORD. For seven years, he temporarily loses his kingdom. This extremely proud man ends up wandering around like an animal, living with the wild animals and eating grass.

After a strange dream, Daniel gave Nebuchadnezzar the interpretation speaking of his kingdom loss. Daniel pleads with Nebuchadnezzar to repent of his sins and wickedness, and to begin to do what was right. Instead, this proud man decided to keep going down his own path. As a result, he lost his kingdom and his mind. Finally, at the end of the seven years, he repents and looks up to the LORD. As a result, his sanity is restored.

His look to the LORD was not just some ordinary glance but Nebuchadnezzar acknowledged the LORD was right and he was wrong. Repentance restored his sanity and kingdom. It also gave him a correct perspective of himself and the LORD as he acknowledged in the above verses.

In Daniel 5:1 and 5:17-6:1 [1-31], we read another perspective. King Belshazzar, the co-ruler, was having a feast with thousands of his nobles. They were in great spirits, getting drunk with their wine, but an upcoming event would bring them back to total sobriety. During his banquet, this ungodly king had gold and silver goblets Nebuchadnezzar took from the temple in Jerusalem brought in to the banquet. When the stolen goblets are brought in, banquet participants drink from them as they praise their gods.

At this point in the story a human hand appears and writes some words on the wall. What was previously a happy and cheerful time now turns into one of tremendous fear and trepidation. At once Belshazzar has all his wise men brought in to interpret the writing. But none can interpret it. Sure, they can read its words but don't know what these words mean.

Finally the Queen mother hears what happened and tells the king to call for Daniel. She says he will interpret the writing for the king. At once Belshazzar sends for Daniel who comes into the banquet. Listen to Daniel's words beginning in Daniel 5:18-23,

> O king, the Most High God gave your father Nebuchadnezzar sovereignty and greatness and glory and splendor. Because of his position he gave him, all the peoples and nations and men of every language dreaded and feared him. Those the king wanted to put to death, he put to death; those he wanted to spare, he spared; those he wanted to promote, he promoted; and those he wanted to humble, he humbled. But when his heart became arrogant and hardened with pride, he was deposed from his royal throne and stripped of his glory. He was driven away from people and given the mind of an animal; he lived with the wild donkeys and ate grass like cattle; and his body was drenched with the dew of heaven, until he acknowledged that the Most High God is sovereign over the kingdoms of men and sets over them anyone he wishes. But you his son, O Belshazzar, have not humbled yourself, though you knew all this. Instead, you have set yourself up against the LORD of heaven. You had goblets from his temple brought to you, and you and your nobles, your wives and your concubines drank wine from them. You praised the gods of silver and gold, of bronze, iron, wood and stone, which cannot see or hear or understand. But you did not honor the God who holds in his hand your life and all your ways.

Daniel proceeds to tell the meaning of the writing on the wall. This foolish king loses his kingdom and life that same night as the Medes take over Babylon and kill Belshazzar. All this happens as a result of his failure to follow his grandfather's example and worship the God of heaven.

Another king during Daniel's lifetime, Darius, learns that false gods don't bring life or save life. From Daniel and his example, he learns there is a LORD in heaven who does both.

Darius is duped into signing a foolish decree into law by some nobles. They want Daniel killed because of their jealousy. As a result of this decree, that Daniel doesn't obey, he is thrown into the lion's den. Not even this king, who likes Daniel very much, can save Daniel's life. Daniel 6 gives this narrative.

After a sleepless night at the break of day, Darius runs to the den of lions and frantically calls to his friend to see if, by some small hopeless chance, the LORD whom Daniel worships spared his servant. And what did this Gentile king discover? He discovered the LORD was very much alive and able to spare his servants. Daniel was not only alive; he was totally unharmed. As a result of all these events, Darius issues another decree and sends it to every part of his kingdom – to the nations. In Daniel 6:26 – 27[27], here's what is says,

> I issue a decree that in every part of my kingdom people must fear and reverence the God of Daniel. For he is the living God and he endures forever; his kingdom will not be destroyed, his dominion will never end. He rescues and he saves; he performs signs and wonders in the heavens and on the earth. He has rescued Daniel from the power of the lions.

Our last reference in Daniel 7:13-14 is a messianic reference that starts by speaking of a night vision,

> In my vision at night I looked, and there before me was one like a son of man, coming with the clouds of heaven. He approached the Ancient of Days and was led into his presence. He was given authority, glory and sovereign power; all peoples, nations and men of every language worshipped him. His dominion is an everlasting dominion that will not pass away, and his kingdom is one that will never be destroyed.

The imagery used here is interesting. One like a son of man who comes with the angels is led into the very presence of the LORD. This mysterious character is given sovereign power, glory and authority. And then we see something even more amazing, something that, at first glance, seems like blasphemy. **This son of man will be worshipped by all ethnicities!** He will receive a kingdom that will never be destroyed or end; in other words, an eternal kingdom. How can this Son of Man receive a forever-kingdom? Only the King of kings and LORD of Lords has a forever-kingdom that will never end; how can this be?

Let me ask another question. "How is it that the above Gentile kings who did not know the LORD and were, at the time, ruling over the Jewish people find it necessary to proclaim the LORD's greatness to the known world?" Here's amazing irony: even as Judah is in the middle of their Diaspora, the LORD still desires to be known, exalted and worshipped by Gentiles!

Why is this true? Does this relate in any way to the purpose of the Jewish people? Or are these references and narratives purely random events? To get proper understanding of The Chosen People, we need to see things from the LORD's perspective.

Over and over when looking at Messianic passages, we see that Israel and the Gentiles are both represented. As a nation of priests, Israel had the responsibility to display God, his greatness and salvation to the nations. This is exactly what we see taking place above in our Messianic references and also in the End of Days references.

Because some don't believe the writings of Daniel are true historical narratives, I inserted the reference below. Even Josephus, living in the 1st century CE, speaks about this man named Daniel. He speaks of him in his writing entitled, The Antiquities of the Jews. Let me quote just a part of what this Jewish priest by the name of Josephus has to say concerning this man named Daniel and about his writings. Josephus, beginning in Antiquities 10.11.7.276-.277 states the following,

> And indeed it so came to pass, that our nation suffered these things under Antiochus Epiphanes, according to Daniel's vision, and what he wrote many years before they came to pass. In the same manner Daniel also wrote concerning the Roman government, and that our country should be made desolate by them. All these things did this man leave in writing, as God had showed them to him, insomuch

*that such as read his prophecies and see how they have been
fulfilled, would wonder at the honor wherewith God honored Daniel.*

Let me end with the closing remarks of Book 10 by Josephus in
Antiquities 10.11.7.280:

*So that, by the aforementioned predictions of Daniel, those men
seem to me very much to err from the truth, who determine that God
exercises no providence over human affairs; for if that were the case,
that the world went on by mechanical necessity, we should not see
that all things would come to pass according to his prophecy.*

Resurrection

Resurrection is another theme in the Hebrew Scriptures that is tied together with Messiah. Let's look at some narratives that address this theme. We looked at a couple references in Psalm 2 and 16. Now let's take a look at four more references.

Isaiah 25:7-8 tells us that something will happen on a mountain. This has to do with death to broaden our view,

On this mountain he will destroy the shroud that enfolds all peoples, the sheet that covers all nations; he will swallow up death forever.

The subject of resurrection in light of Messiah is again broached in Isaiah 26:19-21. This section also speaks of the end-of-time judgment; verse 19 begins,

But your dead will live; their bodies will rise. You who dwell in the dust, wake up and shout for joy. Your dew is like the dew of the morning; the earth will give birth to her dead. Go, my people, enter your rooms and shut the doors behind you; hide yourselves for a little will while until his wrath has passed by. See, the LORD is coming out of his dwelling to punish the people of the earth for their sins. The earth will disclose the blood shed upon her; she will conceal her slain no longer.

Hosea 13:14 also speaks of this time of redemption. Hosea speaks of a coming redemption with a different slant,

I will ransom them from the power of the grave; I will redeem them from death. Where, O death, are your plagues? Where, O grave, is your destruction?

Job is seen by many scholars as being written around the time of the patriarch Abraham – maybe before. In chapter 19, Job also speaks of the end and one thing that will happen at that time. Let's start in verse 25 and go through 27; Job says,

I know that my Redeemer lives, and that in the end he will stand upon the earth. And after my skin has been destroyed, yet in my flesh I will see God; I myself will see him with my own eyes – I, and not another. How my heart yearns within me!

These words may seem a little graphic, but Job speaks about what will happen to his decomposed body at the last day. He says, even though his flesh has been destroyed – in his flesh, with his own eyes he will see the Lord. This is significant as Job says his body will be resurrected and changed.

Aspects of Messiah

The King, The Prophet, The Servant, The Shepherd

At this point, I want to delve into the One who would bless Israel as well as the Gentiles, the One called Messiah.

We will look at what the prophets of Israel said about these themes. **First,** we will touch on the references pointing to this coming *King of Israel*. **Second,** I want to look at *The Prophet* referred to by Moses in Deuteronomy 18. **Third,** will be the *Servant of Israel*. **Fourth,** we'll look at the *Shepherd of Israel*. Let's take a look at these four themes as seen through the aspect of the coming Messiah.

Please stay with me while we travel through these narratives and references. Sometimes these references will come one right after another without much dialogue. However stay with me as I lay the groundwork for what I will be showing later concerning Messiah – using these very same aspects of Messiah. Let's see what we can discover next.

The King

In I Samuel 2 we find our first and early prophetic reference to Messiah. We read of Samuel's mother, Hannah, and her prayer of thanksgiving to the Lord. She gives praise because of the son the LORD gave her.

Earlier we talked about this woman's bitter struggle with her husband's other wife, Peninnah, who continually provoked Hannah to tears as she ridiculed her because of her inability to bear children. Listen to this amazing woman's prayer as she speaks of who the LORD is, what He knows, how He weighs thoughts and deeds, and who He exalts. This is found in 1 Samuel 2:1-10,

> *My heart rejoices in the LORD; in the LORD my horn is lifted high. My mouth boasts over my enemies, for I delight in your deliverance. There is no one holy like the LORD; there is no one besides you; there is no Rock like our God. Do not keep talking so proudly... for the LORD is a God who knows, and by him deeds are weighed. The bows of the warriors are broken, but those who stumbled are armed with strength....She who was barren has borne seven children, but she who has had many sons pines away....The LORD ...brings down to the grave and raises up... He raises the poor from the dust and lifts the needy from the ash heap....He will guard the feet of his saints, but the wicked will be silenced in darkness. It is not by strength that one prevails; those who oppose the LORD will be shattered. He will thunder against them from heaven; the LORD will judge the ends of the earth. He will give strength to his king and exalt the horn of his anointed.*

Verse 10 speaks of the LORD giving strength to <u>his king</u> and exalting the horn of <u>his anointed</u>. Who is this king who receives strength and exaltation? Could this king be Messiah? I believe so since the LORD doesn't need to give himself strength or exaltation. Also, at the time of this Scriptural reference, Israel's leaders are their judges rather than their later kings.

Two other quotes in the book of Samuel fall in line with verse 10 above. These quotes are found in 2 Samuel 22 and 23. These references tell us a lot about the coming one, Messiah. The first reference is King David's song of praise to the Lord in 2 Samuel 22:44 to 51. David says,

> *You have delivered me from the attacks of the people; you have preserved me as the head of nations. People I did not know are subject to me, and foreigners come cringing to me; as soon as they hear me, they obey me….The LORD lives! Praise be to my Rock! Exalted be God, the Rock, my Savior….Therefore I will praise you O LORD among the nations….He gives his king great victories; he shows unfailing kindness to his anointed, to David and his descendants forever.*

Our next reference is 2 Samuel 23:1 as David uses prophetic words and imagery to speak of his house,

> *The oracle of David son of Jesse, the oracle of the man exalted by the Most High, the man anointed by the God of Jacob, Israel's singer of songs: The Spirit of the LORD spoke through me; his word was on my tongue. The God of Israel spoke, the Rock of Israel said to me: When one rules over men in righteousness, when he rules in the fear of God…Is not my house right with God? Has he not made an everlasting covenant arranged and secured in every part….But evil men are all to be cast aside like thorns.*

Many of the next quotes concern Messiah spoken by the prophets. Just as David was, Messiah will be attacked but also delivered from his enemies. He will conquer and rule over the Gentiles. The Gentile nations will be placed under the feet of Messiah. As David was, Messiah will be exalted above his foes, the violent men who desire his demise. David's son, Messiah will be the Bright Morning Star, and a light to the Gentiles. Messiah will praise the Lord before all nations as he fulfills the LORD's promise to Abraham and David by continuing the rule of David promised above. His rule will be one of Righteousness, Peace and in the fear of the LORD.

Notice also in 2 Samuel 23:2 that David speaks as the prophets of Israel did. He says,

> *The Spirit of the LORD spoke through me; his word was on my tongue. The God of Israel spoke, the Rock of Israel said to me.*

Isaiah 7 speaks of one of King David's descendants by the name of King Ahaz of Judah. Unlike David, Ahaz did not follow the LORD. From this narrative we see this king was not concerned about

what the LORD thought or about his word. In this narrative two evil kings have a terrible agenda, from the LORD's perspective. Their agenda is to defeat Judah at all cost. These two kings are King Rezin of Aram and King Pekah of Israel. However, before going to Isaiah 7, let's gain more insight about this descendent of David by looking at what 2 Kings 16 and 2 Chronicles 28 has to say about King Ahaz.

Listen to what the Hebrew Scriptures say about this king of Judah in 2 Kings 16:2, *"Ahaz was twenty years old when he became king, and he reigned in Jerusalem sixteen years. Unlike David, his father, he did not do what was right in the eyes of the LORD his God."* Verse 3 tells us he walked in the ways of the evil kings of Israel, and even sacrificed one of his sons in the fire.

A look at 2 Chronicles 28 gives more details concerning this above king of Judah and his fight against both the kings of Aram and the Northern Kingdom of Israel. Here, King Aram had already defeated Judah and taken many of them as prisoners to Damascus. King Pekah of Israel also defeated King Ahaz and took prisoners, some 200,000 women and children. After these events, King Ahaz pleads with Tiglath-Pileser, the king of Assyria to come and help him in his fight against these two kings.

These events provide some backdrop to our Isaiah 7 narrative. Both King Rezin and King Pekah marched up to Jerusalem and attacked her but couldn't overpower her.

When Ahaz and the people of Jerusalem hear that these two kings allied themselves together, both the king and his people feared for their lives. After all, we already know of the large toll these two kings inflicted upon Judah.

King Ahaz takes the silver and gold from the Temple and what was in the Palace treasuries and sends it to Tiglath-Pileser so he will come to his aid. King Ahaz never once thought about asking the LORD for His help. Tiglath-Pileser came and defeated both kings, but according to the Scriptures, Tiglath-Pileser didn't provide King Ahaz with the help he so desired.

Without looking to the LORD, it was foolish for King Ahaz to imagine Tiglath-Pileser would do exactly as he wanted. Whereas King Ahaz wanted protection for his country, Tiglath-Pileser conquered the two troubling kings but then laid siege against Jerusalem for the expansion of his own kingdom. This is where things really fall apart for King Ahaz as he sought help from false gods. His stubbornness built a high wall against the leading of the LORD he should have followed.

As a result of these happenings the LORD tells the prophet Isaiah, "*Go with your son and meet Ahaz at the end of the aqueduct of the Upper Pool.*" Here are the words the LORD gave Isaiah to relay to King Ahaz of Judah, found in Isaiah 7:4-6,

> *Be careful, keep calm and don't be afraid. Do not lose heart because of these two smoldering stubs of firewood – because of the fierce anger of Rezin and Aram and of the son of Remaliah. Aram, Ephraim and Remaliah's son have plotted your ruin, saying, let us invade Judah; let us tear it apart and divide it among ourselves, and make the son of Tabeel king over it.*

After everything that happened, especially knowing Ahaz' lack of trust in the LORD, I don't know if I would be comforted by Isaiah's words of calm. After all, these two kings were not men who said they were going to do something without following through. They both made good on their threats of conquest. But evidently the LORD was not too impressed with these king's abilities of warfare. The LORD had something else in store to demonstrate His power.

The prophet Isaiah has more to say. He doesn't just tell Ahaz to keep calm; he has words of assurance to relay to this king of Judah. His words in Isaiah 7:7-9 are,

It will not take place, it will not happen, for the head of Aram is Damascus, and the head of Damascus is only Rezin. Within 65 years Ephraim will be too shattered to be a people. The head of Ephraim is Samaria, and the head of Samaria is Remaliah's son. If you do not stand firm in your faith, you will not stand at all.

The LORD doesn't stop there though; he tells Ahaz to ask him for a sign to prove to him that what He just said will happen exactly as He said. But King Ahaz, because he does not really care about the LORD, says something that may sound religious and the right thing to say, when in reality it's just the opposite. To Isaiah's challenge from the LORD, to ask for a sign, no matter what it is, Ahaz replies, in Isaiah 7:12, *"I will not ask; I will not put the LORD to the test."*

Deuteronomy 6:16 tells us not to put the LORD to the test so Ahaz's response sounds religious, correct and obedient. In reality, when the LORD or one of His angels speaks, His word should be the end of the matter. However, this is the LORD himself who gives Ahaz opportunity to ask Him to prove His word with a miracle. This isn't the first and only time the LORD allows this testing and proof.

In II Kings 20:9, another narrative that includes Isaiah, another king of Judah, King Hezekiah deals with an illness. The LORD promises to heal Hezekiah. But Hezekiah asks the LORD for a sign in this story. As a result, the LORD provides him with one, and does exactly what he said he would do. There is a big difference when we ask with a believing heart rather than ask with a rebellious or disbelieving heart.

No matter, King Ahaz will not ask the LORD for a sign. This lack of obedience to the LORD's command doesn't sit well with the LORD as he tells Ahaz he is trying His patience. But the LORD gives Ahaz and the House of David a sign anyway. The sign is that a young woman will have a son and his name will be Immanuel, God with us! The LORD wants Ahaz to know He Himself will be with Judah to keep his promise to King David. Because of the LORD's promise to David, neither Judah, nor David's line would be wiped out – despite King Ahaz's blatant disbelief.

These measly little kings of Aram and Samaria would not interrupt or destroy the purposes or promises of the LORD concerning His word to David and of His coming Messiah. This sign of Immanuel was to the King of Judah and the people of Judah. They needed to know the LORD cared about them and his promises. As the LORD promised, Jerusalem and the House of David survived, and were not destroyed by these two kings.

The first 7 verses of Isaiah 9[8:23-9:6] are full of many images and names that will be a part of Messiah,

> *Nevertheless, there will be no more gloom for those who were in distress ... he will honor Galilee of the Gentiles, by the way of the sea, along the Jordan: The people walking in darkness have seen a great light; on those living in the land of the shadow of death a light has dawned. You have enlarged the nation and increased their joy....you have shattered the yoke that burdens them, the bar across their shoulders, the rod of their oppressor ....For to us a child is born, to us a son is given, and the government will be on his shoulders. And he will be called Wonderful Counselor, Mighty God, Everlasting Father, Prince of Peace. Of the increase of his government and peace there will be no end. He will reign on David's throne and over his kingdom establishing and upholding it with justice and righteousness....The zeal of the LORD Almighty will accomplish this.*

This Messiah will be a light who will dawn. His light will shine especially in the region of Galilee. Notice also this child is born but the reference to this Son says he is given. What do we make of the above terms describing Messiah?

In Isaiah 11, we are given more clues about this coming King of David, Messiah. We learn important and interesting things in these verses. First, we learn that when Messiah comes he will come from the House of David. Per this narrative, at this time in history, Israel is not a conquering, dominating power on their side of the world. In fact, Messiah will be a branch that sprouts from Jesse's stump, but he will bear fruit. This tells us that, just as the cedars of Lebanon were cut down (from Isaiah 10) the House of David will actually be in decline when Messiah comes on the scene.

Nevertheless, when Messiah comes on the scene, the Spirit of the LORD will rest on him. He will also have the Spirit of wisdom, understanding, counsel, power, knowledge, and the fear of the LORD. He delights in the fear of the LORD. Messiah will not judge by what he sees and hears; instead his decisions will be made by his righteousness.

In fact, Isaiah 11:5 says, *"Righteousness will be his belt and faithfulness the sash around his waist."* Verse 10 says this, *"...Root of Jesse will stand as a banner for the peoples; the nations will rally to him."* In this verse we once again see Gentiles in the context of Messiah.

Next we encounter the branch, the shoot; his righteous reign is spoken of in Jeremiah 23:5-6,

> *The days are coming, declares the LORD, when I will raise up to David a righteous Branch, a King who will reign wisely and do what is just and right in the land. In his days Judah will be saved and Israel will live in safety. This is the name by which he will be called: The LORD Our Righteousness.*

Ezekiel has an interesting pronouncement that carries the same imagery as Isaiah 11. We are told of a thing the LORD will do to a tall, proud cedar in Ezekiel 17:22-23,

> *I will break off a tender sprig from its topmost shoots and plant it on a high and lofty mountain. On the mountain heights of Israel I will plant it; it will produce branches and bear fruit.*

Notice the shared imagery of the shoot, the cedar, the branch, and the fact that fruit is being produced. Our next Messiah reference gives us his birthplace. Micah 5:2[1] says,

> *But you, Bethlehem Ephrathah, though you are small among the clans of Judah, out of you will come for me one who will be ruler over Israel, whose origins are from of old, from ancient times.*

Now we know! The Messiah will come from Judah and his birthplace will be Bethlehem Ephrathah. Why is the addition of Ephrathah important, you ask? Well, because there were two

Bethlehem's and Micah lets us know which one will be the birthplace of Messiah. Is this fact important still today?

Zechariah speaks of this Branch in our next Messiah reference. Not only that but he speaks symbolically of Joshua as the High Priest in Zechariah 3:8,

> Listen, O high priest Joshua and your associates seated before you, who are symbolic of things to come. I am going to bring my servant, the Branch.

In this narrative, we find the high priest and other men around him who are symbolic in some way concerning Messiah. We also learn that Messiah is the LORD's servant. Is the name Joshua relevant in our discussion concerning Messiah today?

Our next narrative in Zechariah 6 provides much more suspense within its Messiah descriptions. The Branch is once more referenced but there's plenty more. Once again the High Priest, Joshua, is mentioned. This time he's seen in reference to two crowns. Zechariah 6:9 begins,

> The word of the LORD came to me: Take silver and gold...make a crown, and set it on the head of the high priest, Joshua...The LORD Almighty says: Here is the man whose name is the Branch, and he will branch out from his place and build the temple of the LORD. It is he who will build the temple of the LORD, and he will be clothed with majesty and sit and rule on his throne. And he will be priest on his throne. And there will be harmony between the two.

Did you notice that the Branch is also the High Priest in this reference? This high priest has a crown on his head, sits on his throne, and rules as king. How can this be? Does this mean Messiah will be both priest and king?

Our next King Messiah reference is found in Zechariah 9. Here the king of Jerusalem is seen in a different light, as a lowly one, as said in verse 9,

> Rejoice greatly, O Daughter of Zion! Shout, Daughter of Jerusalem! See your king comes to you, righteous and having salvation, gentle and riding on a donkey, on a colt, the foal of a donkey.

This scene opens with Messiah riding in his Coronation Parade. Once again righteousness is mentioned and salvation is also found here in reference to Messiah.

The book of The Psalms contains more scenes of messianic imagery. Psalm 2 is written for the King's Coronation; it speaks of a conspiracy of nations against the son who is the king and reigns in Zion on the LORD's holy hill. Listen to Psalm 2:1-12

> Why do the nations conspire and the peoples plot in vain? The kings of the earth take their stand and rulers gather together against the LORD and against his Anointed One ....The One enthroned in heaven laughs...I have installed my King on Zion, my holy hill. I will proclaim the decree of the LORD: He said to me, You are my Son; today I have become your Father. Ask of me, and I will make the nations your inheritance, the ends of the earth your possession. You will rule them with an iron scepter; you will dash them to pieces like pottery... Therefore, you kings, be wise; be warned, you rulers of the earth. Serve the LORD with fear and rejoice with trembling. Kiss the Son, lest he be angry and you be destroyed in your way, for his wrath can flare up in a moment. Blessed are all who take refuge in him.

We again encounter the imagery of the Gentiles, the LORD's Anointed, David's exaltation, and rule over the nations in Psalm 18:46-50[47-51],

> The LORD lives! Praise to my Rock! Exalted be God my Savior! He is the God who avenges me, who subdues nations under me, who saves me from my enemies. You exalted me above my foes; from violent men you rescued me. Therefore I will praise you among the nations, O Lord; I will sing praises to your name. He gives his king great victories; he shows unfailing kindness to his anointed, to David and his descendants forever.

Next, let's take a look at how Messiah, the righteous ruler is depicted. Even his words are talked about here in Psalm 45:2[3] through 17[18],

> You are the most excellent of men and your lips have been anointed with grace, since God has blessed you forever. Gird your sword upon your side, O mighty one; clothe yourself with splendor and majesty....let the nations fall beneath your feet. Your throne, O God, will last forever and ever; a scepter of justice will be the scepter of your kingdom. You love righteousness and hate wickedness;

therefore God, your God, has set you above your companions by anointing you with the oil of joy…. I will perpetuate your memory through all generations; therefore the nations will praise you for ever and ever.

The themes of the LORD's servant, House of David, and generations continue in Psalm 89:3-4[4-5]:

…I have made a covenant with my chosen one, I have sworn to David my servant, I will establish your line forever and make your throne firm through all generations.

We see Messiah as God's son in verses 23[24]-28[29]:

I will crush his foes before him and strike down his adversaries. My faithful love will be with him, and through my name his horn will be exalted….He will call out to me, You are my Father, my God, the Rock my Savior. I will also appoint him firstborn, the most exalted of the kings of the earth. I will maintain my love to him forever, and my covenant with him will never fail.

Another depiction of King Messiah is found in Psalm 110 where Messiah sits at the Lord's right hand. Psalm 110:1-4 shares the following words:

The LORD says to my Lord: Sit at my right hand until I make your enemies a footstool for your feet. The LORD will extend your mighty scepter from Zion….Arrayed in holy majesty, from the womb of the dawn….The LORD has sworn and will not change his mind: You are a priest forever, in the order of Melchizedek.

Once again a priest is mentioned in connection with Messiah. This time it's *the priest*, the one who received a tithe from Abraham in the book of Genesis. That priest is Melchizedek.

Our last Psalm-mention with King Messiah is Psalm 132:11 that speaks of the LORD as he swears to David, "*The LORD swore an oath to David, a sure oath that he will not revoke: 'One of your own descendants I will place on your throne.'*" He also speaks of the shoot, or horn, in verse 17,

Here I will make a horn grow for David and set up a lamp for my anointed one. I will clothe his enemies with shame, but the crown on his head will be resplendent.

Ruth and Boaz are David's great-grandparents. Ruth speaks of King Messiah in Ruth 4:11 and 17,

> *May you have standing in Ephrathah and be famous in Bethlehem .... And they named him Obed. He was the father of Jesse, the father of David.*

This ruler is seen also in I Chronicles 5:2 which speaks of the prince and the ruler when it says, "...*Judah was the strongest of his brothers and a ruler came from him.*"

As we saw above, we see in I Chronicles 17:13-14 the LORD once again promises David a continuing house. He says,

> *I will be his father, and he will be my son. I will never take my love away from him, as I took it away from your predecessor. I will set him over my house and my kingdom forever; his throne will be established forever.*

Every verse contained some aspect of the LORD's Messiah being King of all nations. Do any of these above verses speak of why this coming king of Israel will be worshipped, and called the Son of Man?

The Prophet

In Deuteronomy 18, Moses speaks to the people of Israel about the subject of a prophet he initiated in chapter 13. Moses begins his prophet-precursor by talking about sorcerers and diviners – people who the nations of Canaan employed to guide them through their lives. The LORD however, chose to speak to the people of Israel through his prophets. He forbids His people from seeking out sorcerers and diviners since these are not people the LORD chose to use and speak through.

As far as Israel is concerned, the LORD's choosing to speak through his prophets began with his friend Abraham, whom the LORD called a prophet way back in Genesis 20:7.

We discover the LORD speaks to Israel concerning a specific prophet in Deuteronomy 18:14-19,

> The nations you will dispossess listen to those who practice sorcery or divination. But as for you, the LORD your God has not permitted you to do so. The LORD your God will raise up for you a prophet _like me_ from among your own brothers. You must listen to him. For this is what you asked of the LORD your God at Horeb on the day of the assembly when you said, "Let us not hear the voice of the LORD our God nor see this great fire anymore, or we will die." The LORD said to me: What they say is good. I will raise up for them a prophet like you from among their brothers; I will put my words in his mouth, and he will tell them everything I command him. If anyone does not listen to my words that _the prophet_ speaks in my name, I myself will call him to account.

Notice that this prophet, whom Moses speaks about is different from the prophets spoken of in chapter 13 who did not follow the LORD. What's so different about this prophet in chapter 18 compared to the prophets in chapter 13? Here's the difference; this special prophet in chapter 18 will be _like Moses, "he will tell them everything I command him."_

This special prophet is someone to whom the nation of Israel must listen. Listening to this prophet is crucial — just as it was crucial for the people of Israel to listen to Moses during the Exodus and wilderness-wanderings. Notice that whoever of the people of Israel decide not to follow this upcoming prophet, it is not the prophet himself who this person will give an account to. Instead, the person will give account for their refusal to listen to the LORD Himself. This is seen during Moses' time when Korah spoke out against Moses, and on another occasion when his sister Miriam spoke against him. One more important piece has been added to our Messiah puzzle.

I think Scripture confirms a *special* prophet is in Israel in each Scriptural generation; take Samuel and Elijah for examples. Another two questions need to be asked, "Which prophet of the Hebrew Scriptures met all the above qualifications of which Moses spoke? Did any prophets do what Moses did?" Maybe this was why many in Israel continued to look for the coming of this <u>*special* prophet like Moses</u> even into the Common Era. And many still look for Messiah to come, even today.

To understand all qualifications of this special prophet would require us to look at Moses' life in its entirety just to start. We'd have to know special circumstances surrounding his birth and continued existence all the way to the end of his life. Some might think it is a waste of time to study Moses since he was not allowed to enter Promised Land. According to the Scriptures, however, Moses was not a failure; rather he was an overcomer.

Let's consider another question. If we can correctly paint a picture, "What would the picture of Moses look like?" We know it's not a photograph; instead, this picture has to do with the type of person Moses was, and what he said and did. A couple more questions: "What type of prophet was Moses?" "What did Moses do; how did he live?" These questions are of major importance when we know that Moses' life points to or resembles the one coming on Israel's horizon, <u>The Prophet</u>, Messiah.

Remember Moses was a shepherd and the LORD called to Moses from the burning bush. This much of his portrait is found in

Exodus 3. The LORD notifies Moses of persons whom he is eternally and currently the God of, beginning in verse 6, "I am the God of your father, the God of Abraham, the God of Isaac and the God of Jacob." The LORD continues in verse 7,

> I have indeed seen the misery of my people in Egypt. I have heard them crying out because of their slave drivers, and I'm concerned about their suffering. So I have come down to rescue them from the hand of the Egyptians and to bring them up out of that land into a good and spacious land, a land flowing with milk and honey.

As we continue in our reading in Exodus 3:10 we discover that Moses doesn't go of his own accord but it's the LORD who sends Moses. Here, the LORD says; "So now, go. I am sending you to Pharaoh to bring my people the Israelites out of Egypt." This prophet is sent to the people of Israel during a time of extreme duress. It was the LORD's desire to save Israel from her enemy at this time – Pharaoh and the land of Egypt.

The LORD gives Moses seven directives in Exodus 3. **First**, Moses is to return to Egypt as his representative. **Second**, Moses' objective is to bring the Israelites out of bondage and to *this mountain*. **Third**, Moses is going to Egypt in the LORD's name; verse 14, "*God said to Moses: 'I Am Who I Am.' This is what you are to say to the Israelites: 'I Am has sent me to you.'*" **Fourth**, Moses is to call the elders of Israel together after his arrival and tell them the LORD appeared to him. **Fifth**, he is to take the elders with him when he goes to the king of Egypt.

The words he is commanded to tell the king are found in Exodus 3:18, "*The LORD, the God of the Hebrews, has met with us. Let us take a three-day journey into the desert.*" The LORD prepares Moses for Pharaoh's stubbornness, saying the king of Egypt won't let them take their journey. Because of Pharaoh's stubbornness, the LORD will stretch out his hand and strike the Egyptians with wonders. These wonders are the ten plagues the LORD will bring to Egypt and its inhabitants.

The **sixth** directive is contained in these wonders found in Exodus 4:1-9. The LORD gives Moses three signs to perform that declare Moses' authenticity as the LORD's representative. The first sign: his staff becomes a snake when he throws it down on the ground. The second sign: Moses' hand becomes leprous after he places it inside his cloak. The third sign: when water is taken from the Nile and poured on the ground, it turns into blood. Collectively these signs declare Moses' authenticity.

The **seventh** directive the LORD gives Moses has to do with plundering the Egyptian people before they leave. This is found in Exodus 3:21-22,

> And I will make the Egyptians favorably disposed toward this people, so that when you leave you will not go empty-handed. Every woman is to ask her neighbor and any woman living in her house for articles of silver and gold and for clothing, which you will put on your sons and daughters. And so you will plunder the Egyptians.

Deuteronomy 18 gives three attributes of this special prophet as we seek to formulate an idea of who he is, what he does, and what he looks like. First, the prophet will be *like* Moses. Second, he will speak to the people as the LORD's representative. Third, the LORD will call anyone to account who doesn't listen to this special man. The verses of Deuteronomy 18:21-22 are important as related to the message,

> How can we know when a message has not been spoken by the LORD? If what a prophet proclaims in the name of the LORD does not take place or come true, that is a message the LORD has not spoken. That prophet has spoken presumptuously. Do not be afraid of him.

Again, the question we need to ask at this point is this: "Just exactly what did Moses look like?" Let's begin to paint his picture with listed features of the man and what he did while shepherding the people of Israel for 40 years.

The Life Picture of Moses

Since we have finished up above with Moses, the first shepherd of Israel. And because he is a type of Messiah, and Messiah, **The Shepherd of Israel**, is who we will shortly be depicting below, let me share Moses' Photograph with you here:

1. **Moses** was dispatched by the LORD to go to the captive nation of Israel and redeem them from their captivity to Egypt to freely worship the LORD.
2. **Moses** had a brass serpent made and placed on a pole that saved all who looked at it from death.
3. **Moses** was the shepherd of Israel in the desert.
4. **Moses** – Aaron was the prophet who went before him.
5. **Moses** – Israel was sustained by manna for 40 years.
6. **Moses** was tested at the waters of Marah and failed the test; as a result, he was not allowed to enter into Canaan. Israel was tested for 40 days and also failed the test.
7. **Moses** gives The 10 Words, The Decalogue, or the Ten Commandments which were written by the finger of the LORD on the mountain with an audience of one.
8. **Moses** taught the perpetual ceremony of Passover with the spotless Passover Lamb, whose blood is sprinkled on the door, the eating of its flesh, and the Death Angel. This involved a substitution for the firstborn of Israel.
9. **Moses** built a "transient" Tabernacle that was made after the reality of the heavenly Tabernacle. This transient model later became "permanent" for the purpose of sacrifice, prayer and worship.
10. **Moses** talked with the LORD face-to-face, and relayed the LORD's message to the people.
11. **Moses** prophesied Israel's demise as a nation because of sin, and also their future return and hope.
12. **Moses** performs mighty signs and wonders: Rod turned to snake; leprous hand; and Plagues of blood, frogs, gnats, flies, livestock, boils, hail, locust, darkness, and death of

firstborn.   He received Water from a rock, crossed the Red Sea, and lead Israel into the Promised Land.

13. **Moses** referred to his wicked generation of Israelites (this doesn't mean that every Israelite of his generation was wicked, it only refers to those who refused to obey the LORD), the ones he taught, who followed him out of Egypt and to the threshold of the Promised Land.

14. **Moses** – During his time of leading, the Firstborn of Egypt died while life and freedom were given to the people of Israel.

Let's examine another Scriptural quotation concerning this great prophet of Israel, Moses.   Deuteronomy 34:10 tells us something both interesting and important,

Since then, no prophet has risen in Israel like Moses, whom the LORD knew face to face, who did all those miraculous signs and wonders the Lord sent him to do in Egypt.

Here's a repeated question: "Which of the LORD's prophets, since Moses, did what we see above in Deuteronomy 34?" While Israel had many great prophets, at a basic level, did any do what Moses had done?

The last Scripture passage we'll examine here is found in Psalm 118:22-26. This narrative speaks of the stone, the one who comes in the name of the Lord,

The stone the builders rejected has become the capstone; the LORD has done this, and it is marvelous in our eyes…O LORD, save us…Blessed is he who comes in the name of the LORD.

Messiah will be the one, like Moses, who also comes in the name of the LORD.

The Servant of the LORD

King David and Moses are both referred to as the LORD's servant on many occasions in the Scriptures. The imagery of the Servant of the LORD is also used to speak of the special Servant of the LORD, the Messiah.

Our first Servant of the LORD reference is taken from the book of Isaiah. Isaiah 42:1-9 speaks of the LORD's servant Messiah. It is called the Servant Song; consider its words,

Here is my servant, whom I uphold, my chosen one in whom I delight; I will put my Spirit on him and he will bring justice to the nations....In faithfulness he will bring forth justice; he will not falter or be discouraged till he establishes justice on the earth. In his law the islands will put their hope...I, the LORD, have called you in righteousness; I will take hold of your hand. I will keep you and will make you to be a covenant for the people and a light for the Gentiles, to open eyes that are blind, to free captives from prison and to release from the dungeon those who sit in darkness. I am the LORD; that is my name! I will not give my glory to another or my praise to idols. See, the former things have taken place, and new things I declare; before they spring into being, I announce them to you.

This reference is full of messianic imagery. The Spirit of the LORD is on Messiah; he is faithful, just and righteous. The LORD calls Messiah in righteousness. Messiah will be a covenant for the people of Israel and a light for the Gentiles.

Imagery that depicts captives, prisoners, dungeons, and darkness are continual themes throughout the book of Isaiah. Other parallels in Isaiah are found in 49:1-13; 50:4-11; 51:12-13; 52:13-53:12; and 61:1-11.

It's no wonder our above imagery is used in Isaiah. During Isaiah's lifetime many from the Northern and Southern Kingdoms of Samaria and Judah respectively had become prisoners and were taken captive. Notice also that Messiah is referred to as a mighty man in Isaiah 42:13-16,

The LORD will march out like a mighty man, like a warrior he will stir up his zeal; with a shout he will raise the battle cry and will triumph over his enemies. For a long time I have kept silent, I have been quiet

and held myself back. But now, like a woman in childbirth, I cry out, I gasp and pant. I will lay waste the mountains and hills and dry up all their vegetation; I will turn rivers into islands and dry up pools. I will lead the blind by ways they have not known, along unfamiliar paths I will guide them; I will turn the darkness into light before them and make the rough places smooth. These are the things I will do; I will not forsake them.

Those who were blind will now see as they are led by Messiah. Verse 22 speaks of the people's current problem,

...this is a people plundered and looted, all of them trapped in pits or hidden away in prisons. They have become plunder with no one to rescue them; they have been made loot, with no one to say, "Send them back."

These are just some of the things that Messiah will remedy upon his arrival. Messiah will free these prisoners from all of these things and from the problems which had bound them.

Because of its similar imagery, let's consider Isaiah 61:1,

The Spirit of the Sovereign LORD is on me, because the Lord has anointed me to preach good news to the poor. He has sent me to bind up the brokenhearted, to proclaim freedom for the captives and release from darkness for the prisoners.

This Servant of the LORD Messiah is also spoken of in Isaiah 49:1-13. He is spoken of as being concealed by the LORD,

Listen to me, you islands; hear this, you distant nations: Before I was born the Lord called me; from my birth he has made mention of my name. He made my mouth like a sharpened sword, in the shadow of his hand he hid me; he made me into a polished arrow and concealed me in his quiver. He said to me, You are my servant, Israel, in whom I will display my splendor. But I said, I have labored to no purpose; I have spent my strength in vain and for nothing...And now the LORD says – he who formed me in the womb to be his servant to bring Jacob back to him and gather Israel to himself...It is too small a thing for you to be my servant to restore the tribes of Jacob and bring back those of Israel I have kept. I will also make you a light for the Gentiles, that you may bring salvation to the ends of the earth. This is what the LORD says – the Redeemer and Holy One of Israel – to him who was despised and abhorred by the nation, to the servant of rulers...In the time of my favor I will answer you, and in the day of salvation I will help you; I will keep you and will make you to be a covenant for the people, to restore the land and to reassign its desolate inheritances, to say to the captives, "Come out; and to those in darkness, "Be free!" They will feed beside the roads and find pasture on every barren hill. They will neither hunger nor thirst, nor will the desert heat or the sun beat upon them. He who has compassion on them will guide them and lead them beside springs of water. I will turn all my mountains into roads, and my highways will be raised up. See, they will come from afar – some from the north, some from the west, some from the region of Aswan. Shout for joy, O heavens; rejoice, O earth; burst into song, O mountains! For the LORD comforts his people and will have compassion on his afflicted ones.

An amazing amount of imagery is packed within these verses. We again see reference to the Gentiles. Messiah, just as the prophet Jeremiah, was called by the LORD before his birth. His revelation is somehow a mystery, even to the people of Israel. The events surrounding Messiah will make his mission seem to be a failure and in vain. Messiah's mission is to bring the nation of Israel back to the LORD and bring salvation to all humanity. Messiah will be rejected and despised by the very people to whom he was sent. He is also referred to once again as a covenant for the people.

Isaiah 52 adds to the imagery of Isaiah 49, as the servant prospers in his message. Let's consider Isaiah 52:13-15,

See, my servant will act wisely; he will be raised and lifted up and highly exalted. Just as there were many who were appalled at him – his appearance was so disfigured beyond that of any man and his form marred beyond human likeness – so will he sprinkle many nations, and kings will shut their mouths because of him. For what they were not told, they will see, and what they have not heard, they will understand.

Here the Servant will be wise, exalted and sprinkle many nations. Sprinkling is a priestly term in this narrative. We see this when reading of Aaron and other high priests of Israel who sprinkle the blood of the sacrifice in order to cleanse the altar as well as the people. Messiah's audiences draw back from him because they are stunned and devastated by his extremely disfigured appearance.

Isaiah 53 ties the above four chapters together to bring meanings of this imagery *home* to enlighten our understanding. The imagery of Messiah in Isaiah 53 is interwoven throughout its entire 12 verses. This chapter ties together a lot of Messianic imagery used elsewhere in the Scriptures. Listen to the words as they speak of this coming Servant of the LORD, Messiah.

Who has believed our message and to whom has the arm of the LORD been revealed? He grew up before him like a tender shoot, and like a root out of dry ground. He had no beauty or majesty to attract us to him, nothing in his appearance that we should desire him. He was despised and rejected by men, a man of sorrows, and familiar with suffering. Like one from whom men hide their faces he was despised, and we esteemed him not. Surely he took up our infirmities and carried our sorrows, yet we considered him stricken by God, smitten by him, and afflicted. But he was pierced for our transgressions, he was crushed for our iniquities; the punishment that brought us peace was upon him, and by his wounds we are healed. We all, like sheep, have gone astray, each of us has turned to his own way; and the Lord has laid on him the iniquity of us all. He was oppressed and afflicted, yet he did not open his mouth; he was led like a lamb to the slaughter, and as a sheep before her shearers is silent, so he did not open his mouth. By oppression and judgment he was taken away. And who can speak of his descendants? For he was cut off from the land of the living; for the transgression of my people he was stricken. He was assigned a grave with the wicked, and with the rich in his death, though he had done no violence, nor was any deceit in his mouth. Yet it was the LORD's will to crush him and cause him to suffer, and though the LORD makes his life a guilt offering, he will see his offspring and prolong his days, and the will of the LORD will prosper in his hand. After the suffering of his soul, he will see the light of life and be satisfied; by his knowledge my righteous servant will justify many, and he will bear their iniquities. Therefore I will give him a portion among the great, and he will divide the spoils with the strong, because he poured out his life unto death, and was numbered with the transgressors. For he bore the sin of many, and made intercession for the transgressors.

How could these words have been penned concerning Messiah, the LORD's servant, before he even came on the scene? Even though all these words may seem almost too much to read and take in, I believe it is vitally important to look again, unpack, or open up what we just read in its entirety.

This narrative tells us Messiah grew up before the LORD as a tender shoot, the same way everyone is born – as a baby. This reference also speaks of a drastic downsizing that occurred within the House of David. Messiah appears on the scene as a root out of dry ground rather than as a great prince arrayed in royalties finest. His very existence was hard, and it required great work and exertion.

What do we do with his appearance? Wasn't Messiah supposed to be royal and beautiful? How is it then that this portrayed man has no beauty or majesty? There was nothing about this man to make one suspect he was someone from the House of David. And instead of being greatly desired at great events and especially as a key note speaker this man is despised and rejected. He is a man totally familiar with sorrows and sufferings of all kinds. But instead of being desired as a friend, people want no part of even being associated with this man.

There's more; Messiah here isn't seen saving the day and delivering Israel from her enemies. Instead he deals with the sins, sicknesses and transgressions of his people. Here is a man who is pierced through, not for some crime or sin that he committed, but for the waywardness of the sheep of Israel and their sin against the LORD. In fact, God himself laid all the iniquity of Israel on Messiah – as the sin-bearer and scapegoat.

Messiah is a man who was cut off in the prime of life; he died and was buried even though he had done nothing wrong. But listen to this; it is vitally important not to miss what's next. Isaiah 53:10 tells us that ***it was the Lord's will to crush him and cause him to suffer***. Not only that but the Lord made this man's life a guilt offering. And even though it seemed that his mission was for no purpose and accomplished nothing of value his mission will actually be a success and prosper.

But, again, there's much more. This man who has been rejected, despised, killed and buried will have his life extended. How can this be? It says that he will also produce offspring. How does one reconcile all of these seeming differences and contradictions? This is just some of the mystery surrounding Messiah.

When we read some Psalms that refer to Messiah and view them against the backdrop of the 5 chapters of Isaiah we just looked at, the differences and seeming contradictions begin to make sense. Because of this I want to group together our next references found in the Psalms.

Do you remember Psalm 2 – what is known as the King's Coronation Psalm? While this definitely refers to David and his descendants, its ultimate fulfillment is found in Messiah, The Son of David. Psalm 2 speaks of nations and peoples who plot against both the LORD and his Anointed One. Their plot is to usurp both the LORD's and Messiah's rule. The LORD responds to their plotting by telling them that their scheme is in vain.

Why will their scheme fail? The reason their scheme will fail is first because the LORD placed his King on Zion, which is his holy hill. A second reason their plot is doomed is because, just as David saw, Messiah is both David's son and the LORD's son, as found in Psalm 2:7. The final reason these rulers' and peoples' conspiracy will fail is because of the LORD's promise to David. Messiah *will* reign on David's throne, in Jerusalem, over all nations and the LORD *will* make sure of this. This is an unconditional promise.

Psalm 16 also ties in with Psalm 2 above and also our previously discussed chapters of Isaiah. Do you remember the imagery of Isaiah 53 where the prophet speaks of Messiah? Isaiah 53:9 tells us Messiah is cut off and assigned a grave in his death; by all accounts, his mission failed.

And yet, there is "a light at the end of the tunnel," just as Isaiah 53:10-11 tell us. After dying, Messiah will see the light and have his life prolonged. This is where Psalm 16:8-11 tie into the picture; let's look at these 4 verses of Psalm 16,

I have set the LORD always before me. Because he is at my right hand, I will not be shaken. Therefore my heart is glad and my tongue rejoices; my body also will rest secure, because you will not abandon me to the grave, nor will you let your Holy One see decay. You have made known to me the path of life; you will fill me with joy in your presence, with eternal pleasures at your right hand.

The Messiah imagery of Psalm 22:1 makes sense when seen in the light of the above Scriptural passages. Here Messiah cries out to the LORD, asking why he was abandoned. Further he claims in Psalm 22:6[7], "*I am a worm* (specifically a red maggot) *and not a man.*" Messiah continues in verse 6[7] to speak of his people's continual rejection; he says I am:

...scorned by men and despised by the people. All who see me mock me; they hurl insults, shaking their heads: "He trusts in the LORD; let the LORD rescue him, since he delights in him."

Again speaking with the same imagery that we saw in Isaiah, Messiah says he is despised and scorned by the people. Even through all this rejection, Messiah speaks to the LORD and tries to make sense of all these things in light of his mission. In Psalm 22:9-10[10-11], he says, "*yet you brought me out of the womb; you made me trust in you even at my mother's breast. From birth I was cast upon you.*" He continues with this same theme in Psalm 22:11[12]-16[17],

Do not be far from me, for trouble is near and there is no one to help. Many bulls surround me...Roaring lions tearing their prey – open their mouths wide against me....Dogs have surrounded me; a band of evil men has encircled me, they have pierced my hands and feet.

Psalm 22:16b[17b] carries the savage imagery of piercing, tearing and infliction of terrible damage. This imagery of death is also found in verse 14[15] that says, "*I am poured out like water, and all my bones are out of joint. My heart has turned to wax....you lay me in the dust of death.*"

He continues to speak of his garments being gambled for in Psalm 22:17[18], *"People stare and gloat over me. They divide my garments among them and cast lots for my clothing."* In his desperation, he once again cries out to the LORD as he speaks of sure, impending death,

> *O LORD, be not far off; O my Strength, come quickly to help me. Deliver my life from the sword....from the power of the dogs. Rescue me from the mouth of the lions; save me from the horns of the wild oxen.*

Listen to his summation of all the events we read about that makes no sense unless something amazing took place after the above events occurred. In Psalm 22:22[23]-24[25] he says,

> *I will declare your name to my brothers; in the congregation I will praise you. You who fear the LORD, praise him! All you descendants of Jacob, honor him! Revere him, all you descendants of Israel! For He has not despised or disdained the suffering of the afflicted one; he has not hidden his face from him but has listened to his cry for help.*

Even in light of all this imagery of conspiracy, attack, rejection, misery and death, according to our above Scriptures, this dead man will not be abandoned to the grave. Neither will the LORD allow Messiah's body to decay. Instead the LORD will show Messiah the path back to light and life.

As we saw above, the LORD did not despise Messiah's suffering nor did He permanently hide from him during his darkest hour. Instead he listened attentively to his cry for help. For further reference see Psalm 69, 109 and 118.

The Shepherd of the LORD

David, The Psalter of Israel, wrote so many amazing Psalms. Some of his most amazing ones speak of Messiah whose coming is seen just over Israel's horizon. Even though the writings of David are not specifically found in the prophets, remember that the Spirit of the LORD was powerfully with him continually from the time of his anointing by Samuel. David also speaks, using prophetic language, tones and imagery.

Listen to David's own words found in I Chronicles 28. Here David speaks to Solomon concerning all the plans and preparations he made for the building of the Temple. David begins with his plans for the portico of the temple and ends with his plan for the cherubim of gold whose wings shelter the ark of the covenant of the LORD. In verse 19 David says; *"All this... in writing from the hand of the LORD upon me, and he gave me understanding in all the details of the plan."* *"His hand being upon him"* signifies what David wrote down including the plans he made for the Temple; these came from and were revealed to David by the Lord himself.

Let's remember David's response to King Saul when Saul told him he couldn't go out to fight Goliath, the Philistine champion. He explained what he did on two occasions when a lion and bear attacked his father's flock to carry off a lamb. This shepherd boy disregarded his safety and put himself in harm's way to strike each animal. When they turned to attack David, he grabbed their hair and killed them. David did not perform these feats of courage on his own. He did these things in the power of the LORD which again proves the LORD was with him.

David used this same approach when he became King. He placed himself in harm's way in order to help the people of Israel. But he went, not in his own strength or name, but in the power of the LORD and in his Name. We always find this imagery when we look at the messianic shepherd references.

Isaiah 40:9 and 11 bring two pieces of messianic imagery together – good tidings and being a shepherd. This messenger of Israel proclaims good tidings and is a shepherd. He truly cares for the flock, especially defenseless and the most vulnerable ones; to these he gives special care and attention,

You who bring good tidings to Zion....You who bring good tidings to Jerusalem....He tends his flock like a shepherd: He gathers the lambs in his arms and carries them close to his heart; he gently leads those that have young.

Ezekiel 34 also speaks of the LORD shepherding people of Israel. We again see Messiah the Prince. Ezekiel 34:13-17 and 22-24 use the imagery of shepherds and their flocks,

I will pasture them on the mountains of Israel....I will tend them in a good pasture and the mountain heights of Israel will be their grazing land. There they will lie down....I will search for the lost and bring back the strays. I will bind up the injured and strengthen the weak but the sleek and the strong I will destroy. I will shepherd the flock with justice ....I will judge between one sheep and another....I will save my flock, and they will no longer be plundered. I will judge between one sheep and another. I will place over them one shepherd, my servant David, and he will tend them; he will tend them and be their shepherd. I the LORD will be their God, and my servant David will be prince among them. I the LORD have spoken.

Again the imagery here is of a good shepherd – one who will feed and care for his flock, and won't abandon any strays. He will search for these wayward sheep until he finds them and then will return them to the fold. This shepherd will heal the injured, nurture the weak, and place them once again back on their feet. He won't allow other sheep to bully, butt, and push weaker sheep aside. He will oppose these bullying sheep face to face. As a shepherd, his determinations will be marked by justice. David's son, Messiah, will be the LORD's servant who brings peace to the flock.

Ezekiel 37:24 also speaks of David and shepherding, "*My servant David will be king over them, and they will all have one shepherd. They will follow my laws....I will make a covenant of peace with them.*" David's son, Messiah, will once again be this flock's shepherd. These people of Israel will follow him and his teachings, and he will provide peace for his flock.

Pasturing of the flock is again our imagery in Zechariah 11. This time, however, the flock is marked for slaughter. The flock is watched over by Messiah the shepherd who gives himself for the people. The LORD begins Zechariah 11:4-14,

> *Pasture the flock...So I pastured the flock...particularly the oppressed of the flock....The flock detested me, and I grew weary of them....Then I took my staff called Favor and broke it, revoking the covenant I had made with all the nations....I told them, if you think it best, give me my pay; but if not, keep it. So they paid me thirty pieces of silver. And the LORD said to me, Throw it to the potter – the handsome price at which they priced me! So I took the thirty pieces of silver and threw them into the house of the LORD....Then I broke my second staff called Union, breaking the brotherhood between Judah and Israel.*

Did you notice the imagery above that pictures people who detest their shepherd? This shepherd was paid for his trouble. He was given 30 pieces of silver; however, that's not a great price. In fact it was a slap in the face, considering that's the price to purchase a slave. This money is then thrown into the house of the LORD, and is given to the potter.

Our next shepherding narrative begins by speaking of the fountain that will be opened to the house of David and the people of Jerusalem. This fountain will cleanse them from sin and impurity. Zechariah 13:7 also uses imagery of the shepherd,

> *Awake, O sword, against my shepherd, against the man who is close to me... Strike the shepherd, and the sheep will be scattered, and I will turn my hand against the little ones.*

Here again, as in other places in the Scriptures, Messiah is the one being struck. But this time the sheep are scattered as a result. Where will their hope come from?

David / City of David / House of David

Now let's take a look at the above Davidic terms and other corresponding terms in light of Messiah.

We learn that David's Fallen Tent will be repaired and restored in Amos 9:11, *"In that day I will restore David's fallen tent. I will... build it as it used to be, so that they may possess... all the nations that bear my name."*

The last part of Amos 9:13 says, *"New wine will drip from the mountains."* The LORD's exiled people will return to Israel and will rebuild the ruined cities. Israel will never again be uprooted from their land that the LORD gave to them.

Did you notice the four images spoken of here in Amos? **First**, the Kingdom of David will be restored just as it used to be. **Second**, Israel will possess all nations. **Third**, new wine will drip from the mountains of Israel and flow from all her hills. **Fourth**, Israel will never again be uprooted from her land.

We touched on Zechariah 13:1 earlier; here we need to notice it says, *"On that day a fountain will be opened to the house of David and the inhabitants of Jerusalem."* An important aspect of this verse has to do with the fact that this fountain will cleanse the House of David and Jerusalem's inhabitants from their sin and impurity.

Jerusalem – Future Hope – The Glory of the Whole Earth

The Hebrew Scriptures tell us that there is a future hope for Jerusalem. This future hope, according to the Scriptures, will not be an, "I hope so!" No, instead it will be a hope that is solid and trustworthy, an anchor in which someone may place their trust. The end result of this hope will be the glory of the whole earth, Israel, and the city of Jerusalem.

Let me share the following scriptural references from Isaiah concerning this future hope. Isaiah 24:23 says, *"The Lord Almighty will reign on Mount Zion and in Jerusalem."*

The picture portrayed in Isaiah 27:6 tells us that Israel is blossoming, *"In days to come Jacob will take root, Israel will bud and blossom and fill the earth with fruit."*

Comfort is conveyed in Isaiah 30:19, *"...O people of Zion, who live in Jerusalem, you will weep no more....As soon as he hears, he will answer you."*

The care of the Lord is seen over Jerusalem in Isaiah 31:5, *"The Lord Almighty will shield Jerusalem; he will shield it and deliver it, he will pass over it and will rescue it."*

Is it just me, or does our above reference bring back a Passover image? Remember the death angel passes over the firstborn of Israel. In passing over them, they are delivered.

We find a kingdom of peace with the LORD reigning as King in Isaiah 33:17-24,

> *Your eyes will see the king in his beauty and view a land that stretches afar. In your thoughts you will ponder the former terror: "Where is the chief officer? Where is the one who took revenue"....Look upon Zion, the city of our festivals; your eyes will see Jerusalem, a peaceful abode, a tent that will not be moved; its stakes will never be pulled up, nor any of its ropes broken. There the LORD will be our Mighty One....For the LORD is our judge.... lawgiver....king; it is he who will save us....No one living in Zion will say, "I am ill;" and the sins of those who dwell there will be forgiven.*

Words of comfort are found in Isaiah 40:1-11,

Comfort, comfort my people, says your God....A voice of one calling: "In the desert prepare the way for the Lord; make straight in the wilderness a highway for our God"....but the word of our God stands forever. You who bring good tidings to Zion....say to the towns of Judah, "Here is your God!" See, the Sovereign LORD comes with power, and his arm rules for him. See, his reward is with him, and his recompense accompanies Him.

Good news is pronounced in Isaiah 41:27, "*I was the first to tell Zion, 'Look, here they are!' I gave to Jerusalem a messenger of good tidings.*"

We learn of declarations related to the Redeemer of Jerusalem, Judah and the temple in Isaiah 44:24-28,

I am the LORD....who says of Jerusalem, "It shall be inhabited," of the towns of Judah, "They shall be built," and of their ruins, "I will restore them" ....he will say of Jerusalem, "Let it be rebuilt," and of the temple, "Let its foundations be laid.

Isaiah 51;3, 11, 15 and 16 all speak of the comfort and joy that will be found in Zion,

...The LORD will surely comfort Zion....The ransomed of the LORD will return. They will enter Zion with singing; everlasting joy will crown their heads....For I am the LORD your God....who laid the foundations of the earth, and who say to Zion, "You are my people."

The LORD's redemption of Jerusalem is in Isaiah 52:1-9,

Awake, awake, O Zion, clothe yourself with strength. Put on your garments of splendor, O Jerusalem, the holy city. The uncircumcised and defiled will not enter you again ....You were sold for nothing, and without money you will be redeemed....How beautiful on the mountains are the feet of those who bring good news....Burst into songs of joy together...for the LORD has comforted his people, he has redeemed Jerusalem.

Isaiah 62:11-12 cry out concerning Zion's Savior, the city, and its people,

The LORD has made proclamation to the ends of the earth: "Say to the Daughter of Zion, See, your Savior comes! See, his reward is with him, and his recompense accompanies him." They will be called the

Holy People, the Redeemed of the LORD; and you will be called Sought After, the City No Longer Deserted.

Isaiah 65:17-19 declares new heavens and a new earth,

Behold, I will create new heavens and a new earth….be glad and rejoice forever….for I will create Jerusalem to be a delight and its people a joy. I will rejoice over Jerusalem and take delight in my people; the sound of weeping and crying will be heard in it no more.

Words of rejoicing are expressed in Isaiah 66:10-23,

Rejoice with Jerusalem and be glad for her, all you who love her; rejoice greatly with her, all you who mourn over her….I will extend peace to her like a river, and the wealth of the nations like a flooding stream….They will proclaim my glory among the nations. And they will bring all your brothers, from all the nations, to my holy mountain in Jerusalem….says the LORD. They will bring them, as the Israelites bring their grain offerings, to the temple of the LORD in ceremonially clean vessels. And I will select some of them also to be priests and Levites, says the LORD. As the new heavens and the new earth that I will make will endure before Me….so will your name and descendants endure. From one New Moon to another and from one Sabbath to another, all mankind will come and bow down before me.

Next, the exclamations and declarations of honor and blessing that will be coming to Jerusalem continue in the book of our next prophet, Jeremiah. Jerusalem, the throne of the LORD, is revealed in Jeremiah 3:17, *"At that time they will call Jerusalem The Throne of the Lord, and all nations will gather in Jerusalem to honor the name of the Lord."*

Blessings are enunciated in Jeremiah 33:10-16,

…there will be heard once more the sounds of joy and gladness, the voices of bride and bridegroom…For I will restore the fortunes of the land to return as they were before….The days are coming, declares the LORD, when I will fulfill the gracious promise I made to the house of Israel and to the house of Judah. In those days and at that time I will make a righteous Branch sprout from David's line; he will do what is just and right in the land. In those days Judah will be saved and Jerusalem will live in safety. This is the name by which it will be called: The LORD Our Righteousness.

The prophet Joel also speaks of future announcements over Jerusalem and Mount Zion. Joel 2:28-32[3:1-5] says,

And afterward, I will pour out my Spirit on all people. Your sons and your daughters will prophesy, your old men will dream dreams, your young men will see visions. Even on my servants, both men and women, I will pour out my Spirit in those days. I will show wonders in the heavens and on the earth, blood and fire and billows of smoke. The sun will be turned into darkness and the moon to blood before the coming of the great and dreadful day of the LORD. And everyone who calls on the name of the LORD will be saved; for on Mount Zion and in Jerusalem...among the survivors whom the Lord calls.

We hear of Zion, the LORD's holy mountain, in Joel 3:17-21[4:17-21],

Then you will know that I, the LORD your God, dwell in Zion, my holy hill. Jerusalem will be holy; never again will foreigners invade her. In that day the mountains will drip new wine, and the hills will flow with milk; all the ravines of Judah will run with water. A fountain will flow out of the LORD's house and will water the valley of acacias. But Egypt will be desolate, Edom a desert waste, because of violence done to the people of Judah, in whose land they shed innocent blood. Judah will be inhabited forever and Jerusalem through all generations. Their bloodguilt, which I have not pardoned, I will pardon. The LORD dwells in Zion!

Micah 4:1-8 speaks of the end of days, the exaltation of the Lord's house, and Jerusalem at that time,

In the last days the mountain of the LORD's temple will be established as chief among the mountains; it will be raised above the hills, and peoples will stream to it. Many nations will come and say, Come, let us go up to the mountain of the LORD, to the house of the God of Jacob. He will teach us his ways, so that we may walk in his paths. The law will go out from Zion, the word of the LORD from Jerusalem. He will judge between many peoples and will settle disputes for strong nations far and wide. They will beat their swords into plowshares and their spears into pruning hooks. Nation will not take up sword against nation, nor will they train for war anymore. Every man will sit under his own vine and under his own fig tree, and no one will make them afraid, for the LORD Almighty has spoken. All the nations may walk in the name of their gods; we will walk in the name of the LORD our God for ever and ever. In that day, declares the LORD, I will gather the lame; I will assemble the exiles and those I have brought to grief. I will make the lame a remnant, those driven away a strong nation. The LORD will rule over them in Mount

Zion…the former dominion will be restored to you; kingship will come to the Daughter of Jerusalem.

The prophet Zechariah weighs in with our next three future prophetic revelations concerning Jerusalem. The first is found in Zechariah 1:14-16,

This is what the LORD Almighty says: "I am very jealous for Jerusalem and Zion" …. Therefore…."I will return to Jerusalem with mercy, and there my house will be rebuilt."

Second, a fountain is revealed in Zechariah 13:1 and 9,

On that day a fountain will be opened to the house of David and the inhabitants of Jerusalem, to cleanse them from sin and impurity….They will call on my name and I will answer them; I will say: "They are my people" and they will say, "The LORD is our God."

Third, Zechariah 14:3-16 answers all of Israel's enemies with this pronouncement,

Then the LORD will go out and fight against those nations, as he fights in the day of battle. On that day his feet will stand on the Mount of Olives…. living water will flow out from Jerusalem…in summer and in winter. The LORD will be king over the whole earth. On that day there will be one LORD, and his the only name…Jerusalem will be raised up and remain in its place…It will be inhabited; never again will it be destroyed. Jerusalem will be secure….Then the survivors from all the nations that have attacked Jerusalem will go up year after year to worship the King, the LORD Almighty, and to celebrate the Feast of Tabernacles.

These are not all of the Jerusalem prophecies that deal with the blessings the Lord will bring on her and her people. At this point you may ask, "When were these tender words of comfort and hope written? Were they written during the golden days of the Kingdom of Judah?" No, they were written during trying and perilous times. These words were written both before and after Judah and Jerusalem's captivity in Babylon.

My questions at this point are these: "Have any of these promises taken place since these prophecies were delivered? If so, which ones? Does the fact that some prophecies are still unfulfilled negate what the Lord said concerning what He will do to and for

Israel, Judah and Jerusalem? Will the Lord still perform what he promised to his people just as he has said?" Only you can decide these answers for yourself.

As we have seen from the Scriptures, going against the Word of the LORD is never a good idea. Also, we should not take the position, "Don't confuse me with the facts; I've already made up my mind!" Please let the LORD open your eyes to see the beauty of his Messiah – so you can experience his salvation.

Remnant

The remnant of Israel and Jerusalem is another topic sprinkled throughout the Hebrew Scriptures. And this term is especially found in the prophets' prophecies of Israel. Isaiah, Jeremiah, Ezekiel, Joel, Amos, Micah, Habakkuk, Zephaniah, Haggai and Zechariah all speak concerning a remnant.

If we ask, "Has a remnant of Israel, Judah and Jerusalem returned to the land the Lord promised to Abraham and his descendants?" honestly I don't think anyone can say no. "Can we say a remnant has been returning to the nation of Israel since it once again became a nation in 1948?" I believe that History and current events tell us this is so!

In speaking of *The Remnant,* something more needs to be said. Do you remember when the prophet Elijah was running scared – scared for his life? He was so scared that he ran all the way to the mountain of God in Horeb. Here, he complained to the LORD against the people of Israel and said 'I am the only one left who worships the Lord.'

Do you remember the LORD's reply to his prophet? The Lord told Elijah in I Kings 19:18, 'I've kept 7,000 in Israel as a remnant – ones who haven't bowed to Baal or kissed his image.' In other words, even though most of Israel was not following the LORD, there was still a remnant in Israel who was following the LORD. This was the righteous remnant. And the righteous remnant is an important topic to realize and consider.

The Angel of the LORD

The Angel of the LORD is another mysterious and unique being mentioned often in Scripture. He is seen with Abraham, Jacob, Moses, Joshua, Samson's parents, Gideon as well as others. This angel is seen as an angel but also as a man. This One is referred to as an angel but also as the LORD and God. We also find this angel in both heaven and on earth.

An introduction for the Angel of the LORD is found in Genesis 16:7-14. In this narrative the Angel of the Lord, the one who spoke to Hagar, is called, *"You are the God who sees me."* Verse 13 continues by saying, *"I have now seen the One who sees me."* This angel was sent by the LORD to speak for him, yet he is referred to as having deity within him.

This same angel deals with Jacob in Genesis 32. How is it that Jacob wrestled with a man until daybreak, yet Jacob says in verse 30[31] this man was the LORD himself? Jacob said, *"I saw God face to face"* yet he was wrestling with an angel.

Our mysterious man in verse 28[29] also told Jacob that his name would be changed because he had, *"struggled with God and with men and have overcome."* Who was it that Jacob was struggling with? Was it a man, an angel or the LORD?

As if the above verses aren't enough to bring confusion, what does one do with the following? Jacob utters a peculiar declaration in Genesis 48:15-16, *"May the God before whom my fathers Abraham and Isaac walked, the God who has been my shepherd all my life to this day, the Angel who has delivered me from all harm."* How is it that Jacob refers to the LORD and this angel as the same being? Does this tell us that there is something more to this being than just angelic substance?

This angel is also found in the book of the Exodus 3 and 4 as he speaks to Moses from the burning bush. However, in this storyline, he is also referred to as both angel and the LORD.

Upon reading Exodus 23:21 we learn the LORD's name is within this angel. Does this reference mention something to imply a different makeup to this angelic being? Does something mysterious and more than angelic explain or define this being?

In Numbers 22:31, we again encounter this angel. Here Balaam bows down to this Angel of the Lord. Some might say, "Balaam, after all, is a Gentile and doesn't know any better."

We also read of this angel in the book of the Judges of Israel. Here too, he's seen as more than just angelic. This time it's by people of Israel! The Angel of the Lord appears to Gideon in Judges 6:22. Listen to what Gideon says about seeing this angel *face to face* in verse 22; "*Ah, Sovereign Lord! I have seen the angel of the Lord face to face!*"

Why such a statement? After all Gideon wasn't the first one to see this angel. Scripture doesn't tell us that a person must die if they see an angel face to face. However, Scripture explicitly says (Exodus 33:20) that anyone who sees the LORD face to face will die. What's going on here?

Two other Israelites also see this angel face-to-face – Samson's parents. We find this encounter in Judges 13 where Samson's father enquires of this angel about how to raise his coming son. This is another amazing narrative. Manoah asks this angel to tell him his name; this angel replies in Judges 13:17-18, "*Why do you ask my name? It is beyond understanding.*" This angels' name is hidden or beyond understanding; that's exactly what the LORD did with His Messiah. But hidden can also mean wonderful – that brings up the picture of a sign, one that makes us sit up to take notice of something amazing that's happening. It's just interesting to me that this is one title of Messiah in Isaiah 9:6 as he's referred to as Wonderful.

Within this Judges narrative we view something seen other places in the Hebrew Scriptures. Judges 13:19-20 says,

And the LORD did an amazing thing while Manoah and his wife watched. As the flame blazed up from the altar toward heaven, the angel of the LORD ascended in the flame. Seeing this, Manoah and his wife fell with their faces to the ground.

The fact that this angel ascends toward heaven in the smoke of the sacrifice is amazing enough, but there's more. In Judges 13:22, Manoah responds similar to Gideon, *"We are doomed to die!...We have seen God!"* Listen to what Manoah's wife says in verse 23, *"If the LORD had meant to kill us, he would not have accepted a burnt offering from our hands."* Once again this angel is referred to as the LORD and God.

Why does Manoah say such a thing? After all, hasn't this couple just seen the angel of the LORD and not the LORD Himself? Or is there something more mysterious to this angel than we realize? After all, many people speak of this angel in the same way. They speak as if this angel is the LORD. He is also referred to as having the LORD's name in him. Why is this?

This story of an angel ascending or descending into or out of heaven is not an isolated one. In many places, Scripture speaks of the LORD as going up from a place back into heaven. Other references speak about ascending/descending as well.

The first one is when Jacob is on his way to meet his mother's family to find a wife for himself. This encounter is in Genesis 28. Since the sun has set, Jacob lays down for the night. As he sleeps, he has a dream where he sees the angels of the LORD ascend and descend to heaven and earth on a stairway. At the top of this stairway stands the LORD himself.

We hear of ascending in Psalm 68:18[19]; we read, *"When you ascended on high, you led captives in your train."*

Proverbs 30:4 also deals with the ascending subject and asks several interesting questions,

Who has gone up to heaven and come down? Who has gathered up the wind in the hollow of his hands? Who has wrapped up the

waters in his cloak? Who established all the ends of the earth? What is his name, and the name of his son? Tell me if you know.

Daniel 7:13 also uses similar imagery when speaking of the son of man coming with the clouds, or angels of God.

In Isaiah 63:9 this unique ascending/descending angel is referred to as the *"Angel of his presence."* In this reference, this angel is also spoken of as saving and redeeming Israel.

Just who is this Angel of the LORD? How can he be described as having the LORD's name within him? How can he be described as being the angel of His Presence? Why do people who see this angel fear for their lives? How can this angel be seen in correlation with the LORD at all? If the links do not reflect truth, isn't this idolatry? We know from Isaiah 42:8 that God won't share his glory with another.

But there are more questions concerning Messiah himself. How can Messiah be the next four things at the same time? How can he be called Mighty God? How can he be seen as a king with an eternal kingdom? How can he be seen as one who rules in Sovereign Power and Majesty? How can Messiah be seen as the LORD's son when the Shema plainly states that the LORD is one?

How Should We See These Prophecies of Scripture?

In what light should the above four prophecies be seen? There are a whole range of answers to consider. Should we see them in the light of sincere hopefulness that is sincerely wrong? Should we treat these prophecies the same as one would treat the prophecies of the false prophets of First Temple Israel? Or should we see these prophecies as only words spoken by men, or simply ones with no meaning or without relevance for today? Maybe we can see these prophecies as having meaning, truth and relevance both for their day, future days, and our times.

Only you can decide how to process these Scriptural passages and questions. I primarily want to present what the Hebrew Scriptures proclaim as true so you can pursue the LORD's truth. After all, **believing** the LORD is what counts for the eternal Kingdom.

Scholars tell us that many prophecies of the Hebrew Scriptures have an initial fulfillment, and ultimately they will have or did have a future fulfillment as well. I believe a hint of this can be found in the LORD's promise to Abraham that he would make him and his descendants a blessing to the nations. This word of the LORD to Abraham has proven true down through the centuries and will stay true throughout history.

The LORD brought blessing to all the nations that his friend Abraham encountered in his travels. This is true if for no other reason than these nations and people had the privilege of knowing Abraham and seeing the LORD of Abraham at work in and through his life. Indeed, it was an amazing work and life.

Israel's Preservation

The Hebrew Scriptures speak of a humanity that places their faith or trust in a very reliable and caring LORD. This is the same LORD who chose Israel for himself and who will always preserve Israel. Listen to what the prophet says about this in Habakkuk 2:4, "...The righteous will live by his faith."

The faith Habakkuk mentions is the opposite of what the children of Israel exhibited many times. Rather than live by the righteous faith from the LORD, they often demanded proof by an action of God before they would believe what He said. The LORD's Word is the ultimate issue. When the LORD or his angels say something, the truth issue is settled! Trust is not just "believing" but acting on the LORD's Word as well!

The book of Deuteronomy speaks of one instance of unbelief when it refers to a specific generation of Israelites. This passage in Deuteronomy 32:20 says, "I will hide my face from them," he said, "and see what their end will be; for they are a perverse generation, children who are unfaithful."

The LORD says he was faithful and had shown himself to be strong, trustworthy and secure. Messiah demonstrates the righteous faith that we are supposed to live by. In contrast, his rebellious people, the ones Moses speaks of above, portrayed the opposite characters of being unfaithful, untrustworthy, weak and helpless.

Even though it is an exciting part of the Hebrew Scriptures, in reality the truly miraculous occurs very rarely. We don't find the miraculous on every page or even in every book. Yet, so much Scripture reveals the preservation of Abraham, Isaac, Jacob, Joseph, David, the Davidic line, and the people of Israel. As far as I'm concerned, these preservations all have to do with the LORD showing himself true to his promises and faithful to the covenant with his friend, Abraham.

When we think of the historical facts of the 20th Century alone, how do we account for so many of the factual accounts of this past century? How do we explain such a small group of people, who were once a nation being scattered to the four corners of the world, only to return to their homeland once again after an absence of almost 2,000 years?

Why weren't these people swallowed up by the very nations wherein they lived? How was it that the Jewish people were able to keep their ethnicity intact? So many other ethnicities of antiquity disappeared without as much as a trace; so many were assimilated into the surrounding peoples. Even when we look at the atrocity of the Holocaust, how do we explain the fact that the Jewish people were preserved at all, even though 6 million Jewish men, women and children died unmercifully?

If we look at the geographic location of the nation of Israel, I am amazed at the location of this small sliver of land. It is barely as big as the State of New Jersey in its current layout. Besides the Mediterranean Sea to the West, Israel is completely surrounded by nations and peoples whose express intent and commitment is the extermination of the Jewish people. But, thanks be to the LORD, Israel will never be exterminated.

How did the current nation of Israel become a nation in the first place? This nation didn't just win its rebirth through its first war in 1948. As a fledgling nation it was victorious in two later major wars. Were the victories of 1967 and 1973 strictly due to superior military planning and strategy? Was it due to the fact that Israel's soldiers had more water than their enemies? Or maybe there was something more to these victories? Certainly it was not by chance that Israel was birthed as a nation!

Even if one doesn't believe in the miraculous as far as the LORD being involved in the creation of this nation and its victories, how does one account for the things mentioned above? The Jewish people are hated without reason and without provocation on their part. How can this hatred that goes back thousands of years be explained? How is it that a religion, with the hatred of Jewish people at its core, fill the countries of those people who now surround Israel with such hatred? Are all these things dumb luck, fate, chance, or is the LORD's hand and his plan for a small, seemingly insignificant, nation being displayed to the world?

I don't believe the LORD's word just because I'm told that I should or must. I believe his word because it is truthful and trustworthy, as shown historically and archaeologically. Neither history nor archaeology has disproven Scripture. While areas of dispute exist, all knowledge of history-past is not yet known. In antiquity, rivers were known to run backwards to their natural flow due to seismic activity. A man was reportedly found inside a beached whale. Do we discount these known facts because they seem miraculous?

Do words of the prophet Isaiah in 51:1-2 say anything to us today? They tell us, *"Look to the rock from which you were cut and to the quarry from which you were hewn; look to Abraham, your father, and to Sarah, who gave you birth."*

In these two verses the LORD reminds his people of the faith and perseverance of Abraham and Sarah. These people of faith in the LORD were not perfect, and both endured doubt. However, they both clung tenaciously to the LORD's word as true in spite of what they saw with their eyes or experienced in their aging bodies. They were eventually rewarded for their faith; they saw the LORD's promise become reality through the birth of Isaac in spite of their bodies being past the age to produce children.

Speaking of preservation, the LORD even told Jeremiah to buy a field just before the Babylonians captured Jerusalem. Why would the LORD have him do such a thing? Did Israel have any future hope? Would Jerusalem rise from the dust? These are good questions. From my perspective, it seems that Israel did and does have a future hope. It seems that Israel did rise from the dust, just as these prophets of Israel predicted.

The blessings that Israel brings to the nations, in my opinion, are still being produced even today. But my opinion isn't the one that counts. In the end, it's the LORD's "opinion" that ultimately counts! Let me ask another question, "How does one account for these above happenings?"

In fact Jeremiah does speak of just that hope in the middle of terrible times for Judah. And he speaks of this hope to the people of Judah who've already been taken captive to Babylon. This reference is Jeremiah 29:11. Here is the promise of hope the LORD gives to the captives, *"For I know the plans I have for you, declares the LORD, plans to prosper you and not to harm you, plans to give you a hope and a future."*

Even though the above message given by Jeremiah must have brought some hope to the captives in Babylon, there's one specific blessing that one specific person would bring. This blessing would come first to his own people and then to the nations. This person, bringing the ultimate blessing to Israel and later to the Gentiles is the Messiah.

Summation of Messiah's Life Puzzle and the Sometimes Puzzling Imagery of Messiah

I hope our journey has been informative, thought-provoking and challenging. I left many questions unanswered and I seemingly left you dangling at the end of some chapters. Here is where I want to try to summarize all of what we looked at in the Hebrew Scriptures. My format is set up to follow what I will shortly reveal concerning Messiah.

I will still, however, leave many questions unanswered. The reasons behind this are one: I am only laying a foundation in this book, one upon which I desire to build upon in a second book. And two: I desire for you to look at these Scriptures, to do your own research, pray to the LORD and ask for his help and direction in your journey of discovery.

In order for a summary to do true justice to these varied subjects of Abraham's call, blessing, only begotten son Isaac, Messiah and all that is entailed within these people and related topics would take many volumes of books. But I will attempt to do this in the most complete and yet brief manner possible.

Out of all the messianic imagery we have experienced as we've traveled through the Hebrew Scriptures, can a true picture of Messiah be retrieved? I think this is a good question that requires much thought, research and prayer.

This requires the contemplation of many things, such as, "Do all of these messianic Scriptures and imagery point to one individual alone?" "How do we understand the messianic narratives that seem to refer to Messiah as more than just a man?" "Do all three specific messianic categories – King, Priest and Prophet – tie in with one person?" "If so, how does this work and what would this look like?" "Are there any historical events, happenings or writings that may be able to shed more light on the Scriptural imagery of Messiah, etc.?"

Atonement

The precursor to Messiah and his mission is found in the first book of Torah, which is Genesis. After Adam and Eve have decided to experience good and evil by eating the forbidden fruit, they find themselves in a quandary. Yes, their eyes are opened but not exactly as the serpent promised them. They have experience alright, and it's firsthand experience, but this experience reveals to them that something has changed; but the change is not one for the better. In fact these two humans now realize nakedness, embarrassment and separation both from each other and from the LORD.

In this after-the-bite narrative, it's the LORD Himself who seeks this couple out and finds them hiding from His presence. Why are they hiding? They're hiding because of another new current experience. This experience is called fear, and they are both afraid. Adam and Eve experienced the separation that sin brings between humanity and the LORD. But the Lord has a plan; and it's not "Plan B!"

Just as what will be experienced later in the Akedah, a substitution is made here in this early Genesis narrative. The backdrop, though not fully in view, is that an animal paid the price for this couple's choice of disobedience. The LORD "sacrificed" an animal and the blood of an animal was spilled "in the stead of" this couples' choice of sin. Through the LORD's substitution of the animal for this couple, they have their nakedness, sin and shame covered by this animals' skins.

Miraculous Birth / The Only

In this same book we find the Akedah, where Abraham offers his son Isaac on an altar in Genesis 22. Please remember that the Lord talks about Isaac as Abraham's only begotten son. As previously presented, we know this isn't because Isaac is Abraham's only son because he already fathered Ishmael.

But this *onlyness* has to do with the fact of Isaac's miraculous birth. Without the LORD working a miracle within Sarah's body, she would never have been able to conceive, and Isaac would not have been born!

The Hebrew Scriptures speak of several other miraculous births as well. These include the conception and birth of Jacob, Samuel and Immanuel to mention just three. In fact, when you look at the LORD's chosen people, you find many significant and even miraculous births.

Father / Son Relationship

There is also a father/son aspect taking place here. Isaac's seed will someday be King David, and eventually King Messiah. Remember that there is also a father/son aspect within David's relationship with the LORD. And there is another father/son relationship between Solomon and the LORD. The possibility of this relationship is available to all of Judah's kings. But this special relationship is ultimately fulfilled in Messiah where there will be an ultimate father/son relationship between him and the LORD.

The *father/son relationship, only begotten son,* and *only son* imagery and connections are aspects that you will need to look at more closely. This is especially true since we see this same imagery and connection in many of the messianic and related narratives. Let's take a broader look at the other places in the Hebrew Scriptures where this above imagery and connection are found to summarize the book's purpose.

In our first reference in II Samuel 7, we learn of the *father/son* relationship that will exist between the LORD and David's son Solomon. Verse 14 begins with the LORD speaking, "*I will be his father, and he will be my son.*" This opportunity for the same *father/son* relationship is given to each succeeding king of Israel and, after King Rehoboam, to the kings of Judah.

The above covenant that the LORD entered with David is that he will always have a son after him who will rule on his throne. Even if this son of David sinned, the Lord would not take his Spirit from him as he had done with King Saul.

Does this mean that we should be looking for a coming Messiah who's from the tribe of Judah? If this is the case, since the genealogies have now been lost, how could we know that he was really a Davidic king? So, the bigger question is: "Are we looking for a future king or one from the past?"

Speaking of King Messiah who would rule on David's throne, Isaiah 9:6[5] tells us the following, *"For to us a child is born, to us a son is given."* The Messiah, David's son, would be a child who would be born at some future time in history. But this son is to be given to the people of Israel. One could ask, "Just who is giving this son to Israel?"

Zechariah 12:10 speaks to the emotions of this future time when the son is given, *"The inhabitants of Jerusalem ....They will look on me...and they will mourn for him as one mourns for an only child...for a firstborn son."*

Psalm 2:7 also speaks of this special son as it proclaims the following: *"You are my Son; today I have become your Father."* Verse 12 continues with these words, *"Kiss the son, lest he be angry....Blessed are all who take refuge in him."*

Psalm 89:26[27] continues in this *father/son* imagery, *"He will call out to me, You are my Father....I will also appoint him my firstborn, the most exalted of the kings of the earth."*

Did you notice the special designation concerning this firstborn son in the above verses? The Scriptures designate that the LORD will appoint him as his firstborn. Just like Isaac, who was not Abraham's first son, a special significant attachment is given to David's son, Messiah. The attachment is this: he will be known as the Lord's firstborn. Just as Abraham received Isaac back after he was non-typically sacrificed to the LORD, David tells us the LORD will receive back his son Messiah as well.

Another mysterious reference, Proverbs 30:4, asks five questions, *"Who has ascended/descended into or from heaven? Who has gathered the wind in his fists? Who has bound the waters in his garment? Who has established all the ends of the earth? What is his name, and what is his son's name?"*

Our last *father/son* reference for summary is found in I Chronicles 28:4-6. This reference, as our first one, deals with David and his son Solomon, the one who would follow David on the throne of Israel. It also speaks of the LORD's choosing of Solomon in verse 6, "...I have chosen him to be my son, and I will be his father" to give more development to this reality.

To recap our above findings; Messiah will have a *father/son* relationship with the LORD. He will be a child who is born, but also one who is given. The people of Jerusalem will look on this son as a special son like Isaac at some point in history. They also will mourn for him, as one would mourn for an only son.

There is also imagery of the LORD speaking of calling this son – His son – at a specific point in time. It also refers to a blessing to all who trust in, rely on, or take refuge in this son. This special unique son of David will be appointed as the LORD's firstborn and as the most exalted of all the kings of earth. We still need to remember all of our above imagery concerning this coming Messiah that also depicts him as being rejected, opposed, beaten and killed.

Mount Moriah / Mount Zion / Jerusalem

Another aspect of Messiah within the above narratives has to do with the mountain where the above sacrifice, the Akedah, took place.

This mountain is eventually called Jerusalem and many sacrifices were offered there. When we return to our Akedah narrative in Genesis 22:14, after the ram is offered in exchange for Isaac, we encounter a specific pronouncement that says, *"So Abraham called that place The LORD Will Provide. And to this day it is said, On the mountain of the LORD it will be provided."*

We talked about how this mountain, Mt Moriah, became known as Jerusalem and the place of the Temple Mount. This is the very spot where so many sacrifices and offerings were provided for so many centuries. As important as it was we need to ask, "Is there more to this place of the special Akedah sacrifice than just the temple?" Does this verse refer to another special event that would take place in Jerusalem at a later time?

The Cost of Sin

Now let me ask you a question that goes all the way back to the initial couple in Genesis 3. In this Garden narrative, "Who paid the price for Adam and Eve's sin?" The animal paid the price. "But who was the one who ultimately took care of this mess and covered these two people's sin and shame?" It's the same one who would tell His friend Abraham, many years later, that He would bless him as a result of his obedience.

The question is: "What would be provided on Mount Zion and in Jerusalem?" Something special and singularly significant would one day be provided on this mountain. Just as the prophets said, sin would be atoned for and an innocent one would pay the price. Just as in the Garden narrative, it would be the LORD who would ultimately be responsible for how this all plays out. He is the one who orchestrates all the details and all surrounding circumstances. According to the Hebrew Scriptures the application of this sacrifice of substitutionary atonement will remove all sin from Jerusalem and the people of Israel.

But there's more to the Once-for-all-time sacrifice by Messiah on Mount Zion in Jerusalem. It will also provide the Gentiles with atonement as well. Just as the people of Israel believed, the life of a righteous person made atonement. It is this coming Messiah, the one who would be a perfectly righteous and sinless person, whose death and blood would Once-for-all-time atone. Some of Israel's sacrifices made atonement for the Gentiles as well. These truths point to the ultimate payment for sin that will be made in Jerusalem on Mount Zion. But you may ask, "Is this really what the Hebrew Scriptures say will happen?"

Exchange: The LORD's Requirement

There is an exchange that has taken place in our above Akedah narrative. A ram is sacrificed in exchange for Isaac. And sacrifices of exchange are seen throughout Scripture.

Besides this narrative of exchange, we see an exchange made in Egypt. In each house of Israel, a lamb was killed in exchange for the firstborn son of that house. Later, as a result of this above exchange, the LORD took the Levites in exchange for the firstborn of Israel. This exchange and the one below are requirements by the LORD for all of Israel.

The Scriptures show us another exchange that is part of what is called the Day of Atonement. During this day, one goat is killed and sacrificed while another goat, the scapegoat, with the sins of Israel placed upon it, removes these sins away from the people of Israel by taking them out into the desert.

Isaiah 53 also speaks of another such exchange in light of Messiah. Let's look at verses 5-7, and then verse 10,

But he was pierced for our transgressions; he was crushed for our iniquities: the punishment that brought us peace was upon him, and by his wounds we are healed. We all, like sheep, did go astray, each of us has turned to his own way; and the LORD has laid on him the iniquity of us all....Yet it was the LORD's will to crush him and cause him to suffer, and thou the LORD makes his life a guilt offering.

Have you noticed something else about some of our exchanges? What stands out – waiting like a sentry at attention – is the word *upon*. In Genesis 22, Abraham places the wood *upon* Isaac. The people of Israel, before the Exodus, place the blood *upon* the doorposts of their dwellings. In the case of the scapegoat, it's the sins of Israel that are placed *upon* this goat before he carries them away into the desert. And in our above Isaiah reference, it was our punishment and iniquity that will be placed *upon* Messiah as this exchange brings us peace.

The Prophet

Most of us are probably very familiar with the Prophet/ King aspects and imagery within the messianic portions of the Hebrew Scriptures. As a result of this granted knowledge, I don't want to rehash these narratives here. However, I do want to look at some of the mysterious and uncommon imagery found in these messianic narratives.

We remember that Messiah is pictured, among other things, as King, Prophet and High Priest. I believe everyone "gets" or understands the Conquering, Ruling and Kingdom- Reigning King imagery. But why would Messiah be a Prophet and, especially, why would he be a High Priest?

Moses, the one who spoke of *The Prophet* who was coming, as a prophet himself, spoke to the people of Israel on many occasions. While this man's instructions to the people covered a wide assortment of topics, many times he spoke to them concerning obedience to the LORD and remaining faithful to Him. He spoke of the sacrifices and offerings that would be provided, and of how sins would be atoned.

This shepherd of the LORD's people, just as a High Priest would do, interceded on behalf of the people before the LORD when they sinned. Moses even asked the LORD at one point to blot his name out of His book in order to save his people Israel. As a true shepherd, Moses laid his life on the line for the people of Israel on several occasions. Near the end of his life, this prophet of Israel was present as the blessings and cursings were pronounced over the people. Moses also predicted the people of Israel's later apostasy and its sad result.

When we think of the prophets of Israel we must remember they repeatedly called both the Northern Kingdom of Samaria and the Southern Kingdom of Judah to turn from their apostasy and return to the LORD. This was a continual theme among these prophets.

Many prophets of Israel also prophesied to the Gentile nations. Jonah was one such prophet; however, his mission was just a little different than most. He not only prophesied to the city of Nineveh in the name of the LORD, he personally traveled to this Gentile city in order to pronounce its doom.

The people of the city of Nineveh, part of Assyria, were one of Israel's most hated enemies. From the text, Jonah went through a harbinger-event to parallel the work of the coming Messiah – he died, was "entombed" (inside a large fish) for three days, and was resurrected. Upon hearing Jonah's words of doom, many Ninevites repented of their sins and turned to the LORD. Sadly, Jonah wasn't happy at all.

Because of the LORD's work in Jonah's message, people in Nineveh repented, starting with the King. As a result of repentance, the LORD's hand of judgment was stayed. His cup of wrath was not poured out upon these Gentile people.

Many of our above prophets of the LORD, even paid with their own lives as they spoke the LORD's words to their brothers. These men paid a tremendous price while they sought to point their people back toward the LORD and his ways.

High Priest

We saw that Moses himself interceded for the people of Israel, just as a High Priest should do. I still believe we must understand why Messiah was seen as a High Priest, especially from today's perspective. Maybe the most puzzling of all the messianic imageries used in relation to Messiah is Melchizedek.

One narrative in Genesis that may seem out of place provides the background for our High Priestly/Messiah imagery. Back in Genesis we encounter a man named Melchizedek who is both king and priest of his city, Salem. This man receives a tithe from Abraham and blesses him even though this man had no relation to Abraham at all. Salem, the city of this king/priest will one day be known by the name of Jerusalem. And, this isn't the only place Melchizedek is mentioned in Scripture.

Later in the Writings we read again concerning this king-priest in Psalm 110:4, *"The LORD has sworn and will not change his mind: You are a priest forever, in the order of Melchizedek."* Why would the LORD choose to use a High Priestly line for Messiah which wasn't from the tribe of Levi? We remember that Melchizedek blessed Abraham in the Genesis 14 narrative. The fact that Melchizedek blesses Abraham brings us to another question. Is it Messiah's function as High Priest to bless both Israel and all ethnicities or Gentiles?

We also find further examples of this messianic King-High Priest in conjunction with the book of Zechariah. This prophet speaks in messianic imagery very definitely concerning the High Priest and his office. Within chapter 3, this prophet speaks some amazing pronouncements.

In this narrative, Joshua is the High Priest of the people. He represents symbolically, with others around him, things that pertain to the LORD's servant – the Branch. Notice also, toward the end of Zechariah 3:9 that we read these words, *"I will remove the sin of this land in a single day."* Another priestly function.

Zechariah 6 is another place in the Hebrew Scriptures that is rich in messianic imagery. We read again of Joshua the High Priest, and two crowns. Zechariah 6:9-15 speaks of this High Priest wearing a crown and goes on to tell us that this one called the Shoot or *Branch* will come and build the temple. But that's not all. This man will be both King and High Priest, thus the two crowns. And there will be total harmony between both of these offices of king and priest.

The servant of the LORD, the Branch, again provides the backdrop to these verses. The Branch is the one who will build the Lord's Temple. He will be clothed with majesty and will rule on his throne. His rule will be one of both king and priest, which is like Melchizedek above.

Some of the above imagery very closely parallels Daniel 7 and its pronouncement concerning the Son of Man as well as another narrative found in Daniel 9:24. Look at these and see what you think.

Last, I want to add references from Isaiah that are spoken about Messiah's priestly functions and duties:

Isaiah 42:6-7 speak of Messiah being a covenant for the people and a light for the Gentiles.

Isaiah 48:17 says that the servant of the LORD will teach them in the way that they should go. The way in the Hebrew Scriptures refers to the "Way of the LORD," which is following Torah with one's heart.

Isaiah 49:5-6 declares the servant of the LORD will bring Jacob back to the LORD, which is both their physical presence in the land and also their turning back to the Way of the LORD. He will also bring the LORD's salvation to the ends of the earth.

Isaiah 52:15 pronounces the sprinkling of many nations by Messiah which is a priestly cleansing ritual.

Isaiah 53:1-12 expresses how Messiah will carry the people's transgressions and iniquities on himself.

Isaiah 59:20 reveals that the Redeemer will come to Zion, to those who repent of their sins.

These verses tell us that our transgressions and iniquities were placed upon an innocent and righteous Messiah. **Isaiah 53:10 and 12** specifically tell us that the LORD made Messiah's life a guilt offering and that he bore sin while making intercession for the transgressors.

The Branch (Shoot)

Next we will take a look at one image we saw above in our Zechariah narratives – the one called *The Branch (Shoot).* We'll also look at other similar imagery that is used when speaking of this man.

Isaiah tells us what will happen on Mount Zion and in Jerusalem in the day of the Branch. Isaiah 4:2 says, *"In that day the Branch of the LORD will be beautiful and glorious."*

Isaiah 11:1 and 10 continues with this Branch,

A shoot will come up from the stump of Jesse; from his roots a Branch will bear fruit....In that day the Root of Jesse will stand as a banner for the peoples; the nations will rally to him, and his place of rest will be glorious.

Jeremiah 23:5 says, *"...The days are coming," declares the LORD," when I will raise up to David a righteous Branch."* Jeremiah 33:15 is almost verbatim of 23:5; it says, *"In those days and at that time I will make a righteous Branch sprout from David's line; he will do what is just and right in the land."*

Zechariah 3:8 also speaks of this *Branch*, *"I am going to bring my servant, the Branch."*

In speaking of Joshua the High Priest, Zechariah 6:12 says, *"Here is the man whose name is the Branch, and he will branch out from his place and build the temple of the LORD."*

Rejection – Then Acceptance

Another part of our summation was seen in the lives of Joseph and Moses. Both of these men are used to save their relatives. There are many more important aspects to both of their lives and missions. But I want to speak here of one aspect in particular. This aspect is how both of these men were initially received by the family of Israel. We know both Joseph and Moses are types of Messiah so I want to demonstrate that these two men's lives typically demonstrate how Israel will initially reject Messiah.

Remember, Joseph had two dreams. In both of these he happens to be in charge. But his family members are not too thrilled by these dreams, especially with the aspect of his being in charge. They rejected him because he told his dreams.

When his brothers first travel to Egypt, they don't even recognize their brother. Not until their second Egypt-journey does their brother reveal his identity to them. Now they realize how both of Josephs' dreams have proved altogether true.

Moses also suffers initial rejection by his people. We remember the day after he rescued a fellow Hebrew, he runs into an issue of rejection. This narrative in Exodus 2:14 tells how, after breaking up a fight between two Hebrews, he hears biting sarcasm from the Hebrew in the wrong, who asks, *"Who made you ruler and judge over us?"*

This great man and prophet of Israel still ran into difficulty and rejection over and over again. Even though he eventually brings his people out of Egypt, he is rejected. He is rejected while he is on the mountain with the LORD. Korah and his followers reject Moses' leadership. Even his own sister and brother speak against this humble man.

At this point we transition from the Messiah-types of Joseph and Moses – knowing the upward progression from rejection to acceptance that is experienced in their lives – to Messiah. Even

Messiah is *despised* and *rejected* as we read in Isaiah 49:7; 52:14; and 53:3. In contrast to Moses and Joseph, Messiah is not really accepted until after His death.

Also in Isaiah, we see Messiah coming from Jesse's stump instead of bursting on the scene in wealth, pomp and power. Messiah is seen as appearing on the scene when the House of David has been cut down, per Isaiah 11:1. He is the twig who grows from this root system. Just a root system is all that is left from the once powerful House of David.

Isaiah gives us the picture of Messiah coming onto the scene from the backdrop of dry hard ground rather than fertile soil. Isaiah 53:2a says, "*He grew up before him like a tender shoot, and like a root out of dry ground.*" Isaiah 53:2b gives us an unflattering description of Messiah's beauty or lack thereof, "*He had no beauty or majesty to attract us to him, nothing in his appearance that we should desire him.*"

This is opposite of the description of Absalom, one of David's sons. II Samuel 14:25 speaks of his appearance. This description is something we might expect of a king's son,

> *In all Israel there was not a man so highly praised for his handsome appearance as Absalom. From the top of his head to the sole of his foot there was no blemish in him.*

Ezekiel 17 also speaks of this Messiah. In 17:22-24, he is the shoot taken by the LORD and planted on the mountains of Israel. This shoot and sprig is spoken of as follows,

> *I myself will take a shoot from the very top of a cedar and plant it; I will break off a tender sprig from its topmost shoots and plant it on a high and lofty mountain. On the mountain heights of Israel I will plant it; it will...bear fruit, and become a splendid cedar.*

Again, though initially it is only a shoot, it will later become splendid – to the salvation and surprise of many.

Resurrection

Resurrection is another issue that may not seem to fit with other messianic imagery. I speak of this issue "not fitting" with other messianic imagery for the following reason: for resurrection to occur, death must first take place.

Let's raise two questions concerning resurrection. "How can Mighty King Messiah succumb to death?" After all, was he supposed to be highly exalted and triumphant, with an eternal kingdom? Yes, he was! "How then can death and resurrection perfectly manifest a highly exalted, triumphant, and eternal King and Kingdom?" There's more to the picture.

The Hebrew Scriptures present us with images of death for Messiah. These are not just pictures of death but horrific depictions of tremendous beating and abuse. Although Messiah is beaten horrifically, pierced through and seen dying a brutal death, he is restored to life once again. Messiah's mission, that seemed to be left unaccomplished, is in fact a success and bears fruit. Can these things really be true? Well, let's see.

Our first reference to speak of these important details of Messiah's suffering, death and resurrection is Isaiah 53:8-11,

> *For he was cut off from the land of the living….He was assigned a grave with the wicked….Yet it was the LORD's will to crush him and cause him to suffer, and though the LORD makes his life a guilt offering, he will see his offspring and prolong his days…. After the suffering of his soul he will see the light of life.*

King David presents the following facts concerning his son Messiah in Psalm 16:9-11,

> *Therefore my heart is glad and my tongue rejoices; my body also will rest secure, because you will not abandon me to the grave; nor will you let your Holy One see decay.*

But is Messiah the only one who receives the *benefit* of resurrection? Isaiah tells us of something that will happen on a mountain in Jerusalem. The Lord will deal with something that plagued people in every generation; he will deal with death once and for all time. Isaiah 25:7-8 begins, *"On this mountain he will destroy the shroud that enfolds all peoples …he will swallow up death forever."*

Isaiah 26:19 reiterates this same message:

> But your dead will live; their bodies will rise. You who dwell in the dust, wake up and shout for joy. Your dew is like the dew of the morning; the earth will give birth to her dead.

The aspect of the earth giving birth to her dead is interesting indeed. And this leads us to another question in the Psalms. In Psalm 2:7, David says, *"the LORD…said to me, You are my Son; today I have become your Father."* Could it be that the LORD refers here to the resurrection of His son Messiah?

In our last reference to resurrection, Hosea 13:14 states in a matter-of-fact way, *"I will ransom them from the power of the grave; I will redeem them from death. Where, O death are your plagues? Where, O grave, is your destruction?"*

We will not properly understand the mission and Good News of Messiah without a proper understanding of the reality of death-to-resurrection seen in seeds. As the LORD caused the bones of Ezekiel 37 to come back to life, Messiah wants this "spiritual resurrection" to occur in His followers. This is one of the realities pictured within the New Covenant that we will examine later.

Cornerstone / Stone of Stumbling

Many know Messiah is referenced as the *Cornerstone* – the ultimate stone builders use to set foundations to build upon. If the cornerstone isn't properly set, the temple will be skewed. Within these same Hebrew Scriptures we again see the tension seen repeatedly throughout Messianic references. We see these tensions when he is referenced as a stone of stumbling.

Our first *Cornerstone* reference, Isaiah 28:16, has this to say, *"See, I lay in Zion, a tested stone, a precious cornerstone for a sure foundation; the one who trusts will never be dismayed."*

The fact that Messiah is referred to as a tested stone, what does that say about him? It tells us this stone, Messiah, went through a trial. This stone was completely examined and passed its inspection; at least from the LORD's point of view.

Our second cornerstone reference is Zechariah 10:4; it says, *"From Judah will come the cornerstone."* This verse once again ties the cornerstone to the Son of David, Messiah.

Our third and final *cornerstone* reference is Psalm 118:22, *"The stone the builders rejected has become the capstone; The LORD has done this and it is marvelous in our eyes."*

We saw early that the cornerstone was tried, tested and officially approved. Here in this verse we find this stone didn't impress the builders at all. Because this stone failed *their* test of approval, it was cast aside. Seemingly it was unable to meet the qualifications for which it was needed. However, we see in Psalm 118:22 that the Lord himself had the correct view of this stone. He made it the pinnacle or foundation stone.

These references show us the tension of perspective in the Hebrew Scriptures concerning messianic references when the cornerstone and stone of stumbling are considered. To the LORD this stone is exalted above all others; to the builders it is insignificant, substandard, and is cast aside as worthless.

We should remember it's the LORD's opinion that counts! Since this stone is precious to the LORD but rejected by the builders, this apparent conundrum causes many issues in humanity. Isaiah 8:14-15 adds some interesting yet puzzling circumstances and pronouncements that relate to this stone. Listen to its qualifiers,

> ...and he will be a sanctuary; but for both houses of Israel he will be a stone that causes men to stumble and a rock that makes them fall. And for the people of Jerusalem he will be a trap and a snare. Many of them will stumble; they will fall...be snared and captured.

Once again we encounter tension; Israel's Messiah is a sanctuary yet a stone of stumbling and a snare. We ask, "How can this stone be both an exalted stone and a rejected stone?" "How can he be both a sure foundation and a stone that many trip over and are ensnared by?" "Why did the builders reject this stone when they examined it?" "Should we regard the evaluation of the builders or the LORD?" Can we trust the LORD's assessment of His Messiah?

Just as we saw the opposite ends of the spectrum in King Messiah – shown as an exalted, triumphant ruler and yet as a rejected-and-killed Messiah – we find a similar contrast here. Again we encounter pole-opposite descriptions used to "frame" Messiah, here spoken of as a stone. "What do these things imply?" For one thing, we are shown things from two different perspectives – one from the LORD's viewpoint and the other from the builders view. But I also believe there's more.

At this point, I think the following question needs asked, "What can be done with the many seeming contradictions or contrasts found in the Hebrew Scriptures concerning Messiah?" This is the very thing I would like to look at now.

Contradictions or Contrasts

All the way back to Abraham and the LORD's promise to him concerning his promised seed Israel, we also have in view Judah, David, Messiah, and the Gentiles. In many of these messianic contexts we find Scriptural similarities and seeming contradictions. Below, as best I can in a side-by-side format, I will show these similarities, contradictions or contrasts. I hope that when you see this format it helps you to discern biblical-narrative-pictures in a better way so that you will not be tripped up by what appears to be contradictions.

Contradictions	Or	Contrasts
Abraham's Seed – Bless Nations		Nations Conspire against His Anointed
Abrahamic Covenant		**New Covenant – Messiah is Covenant**
Sacrifice of Promised Son		Promised Son Received Back Again
Animal sacrifice		**Body Prepared for Messiah**
Rule the Nations		King David's fallen Tent
The Branch – Obedience of Nations		**The Stump of Jesse – the Root**
King comes in exaltation		King lowly – bringing salvation
Higher than kings of earth		**Born in little Bethlehem Ephrathah**
Defeats the Nations		Beaten, Dies and is Buried
Son's Kingdom established		**Rulers conspire against the Son**
He'll re-build the temple		Stone the Builders rejected
LORD will be his Father / he will be the Son		**My God, My God why have you forsaken Me?**
Establish Throne Forever		Never Rules, Despised, Rejected & Dies
The Branch		**Tender plant – Root from Dry Ground**
Son of David		Riding on donkey, colt; foal of donkey
Solomon —Loved of the LORD		**No Form, Comeliness or Beauty — Stricken by God**
Goings forth from old, from eternity		David's son, Just – Lowly, Coming to Jerusalem
House of David		**Stump of Jesse**
Spirit of grace/supplication		Mourn for Him as First Born Son
Set son of David on his throne		**Hated w/o cause – Enemies are mighty**
Make Horn of David bud		Imminent Death-Surrounded by goring enemies
Ordained lamp for my Anointed		**Bore Shame for the LORD's Sake/ Covered in Shame**

His enemies covered in shame	Enemies Surround Him
Paid for his work	**Repaid with Hatred For His Love**
On LORD's Right Hand	His Enemies Are Strong and Fight against Him
Make Enemies His Footstool	**Reproach to Israel – They Shook their Heads**
Known by the LORD	Stranger to his Own People and his own brothers
Eaten up w/ Zeal for Temple	**His Wage is thrown to the Potter in the Temple**
Highly exalted	Heart broken by reproach none pity him
Led to the Ancient of Days	**Led to the Cross**
Son of David	Son of Man – Mighty God – The LORD's Son
Thy throne O God	**Human, lowly, rejected**
The LORD our Righteousness	**Thought stricken by God because of his sin**
Given Authority, Glory, Sovereign Power; All ethnicities, nations worship him; Dominion is everlasting; Won't pass away; Kingdom will never be destroyed; Sovereign Power	Never Rules on David's Throne; No Kingdom
Covenant w/Chosen – David my Servant will stand fast w/him Scepter of Righteousness	**Covenant Broken w/ Israel and Judah Covenant**
The Prince	The Servant
Exalted	**Despised – Esteemed not – Rejected**
Exalt Horn	Rejected – Man of Sorrows
The LORD	**Servant of the LORD**
Sent by the LORD – by His Spirit	Astonished by His Appearance / Visage Terribly Marred
Exalted –Extolled – Very High	
The Prophet – People Must Listen	**The people would not hear**
All Who Don't Listen Judged	We esteemed him Smitten of God
Bearer of Good Tidings	**Who has believed our Report?**
Light of Morning	Cut off from the Land of the Living
Immanuel – God with Us	**Assigned a Grave with the Wicked**
Redeemer Comes to Zion	To those who turn from Transgression
Sanctuary; Head of Corner; Tried Stone	**Stumbling stone; Rock of Offence; Snare**
Foundation Stone, Precious, Cornerstone	Stone Refused by builders

Gentiles look to his signal fire, to His Standard	Rejected by Leaders/Despised by people
Swallow up Death forever, Dead will live and rise; Ransom from power of Grave; Redeem from death	Beaten, dies and is buried. Assigned Grave Assigned Grave w/ Rich in His Death
Believeth, Trusts, Looks to Him	**Who believed? / Despised, Abhorred**
Blind eyes opened /Deaf hear	Eyes would be blind, ears be deaf
Bring out prisoners from darkness; Proclaim liberty to captives, open prison of bound	**Prisoner, taken from prison and justice**
Shepherd – Gather flock and young	Despised by the flock – Shepherd is disgusted by the sheep
Feed the flock	**Stopped feeding flock**
Shepherd flock on Mts. of Israel	Flock marked for slaughter
Paid 30 pcs of silver as wage	**This is how much he was valued — Thrown to the Potter**
My fellow, familiar friend lifted up heel against me	Sword against him by the LORD
Call on the LORD's Name & delivered	**Smite shepherd – sheep scattered**
The LORD's Spirit on Him	LORD smote him
Anointed to preach	Who has listened
Jewish people	**Gentiles**
Desire of All Nations	Heathen rage – Gentile kings take counsel against the LORD and against His Anointed
Priest – Sprinkle	**Made his soul an offering for sin**
Priest forever – Order of Melchizedek	Justify many – Bear their iniquities
Made Intercession for Transgressors	LORD laid our Iniquity on Him — Guilt Offering
High Priest Joshua	**Builder of Temple**
King/Priest Joshua reigns on throne	Remove iniquity of land in one day
Unity between positions of King & Priest / Crowned	**Rulers Conspire against him and the LORD**
Former Things	New Things
Revealed	**Hid – Possessed him in the beginning before works of old**
Set up from everlasting Brought forth before mountains	David's descendant
Word – Words – Tongue	**Silent**

Sharp sword	Words didn't break bruised reed
Witness to the people	**Silent – Opened not his mouth**
Mission – Bring back Jacob to Him	Mission failed —Who believed report
LORD's Will Prospers in his Hand	**Labored in vain**
Preserved – Days prolonged – Soul shall live	Dead – Cut off – Grave – Death
Pleased the LORD to bruise him –	**Beard Plucked / Spit upon / Stripes / put to grief**
Righteous – Innocent – No Guile	Numbered w/Transgressors
At the LORD's Right Hand – Pleasures forever	**Offered my Back to those who beat Me, pulled out beard**
Flesh rests in hope; Soul not left in hell	Holy One will not see corruption
Messenger of Messiah sent	**Prepare way for Messenger of the LORD's Covenant**
Delighted in	Forsaken by the LORD
Preached righteousness in congregation	**People say, he trusted in the LORD, let him deliver him**
Declared LORD's faithfulness, salvation truth	Surrounded by bulls of Bashan – Roaring Ravening Lion
Lovingkindness to congregation	**We esteemed him stricken of God**
The LORD didn't despise or abhor him	Assembly of wicked, Dogs encircled him
LORD's Anointed One – The Ruler	**Anointed One is cut off and dies**
70 sevens decreed – 483 yrs after Decree to Build Temple	Messiah is announced to his people
Jerusalem's rebuilt in times of trouble	**Destruction of Temple and Jerusalem**

New / New Covenant

Another term tied in with the messianic concepts is the term *new*. We find this term used in many below references. In this section, only a few references are quoted. Please take the time to look up and evaluate the listed references.

Let's start in Isaiah 42:9 and discover what is seen in the backdrop of Messiah, *"See, the former things have taken place, and new things I declare; before they spring into being I announce them to you."* Verse 10 continues, *"Sing to the LORD a new song, his praise from the ends of the earth."*

Two other new things, a *way* and *streams* are found in the words of Isaiah 43:18-21,

> *Forget the former things; do not dwell on the past. See, I am doing a new thing! Now it springs up; do you not perceive it? I am making a way in the desert and streams in the wasteland, to give drink to my people, my chosen, the people I formed for myself that they may proclaim my praise.*

Did you notice what verse 21 says in regard to what occurs here in the time of Messiah? The LORD's people, as a result of these new happenings, will speak of the LORD's praise.

Again, new things appear in Isaiah 48:3; 6-7,

> *I foretold the former things long ago....From now on I will tell you of new things, of hidden things unknown to you. They are created now, and not long ago; you have not heard of them before today.*

A new name is the new thing found within Isaiah 62:2, *"You will be called by a new name."*

New heavens are declared 65:17-25, *"...Behold, I will create new heavens and a new earth. The former things will not be remembered."* Isaiah 66:22 says, *"...As the new heavens and the new earth that I will make will endure before me, declares the Lord, so will your name and descendants endure."*

When we continue on in Jeremiah 31:22 we find this newness, *"The Lord will create a new thing on earth — a woman will surround a man,"* or protect a man.

We hear about a _new covenant_ in Jeremiah 31:31-34,

> The time is coming, declares the LORD, when I will make a new covenant with the house of Israel and with the house of Judah. It will not be like the covenant I made with their forefathers when I took them by the hand to lead them out of Egypt....This covenant I will make with the house of Israel after that time, declares the LORD. I will put my law in their minds and write it on their hearts. I will be their God, and they will be my people....For I will forgive their wickedness and will remember their sins no more.

In the above reference we see the word covenant in relation to something new that the Lord is going to do. Within this new covenant we once again find forgiveness of iniquity or sin.

From these verses, it is easy to make quick conclusions that might be misguided. When the LORD says, *"I will put my law in their minds and write it on their hearts. I will be their God, and they will be my people ....I will forgive their wickedness and will remember their sins no more"* we should realize several necessary differences. A huge difference exists between implicit versus explicit understanding; an assumed versus actual application; and a mere given-ness versus a radically-received-given-ness. As we continue to examine what the LORD desires from those on His Way, please keep these contrasts in mind. This will be talked about below in relation to "Trust".

Do you remember when Messiah is mentioned as being given as a covenant to the people? We find references to this theme in Isaiah 42:6 and 49:8. 42:6 says, *"I, the LORD, have called you...I will keep you and will make you to be a covenant for the people."*

The new covenant is also seen in Isaiah 54:10; 55:3; 59:21; 61:8; Jeremiah 32:40 and in Malachi 3:1 that says, *"I send my messenger....Then suddenly the LORD you are seeking will come to his temple; the messenger of the covenant, whom you desire will come."*

It is important to gain a *new spirit* and *heart*. Both are envisioned in Ezekiel 11:19, "...*I will give them an undivided heart and put a new spirit in them; I will remove from them their heart of stone and give them a heart of flesh.*" This same <u>new</u> imagery continues in Ezekiel 18:31 where it declares, "*Rid yourselves of all the offenses you have committed, and get a new heart and a new spirit.*"

Once again, the imagery of a <u>heart of stone</u> and a <u>heart of flesh</u> are used as the backdrop of forgiveness of sin. Both of these new things are expressed in Ezekiel 36:23-29,

> *I will show the holiness of my great name, which has been profaned among the nations, the name you have profaned among them. Then the nations will know that I am the LORD,* declares the Sovereign LORD *when I show myself holy through you before their eyes. For I will take you out of the nations; I will gather you from all the countries and bring you back into your own land. I will sprinkle clean water on you, and you will be clean. I will cleanse you from all your impurities and from all your idols. I will give you a new heart and put a new spirit in you; I will remove from you your heart of stone and give you a heart of flesh. And I will put my Spirit in you and move you to follow my decrees and be careful to keep my laws. You will live in the land I gave your forefathers; you will be my people, and I will be your God. I will save you from all your uncleanness. I will call for the grain and make it plentiful and will not bring famine upon you.*

As these verses say, we need our heart and eyes opened to the glory of the LORD's salvation. It's amazing at how many things the LORD reveals he WILL do in this brief passage.

Angel of the LORD / The LORD

Many times we've examined our mysterious angel but I want to delve even deeper into this angel of mystery. In our deeper look, "How do we handle the appearances of the LORD, the Angel of the LORD, and the three men who appeared to Abraham as revealed through the Hebrew Scriptures?"

Do you remember back to Exodus 23:20-21 where the LORD warns the people of Israel about the angel he would send with them? Verse 21 tells us many interesting things, "*Pay attention to him and listen to what he says. Do not rebel against him; he will not forgive your rebellion, since my name is in him.*" How do we deal with all these variables of the same angel not just to understand this angel but our response to Him? We can learn much if we deeply consider the LORD.

Some messianic Scriptural references present us with similar challenges especially when Messiah is referenced as being eternal. How do we process the many narratives where Messiah is referenced as Immanuel, Mighty God, Father of Eternity, the LORD, your throne O God, my LORD, and the Son of Man who stands in the presence of the Ancient of Days and is given an eternal kingdom? Is it possible for a mere human being to receive and handle an eternal kingdom?

And how can this Son of Man receive a kingdom that seems identical to the Living God's Kingdom in Daniel? Is this hyperbole or a divine connection that we must realize and personalize? Daniel 6:26[27] tells us that the LORD's kingdom; "*Will not be destroyed, his dominion will never end.*" Now listen to the Daniel 7:14 pronouncement that concerns the Son of Man, "*His dominion is an everlasting dominion that will not pass away, and his kingdom is one that will never be destroyed.*"

Other messianic references like Micah 5:2[1] also speak as if Messiah is eternal. Yes, this verse even speaks of the place where

Messiah will be born, but it says much more. We read in the last part of this verse; *"Out of you will come for me one who will be ruler over Israel, whose origins are from of old, from ancient times,"* or days of eternity. Can we honestly miss the reference to his eternality? How should we receive this?

In Isaiah 9:5[6] Messiah is referred to as *Father of Eternity*. Again, in Psalm 45:6-7 we see that Messiah rules an eternal kingdom. Are we included in His Kingdom because of Abraham's bloodline or Abraham's faith and trust-line?

We should all know that Messiah, like King David is seen as a mighty man and warrior. Messiah will overcome enemies of the LORD and Israel just as David overcame the giant Goliath and his other enemies. We also know he will do more! Speaking of Messiah's might, I Samuel 2:10 shares the following, *"...He will give strength to his king and exalt the horn of His anointed."*

Isaiah 9:6[5] tells us Messiah will be called *el-gibbor*, which can also be seen as *Mighty God.* Isaiah 11:2 says that the Spirit of the LORD will rest on him and, *"The Spirit of...power."* Isaiah 42:13 says that Messiah will, *"March out like a mighty man, like a warrior he will stir up his zeal; with a shout...he will triumph over his enemies."*

Just when we were "totally secure" in his strength and might, we encounter our next narrative and their messianic descriptions. Isaiah 49:4 says, *"I have labored to no purpose; I have spent my strength in vain and for nothing."* How do we process this striking contrast of words and applied meaning?

Messiah's Words

I know it's been a while but can you remember Moses' reference to *The Prophet* in Deuteronomy 18? Moses would speak the words that the LORD placed in his mouth. It was vital that the people of Israel listened to his words to obey them. It is one thing to "hear" the LORD's words but we must obey them if we are to truly follow Him. Other messianic references also discuss his words and what he had to say.

One is found in Isaiah 42:2-3 that says this man will not be one found shouting in the streets. In fact, "*He will not shout or cry out, or raise his voice in the streets. A bruised reed he will not break, and a smoldering wick he will not snuff out.*"

But Isaiah 49:2 tells us this man is no wimp, "*He made my mouth like a sharpened sword.*" Evidently, according to this reference Messiah's words are ones that will cut much, as many of the words of Israel's prophets *cut* their audiences.

Isaiah 50:4 continues in this vein, "*The Sovereign LORD has given me an instructed tongue of them that are taught, that I should know how to sustain with words him that is weary.*"

Israel is given an invitation in Isaiah 55:3-4,

> *Give ear and come to me; hear me, that your soul may live...See, I have made him a witness to the peoples, a leader and commander of the peoples.*

Good news that heals the brokenhearted, proclaims freedom to those in bondage, releases prisoners from darkness and declares the LORD's favor is proclaimed to Israel in 61:1-2:

> *The Spirit of the Sovereign LORD is on me, because the LORD has anointed me to preach good news to the poor. He has sent me to bind up the brokenhearted, to proclaim freedom for the captives and release from darkness for the prisoners, to proclaim the year of the LORD's favor.*

Malachi 3:2-3 sends notice that this man is not just the gentle silent type. These verses begin by asking,

But who can endure the day of his coming? Who can stand when he appears? For he will be like a refiner's fire or a launderer's soap. He will sit as a refiner and purifier of silver; he will purify the Levites and refine them like gold and silver.

Psalm 45:2[3] speaks of the graciousness of <u>this man's</u> words, "*You are the most excellent of men and your lips have been anointed with grace.*"

Psalm 78:2 reveals that <u>this man</u> will speak in parables, "*I will open my mouth in parables, I will utter hidden things, things from of old.*"

Our last reference of this type is found in Psalm 22:1 where Messiah cries out to the LORD in desperation with these words, "*My God, my God, why have you forsaken me? Why are you so far from saving me?*"

Even though we read so many references that convey rejection, in the attack of his enemies and seeming failure of his mission we find it is the LORD himself who protects his Messiah. As we read in Isaiah 49:2, the LORD hid Messiah in the shadow of his hand; he, "*Concealed me in His quiver.*"

We also find as we continue to read from Psalm 22 that those who watch these horrific events unfold upon Messiah, including him being in the throes of death, are sure God in fact rejects this dying <u>man</u>. But Psalm 22:24 tells us something totally different. To our surprise, we find that God has not forsaken Messiah. Actually, He is the One who listened to Messiah's cry for help and will restore him to life. This would seem impossible to the hostile crowd that surrounds him. Here again is the Resurrection we saw earlier.

The Spirit of the LORD

The Lord's Spirit is referenced in many of the messianic Scriptures as well. Isaiah 11:2 is one such reference,

> *The Spirit of the LORD will rest on him – The Spirit of wisdom and of understanding, the Spirit of counsel and of power, the Spirit of knowledge and of the fear of the LORD.*

Isaiah 42:1 also speaks of the LORD's servant in relation to the LORD's Spirit, *"Here is my servant, whom I uphold, my chosen one in whom I delight; I will put my Spirit on him."*

Isaiah 48:16 says, *"And now the Sovereign LORD has sent me, with his Spirit."* Isaiah 61:1 tells us, *"The Spirit of the Sovereign LORD is on me."*

Not only is the Spirit of the LORD on Messiah, God wants us to have the Spirit of the LORD on our lives as we will soon see. If we have not yet noticed, the Spirit of the LORD has been on His chosen ones. The real sense of Scripture is that if the Spirit of the LORD does not abide on and in our life, we should pursue a different path. Messiah tells us this path is not one of many "ways" leading to eternal life and into His Kingdom. In fact He invites us to walk on "This Way of Holiness", in Isaiah 35:8. This is the path where no one who is unclean may walk, no deadly animals or snakes will cross this path. It is only those who are redeemed who will walk on this road. As we will see below, and as David exhibited above, it is the Lord's Spirit who gives us the power and ability to walk on His Path.

Signs and Wonders

Now I want us to quickly look at the fact of the signs and wonders Messiah will perform. Once again, remember that Moses is seen as a type of Messiah. Remember also how Moses provides proof before Aaron and the Israelite elders that it is the LORD who sent him. Moses shows these men the signs that the LORD gave him to use as proof of his authenticity. These are the same signs that he later displays before Pharaoh.

Moses also spoke of the signs of *The Prophet* and how the people will know whether or not the prophet is from the LORD in Deuteronomy 18:21,

> *How can we know when a message has not been spoken by the LORD? If what a prophet proclaims in the name of the LORD does not take place or come true, that is a message the LORD has not spoken.*

Isaiah 35:5-6 speaks of Messiah healing the blind, deaf, lame and the mute. According to Isaiah 42:7, he will, "*...Free captives from prison and release from the dungeon those who sit in darkness.*" Isaiah 53:4 says, "*Surely he took up our infirmities and carried our sorrows.*"

The fact that Gentiles accept Messiah, see his light, and turn to him is also found throughout the prophets. This brings us to another question, "What was and is Israel's mission as the *Chosen People*?" The answer brings us closer to understand and practice the LORD's Truth and Good News.

Israel's Mission

King David says on more than one occasion that he will praise the LORD among the nations. The fact that nations are responsible to praise the LORD is also found within the Scriptures. Why are these things a part of the Scriptures? Why are they important at all; besides the fact that God desires praise?

We will now examine these two questions. These things actually tie in with our first reference to Abraham which is the fact of his descendants being a blessing to the nations. Moses tells Israel in Deuteronomy 28:9-10 why it's important for the Gentiles to know of the LORD's greatness,

> *The LORD will establish you as his holy people....Then all the peoples on earth will see that you are called by the name of the LORD, and they will fear you.*

The LORD wanted to be known to the nations. Without the Jewish voice of support, the nations *did not* know of the LORD and His fame as mentioned in the story of Rahab. They clearly heard of His Works and Fame! They saw and heard of the LORD and his power as a result of his rescuing His people from Egypt and through the Exodus. The LORD wanted His people to boldly declare His Works and Good News. This is also why David speaks of praising the LORD to the nations because, as a nation of priests, Israel was to reflect the LORD and his ways to Gentiles. As Israel followed the LORD they would receive all the *Blessings* that were proclaimed in Deuteronomy 28:1-14. These blessings would be a sure sign to all nations that the LORD was the only God of heaven and earth.

Our above narrative can be seen as the backdrop of Isaiah 26:17-18,

> *As a woman with child and about to give birth writhes and cries out in her pain, so were we in your presence, O LORD ... We have not brought salvation to the earth; we have not given birth to the people of the world.*

I want to leave one last promise the LORD made to the people of Israel before going on. This scriptural reference in Isaiah

49:15-16 and 22-23 speaks to us of the LORD's mercy, love and continual, even future, remembering of his people Israel. Listen to the compassion,

> *Can a woman forget the baby at her breast and have no compassion on the child she has borne? Though she may forget, I will not forget you! See, I have engraved you on the palms of my hands; your walls are ever before me….See, I will beckon to the Gentiles, I will lift up my banner to the peoples…Then you will know that I am the LORD; those who hope in me will not be disappointed.*

This above reference shows how much the LORD loves and cares for his people. Even in the times of severest devastation, when it may have seemed the LORD had totally abandoned and forgotten the Jewish people, He had not! He still remembered them and His promises to Abraham, Isaac and Jacob. No matter what, these promises will be fulfilled!

All the things above provide the backdrop for Messiah, his mission and message. These also lead us to my next point.

The Portrait of Messiah Semi-Completed

Okay, in order for us to finish we need to see the picture that all our messianic puzzle pieces have produced. At this point I want to look at two groups of narratives that will combine to form one photograph of the Scriptural Messiah.

Let's take two Scriptural characters that form our first group of puzzle pieces – King David and his son King Solomon. As we saw above, the Scriptures speak of the *Messianic Warrior King* and the *Time of Peace*. These characteristics are found in the respective lives and characters of David and Solomon.

David is the Shepherd of Israel, the killer of Goliath. He is the one who subdues Israel's enemies and proclaims to the Gentiles the fact that Israel's God is The Only God. Here is one of the LORD's chosen ones declaring the Good News to the Nations. The Scriptures also portray David as being a prophet; this can be seen in the Psalms where he speaks using the same words and imagery as the prophets of Israel.

This man after God's own heart also has an innate sense of God's presence and Spirit. We see him constantly pray and cry out to the LORD for help. David's modus operandi is being in constant communion with God. As a result, the LORD promises David an enduring legacy, an eternal house. One of his descendants will always reign on Judah's throne. While Solomon is one of David's descendants, the LORD looks beyond this man graced with wisdom to another King.

David's son Solomon inherited the kingdom after David subdued Israel's enemies. Solomon's reign was one of peace and prosperity, with the enemies of Israel paying tribute to and being in subjection to him. Solomon is the king that the LORD said He would adopt as His son, and the LORD Himself says he will be Solomon's Father.

There was no one wiser in Solomon's lifetime than King Solomon himself. In fact the Scriptures tell us in I Kings 4:31 that Solomon "was wiser than any other man." Even the Queen of Sheba came to Israel to gain an audience with this great man. This queen was totally amazed at his brilliance, knowledge and wisdom that the LORD, his Father, had given to him.

These above two characters form our triumphant Warrior King and King of Peace; so after subduing Israel's enemies, an era of peace and prosperity began. War, victory, peace and prosperity will also be true of Messiah.

In our second group, we have four references. These references are 1) the Akedah, 2) the narrative of Isaiah 53, 3) the life of Joseph and 4) the life of Moses.

First, the **Akedah** is all about Abraham, the father, and Isaac, the son. It is also about the Father and Son. In this narrative we also hear about and from God the Father whose response that concerns his promised son is very important. The Responsible One is the Father; the Submissive one is the Son.

A Sacrifice of Substitution takes place as one Ram is substituted for The One and Only Son. One day an Ultimate sacrifice of Substitution will take place on this same mountain range. This sacrifice of substitution will also include a Father and a Son and within this substitution both Israel and the Gentiles will be blessed and changed.

Second, **Isaiah 53** has such vivid imagery to make one's stomach churn. The almost-unseen One who is responsible for this whole scene of carnage is <u>God the Father</u>. We can see his responsibility in Isaiah 53:1 when the question is posed, "...*To whom has the arm of the Lord been revealed?*"

The person of whom this speaks is revealed in Isaiah 53: 2, "*He grew up before him like a tender shoot, and like a root out of dry ground.*" <u>This man</u> is the Root of Jesse, the Branch, the Son of David;

Messiah. This son of David, unlike Absalom, has no beautiful flowing locks. He doesn't even have looks to attract anyone to him. This man is also despised and rejected; no one even wants to be acquainted with this guy.

Messiah also personally experiences many sorrows and griefs. In fact, he doesn't just experience these things; he bears and carries Israel's griefs and sorrows. But Israel as a whole doesn't even take notice. Why, you may ask? Israel doesn't take notice of this man and believe him to be Messiah because they assume this man suffers for sins he himself committed, but we find out this assumption is false.

This Isaiah 53 narrative now tells us that instead of The Branch suffering for his own sin, he willingly suffers for Israel's iniquities. Because Israel went astray, the LORD laid all Israel's waywardness and sins on His Servant.

Though this man suffered so much while he was being accused and examined, this innocent man didn't even offer a defense. In the prime of life, this man's light was snuffed out even though he did nothing to deserve death or punishment. In fact, this man was righteous and full of integrity.

We learn even more as we go on; the LORD himself was the one responsible for this man's crushing and grief. But his crushing was essential. Without the snuffing out of this Lamb, his Resurrection could not occur. Remember too that His life was a sacrifice of exchange; a spotless lamb was given as a sin and guilt offering.

Because this innocent man's sacrifice was accepted by the LORD, his death was not the end. Although he died, this man will "live again to fight another day." And fight as a Mighty Warrior is just what he will do! He will again see the light of life and his days will be prolonged! Great results come out of this man's death. Many in Israel are justified before the Lord as a result of this man's sacrifice of exchange.

We see the Warrior image in Isaiah 53:12 as Messiah is depicted as dividing the booty that is won in battle. Because of what this accomplishes he will be assigned his portion along with those who are great. He intercedes for those who were the transgressors, just as a High Priest would do.

Third – Joseph – What an amazing story and an amazing man. He is the much loved son. This man is one of less-than-a-handful of Scriptural characters whose narrative is void of any personal sin; his whole life is seen as one of righteousness.

Joseph is a man whom the LORD gives the ability to see and predict the future. Instead of his family being happy and attracted to him, just the opposite result is produced. His family rejects his predictions, especially the tale of their submission to his rule. In fact, they proudly proclaim they will not bow to this son. However, the narrative reads differently; they definitely bow down to this much loved son of their father.

This man, rejected and sold by his family, is eventually promoted to be the second in charge over the land of Egypt. In the end, he was in submission only to Pharaoh himself.

Eventually, Joseph's family finds themselves in great need due to a famine. So, his brothers travel all the way to Egypt where they heard food is plentiful. Upon their arrival they bow down to their own brother just as he predicted so many years before. On their first visit they don't even recognize who this ruler happens to be. But on their second visit their eyes will be fully opened and they will be totally amazed at the revelations of this ruler.

After returning home and eventually consuming all their food supply, a return to Egypt once again becomes necessary for Israel's family. Upon their return, they are once again led into the presence of their ruling brother. This time, after a prolonged delay, he reveals his true identity to his brothers.

Shock doesn't begin to describe their feelings of awe. Joseph, this once rejected slave became a ruler who saves not only Egypt and the Gentile nations of that part of the globe but his family of Israel as well.

Fourth – Moses – This shepherd of Israel had an almost continual life of ebb and flow. When he was an infant, the king of Egypt wanted him dead, but his family saved his life. He was adopted as a king's son and lived a life of privilege. However, all the while – at least until he became the Liberator – his ancestral family lived a life of bondage.

He eventually chose to be like his own people rather than live in the luxury of being a prince under Pharaoh's roof. Knowing his mission in life was to be his people's deliverer he set out to do just that. However, on his first attempt he was rejected. As a result of this rejection he had to leave the land of his birth and reside in a foreign land for 40 years. His own people were totally ignorant of his existence for a long time.

On his return to the land of his birth, he was received by Israel's elders. The reason for their acceptance of Moses was because he came to his own people in the name of the LORD, not in his own might. He proved the authenticity of being sent to them by the LORD by showing them the miraculous signs that the LORD had given to him.

After many more miraculous signs he delivered his people Israel from their bondage. The people of Israel marched out in the presence of their defeated enemies in glorious triumph after plundering the Egyptians.

Just before their departure the Israelites went through a sacrifice of exchange involving their firstborn sons and lambs. This exchange required the shed blood of a lamb and the eating of its meat or flesh. Its blood was then placed on the mantle and doorpost of each house of Israel and the flesh was eaten; therefore, each family was preserved from the effects of the death angel by this Passover exchange.

Just when one might think it couldn't get any better, you're right; things get much worse when they ultimately leave Egypt. Instead of listening to their LORD Shepherd and Moses' instructions, these people of Israel decide to disobey. Because of their sin, they do not enter the Land of Promise. During the subsequent wanderings, Moses' generation dies out in the wilderness, never to experience God's promised peace and rest – because of their unbelief and refusal to trust in the LORD.

This Wicked Generation, as Moses called them, was one who had eyes to see and ears to hear but refused to see, hear or understand what the LORD had done. They relied instead on their own ideas and perceptions. Even though this generation saw all the miracles of Moses in Egypt and in the Wilderness, they never took them to heart and thereby missed out on God's plan of deliverance and rest. They even rejected Moses as their leader and God as their God; they chose a gold calf instead. Moses even predicted Israel's future apostasy and their rebellion with the devastating results. Deuteronomy 34:10-12 speaks of this great man's life; it ends with these words,

> Since then, no prophet has risen in Israel like Moses, whom the LORD knew face to face, who did all those miraculous signs and the wonders the LORD sent him to do…For no one has ever shown the mighty power or performed the awesome deeds that Moses did in the sight of all Israel.

Okay the portrait of the Mighty Triumphant Warrior King who brings peace and prosperity to Israel and rules on David's throne is coming into view. This is not merely the picture of Messiah but the reality of Messiah that is coming into full view. We have the Sacrifice of Exchange of the Submissive Son by the Responsible Father. We see the Branch who is the Son and God who is the Father. This Son – that we will soon see – takes all Israel's sin upon himself to provide Atonement for Israel through his obedience and death.

For his mission as shepherd of Israel, he is paid the price of a slave. He is adopted by the Royal family but chooses the hard life of his people instead of the trappings of Royalty. As he is received by the elders of Israel during his return to his people, he performs many mighty miraculous signs and wonders.

While he leads his people out of bondage, his entire generation, with Joshua and Caleb being the exceptions, dies off without entering into their promised peace. As a prophet, he not only speaks of *The Prophet* who is coming but also predicts Israel's apostasy and their eventual captivity.

What do you think? Can you see how anyone could match our picture of Messiah shown above? I believe that even though no one in the Hebrew Scriptures meets all our messianic criteria, not even King Hezekiah, there is One on Israel's horizon who will meet every criterion of Messiah as we will see.

But before that introduction, let me next introduce you to four Jewish men from the 1st Century CE who all lived in the land of Israel.

Four Messianic Contenders of First Century CE

Four somewhat prominent Jewish men from the First Century CE are what I call Messianic Contenders. All these men were seen as the Jewish Messiah by some segment within the Jewish people of their time. Each man had dealings with the Romans; three of them even fought against the Romans.

The historian Josephus speaks of all four in his writings, including *The Wars of the Jews*. The three he mentions within his *Wars* pages 2.21.1; 2.19.2.521 and 2.17.8 are: "<u>John of Gischala</u>, <u>Simon the son of Giora</u> and <u>Manahem, the son of Judas [of Masada]</u>." All 3 died as a result of this 66-73 CE conflict. The fourth died about 30 years before the war, but his life was not without conflict. The Romans killed the fourth man outside the city of Jerusalem.

Before going on, let me give a short list of Scriptural qualifications for Messiah in no particular order: The Prophet, Descendant of King David, High Priest, Bringer of Good News, Redeemer, Israel and Gentiles follow his Torah, Worshipped by both Israel and Gentiles, More than a Normal Man, Triumphant over Death and Grave, Rejected by Jewish leaders and people, Gentile & Jewish conspiracy against him, Trust in him gives one Atonement from sins, Branch Born in Bethlehem Ephrathah, Beaten and Killed, Comes to Speak in the Name of the LORD, Shepherd, Speaks New Covenant to Israel, Performs Miraculous Signs and Wonders, Meek and Humble, Mission appeared to Fail but was a real Success, Comes in power and Spirit of the LORD. Only One of the four men can claim these titles and works.

Not one of our first three contenders qualifies as a descendant of David. However they definitely lived in the first century CE, to fulfill one qualification from the book of Daniel. They were definitely warriors, seen as kings and "messiahs" to fulfill two other messianic qualifications but they didn't triumph over Rome.

Also none of the three were spoken of by Josephus as even being righteous men; in fact, he says just the opposite. None of the three produced any signs or miracles as Moses did to prove their authenticity of being the Messiah. Also there is no historical record to indicate their birth was in the town of Bethlehem of Ephrathah.

What about our fourth contender – the one with the same name as the High Priest from Haggai and Zechariah, the one named Yeshua (Joshua)? Josephus also speaks of him but does he perform any better? Yes, I believe he does. Let me show you why. Josephus calls him a righteous man; besides, this descendant of King David meets messianic qualifications in the following Scriptural ways. Again, many given references are not quoted. For your benefit, please read the ones that are not quoted in this book.

Before going on to our below Scriptural references, let's take a look at the comparison of the life and Mission of Moses and one of our four 1st Century CE Messianic Contenders; the 4th one named Yeshua.

Moses /Yeshua Comparison

With examination of our four 1st Century CE characters complete, let's put together the bigger picture of Messiah. To help us bring the picture into better view, allow me to offer a point-by-point comparison between Moses and Yeshua (Jesus). The format I will use is to present the Moses point next to the Yeshua point underneath. It is my hope that you better see Yeshua in the proper eternal Light.

1. **Moses** was dispatched by the LORD to go to the captive nation of Israel and redeem them from their captivity to Egypt to freely worship the LORD.

   Yeshua was dispatched by the LORD to go to the nation of Israel that was oppressed by Rome, to redeem them from their captivity to sin so they would follow Him as the proclaimer of His Good News.

2. **Moses** had a brass serpent made and placed on a pole that saved all who looked in trust from death.

   Yeshua was placed on a pole (tree) and saved all who looked at him by trust (faith).

3. **Moses** was the shepherd of Israel in the desert.

   Yeshua was the shepherd of Israel who was promised by Ezekiel and Zechariah.

4. **Moses** – Aaron was the prophet who went before him.

   Yeshua – John the Immerser was the prophet who went before him.

5. **Moses** – Israel was sustained by manna for 40 years.

   Yeshua – Israel was promised eternal life from his manna per John 6:33.

6. **Moses** was tested at the waters of Marah and failed the test; as a result he was not allowed to enter into Canaan. Israel was tested for 40 days and also failed the test.

   Yeshua was tested in the wilderness for 40 days and He passed the test; as a result he started his Messianic Mission. Some in Israel failed the test. But other's passed the test and entered into the New Covenant, the one promised by the prophets of Israel.

7. **Moses** gives The 10 Words, The Decalogue, or the Ten Commandments written by the finger of the LORD on the mountain with an audience of one.

   Yeshua gave His Words – God's Very Words – of Good News to the people of Israel on the mountain to His Talmidim (Disciples) and the masses.

8. **Moses** taught the perpetual ceremony of Passover with the spotless Passover Lamb, with its blood on the door, eating of its flesh, and the Death Angel. This involved a substitution for the firstborn of Israel.

   Yeshua was The Passover Lamb. Once-for-all-time, through His Holy sacrificed body with its spilled blood, He provided atonement for all Israel, who looked to him through trust, to keep them from sins' consequence, which is spiritual death.

9. **Moses** built a "transient" Tabernacle that was made after the reality of the heavenly Tabernacle. This transient model later became "permanent" for the purpose of sacrifice, prayer and worship.

   Yeshua's body was the Lord's Tabernacle on earth. As the perfect Image of God, it is His sacrifice that alone provides atonement for Israel and the world.

10. **Moses** talked with the LORD face-to-face, and relayed the LORD's message to the people.

    Yeshua talked with the LORD face to face, and relayed the LORD's message to the people.

11. **Moses** prophesied Israel's demise as a nation because of sin, and also their future return and hope.

    Yeshua prophesied Israel's & Jerusalem's demise because they rejected God's Messiah. But he also spoke about Israel's return and God's coming Kingdom. Physically and humanly, He didn't triumph over Israel's enemies because his people rejected him as Messiah; therefore He waits for Israel to accept Him as their Messiah and say, "Blessed is he who comes in the name of the LORD", spoken in Matthew 23:39. Spiritually and eternally, He triumphed over Israel's enemies – Satan, sin and death – to win the Ultimate Eternal War by unleashing His Good News to save those who trust in Him.

12. **Moses** performs mighty signs and wonders **Moses** performs mighty signs and wonders: Rod turned to snake; leprous hand; and Plagues of blood, frogs, gnats, flies, livestock, boils, hail, locust, darkness, and death of firstborn. He received Water from a rock, crossed the Red Sea, and led Israel into the Promised Land.

    Yeshua This prophet performed mighty signs and wonders as follows: Healed all diseases, blind, paralyzed, deaf, dumb, drove out demons, raised the dead back to life and changed water to wine.

13. **Moses** referred to his wicked generation of Israelites (this doesn't mean that every Israelite of his generation was wicked, it only refers to those who refused to obey the LORD), the ones he taught, and who followed him out of Egypt and to the threshold of the Promised Land.

Yeshua taught his wicked generation of Israelites to lead them out of sin and into the LORD's Kingdom.

14. **Moses** – During his time of leading, the Firstborn of Egypt died while life and freedom were given to the people of Israel.

    Yeshua – During his time on earth, eternal life and freedom from sin were given to the people of Israel, and to all who place their trust in him.

Now let's look at the 21 different titles and depictions of Messiah from the Hebrew Scriptures that I mentioned above. Below I will tie these in to the life and mission of our fourth contender.

The Prophet spoken of by Moses in Deuteronomy 18:15-19; it says this prophet will be like Moses. Also, all who don't heed his words will be dealt with by the LORD Himself. Other messianic prophet-references are: Isaiah 49:2-7; 50:4; 55:3-4; Zechariah 11:4-11; Malachi 3:1-3; Psalm 45:3; 78:1-2.

Son of David is found in I Chronicles 28:7 and other references: I Samuel 2:10; II Samuel 7:11-12; Micah 5:1; Zechariah 9:9; 12:10; Psalm 89:24,27-28; Proverbs 30:4.

High Priest/Priest from Psalm 110:4 concerns King Melchizedek. Other messianic references: Genesis 14:17-20; Leviticus 16:15-22; 16:32-34; 17:11; Isaiah 52:15; 53:1-12.

Good News that gives a prophetic reference to the Gospel; others are: Isaiah 40:9-11; 41:27; 52:1-12; 61:1-2.

Redemption from *Sin* as seen in Isaiah 53:1-12 and throughout other prophets: Isaiah 49:5-6; 59:1-20; Ezekiel 36:23-29; Zechariah 3:9; Daniel 9:24.

Law of the LORD being spoken to Israel and the Gentiles seen in the following: Isaiah 2:2-4; 42:1; 48:17.

Gentiles follow Messiah: Isaiah 8:23-9:1; 11:5-10; 42:1,6-7; 49:1,6; 52:15; 55:4; Zechariah 2:14-16; 9:10; Psalm 22:28-29; 72:11; 86:9; and 117:1 all speak of this.

More than a normal man in the following references: Isaiah 9:5; Jeremiah 23:6; Micah 5:1; Daniel 7:13-14; Psalm 89:27; 110:1 and Proverbs 30:4.

Triumphed over *Death* and the *Grave;* spoken of in: Isaiah 25:7-8; 26:19; Hosea 13:14 and Psalm 16:9-11.

Rejected by the Jewish leaders and the people as found in Isaiah 8:14; 49:7; 53:1 and Psalm 118:22-26.

Gentile and Jewish conspiracy against him and the LORD. Psalm 2:1-12 speaks of this very thing.

Forgives all who *Believe and Trust* in him as follows: Isaiah 28:16; Joel 3:1-5 and Psalm 2:12.

The *Branch, Root, Shoot, and Twig* are located in: Isaiah 53:2; Ezekiel 17:22 and Zechariah 6:12-13.

Beaten and **abused** as told by Isaiah 52:13-14; Zechariah 12:10 and Psalm 22:7-22.

Speaks in the *Name of the LORD* in: Isaiah 7:13-14; 9:1-6; 49:1-7; Psalm 18:47-51; 22:23; and 118:22, 26.

The *Shepherd of the LORD*; we see this picture in: Ezekiel 34:12-25; Zechariah 11:4-14 and 13:7.

The *New Covenant* for Israel and the Gentiles is seen in: Isaiah 42:6-7, 9-10; Jeremiah 31:33-34; and Ezekiel 34:23-25.

Signs and *Miracles* are done by Messiah, mentioned in: Isaiah 9:1; 35:5-6; and 42:7.

Meek and *lowly*; Isaiah 42:2-3; 61:1-2; and Zechariah 9:9 all speak of his humility.

Messiah's *Mission* seems to those watching a mission of failure. Both Isaiah 49:4 and 53:1-12 speak of this issue.

The **Spirit of the LORD** is the power behind Messiah, as seen in: Isaiah 11:2; 42:1; 48:16; and 61:1.

Okay, you might say, "While all these Scriptures and Finale: statements are nice and all, just how do these characteristics and titles relate to a Jewish man from the First Century CE?"

Well, I'm glad you've asked. Let me share what a Jewish book from the 1st Century CE, written by Jewish authors has to say about this Jewish man from the Galil (Galilee).

This book is called the New Testament, which in Hebrew means New Covenant. An important point to remember is the fact that it is a Jewish book, written by Jewish authors, who were eye witnesses of this man's life and mission.

The Prophet: Levi, the once hated Tax Collector and now a follower of this prophet from the Galil tells how Yeshua, The Prophet whom Moses promised, told his talmidim of the 2nd Temple's coming destruction; he said that not one stone would be left on another. This prophecy came true in 70 CE when the Romans tore apart this Temple and threw the massive stones down into the valley below. For more on this prophet from the Galil see Matthew 24:1-2; Luke 21:20-24, John 4:19, 44; 6:14; 7:40; and 9:17.

Son of David: The Son of David was a typical title that the people of Israel used to address Yeshua when desiring his help and intervention on their behalf. In Matthew 9:27, as Yeshua departs from a home, two blind men begin to follow him. They call out to him, "*Have mercy on us, Son of David!*" Yeshua does just as they request; he gives them their sight. For more on this descendant of King David see Matthew 1:1-20; 12:23; 15:22; 20:30 and 21:15.

Priest/High Priest: Again in Matthew 9:1-7, Yeshua heals a paralyzed man. But before healing this man, Yeshua speaks words that even today are controversial, "*Take heart, son; your sins are forgiven.*" This pronouncement of course brought consternation from some Rabbis who were present; but to prove that He, as the Son of Man, had authority on earth to forgive sin, He told this man,

"Get up, take your mat and go home." That's exactly what this newly healed man did!

Right before Yeshua's death, he showed and explained to his talmidim how his body and blood would be a sacrifice of atonement for sin. After he took the cup of wine during their final Passover Seder together, he said in Matthew 26:27, *"Drink from it, all of you.* **This is my blood of the covenant, which is poured out for many for the forgiveness of sins.**" Matthew 9:1-2 and 26:17-30 also speak of Yeshua's priestly efforts.

Good News: Luke 8:1 tells us the following about this Rabbi, *"Jesus traveled about from one town and village to another, proclaiming the good news of the kingdom of God."* John 10:11 and Acts 10:38 also tell us about this good news.

Redemption from *Sin*: This really ties in with the High Priest distinction. Yeshua's forerunner, John the Baptist, says this concerning the Rabbi from the Galil (John 1:29), *"Look, the Lamb of God, who takes away the sin of the world!"* Yeshua's bewildered and despondent talmidim, said this about their dead Rabbi after his death in Luke 24:21, *"But we had hoped that he was the one who was going to redeem Israel."* For more on Yeshua's redemption from sin see John 10:11 and 16:8-9.

Law (Torah): The prophets speak of Messiah's Torah, and in Matthew 5-7 we find the foundation of Yeshua's Torah laid out. In response to a Pharisee's question concerning the greatest commandment in Torah, Yeshua said in Matthew 22:40, *"All the Law and the Prophets hang on these two commandments."* These two greatest commands in Torah are to love the Lord God with all your soul, heart and mind, and love their neighbor as themselves.

Gentiles follow Messiah. New Covenant Jewish writers speak of many Gentiles who come to Yeshua to place their trust in him. We see three Gentiles: a woman of Canaan, a Roman Centurion and a Samaritan woman found in Matthew 8:5-13, 15:21-28 and John 4:9-42. Here's a short version of John 4:7-26,

*When a Samaritan woman came to draw water, Jesus said to her, Will you give me a drink?....The Samaritan woman said to him, You are a Jew and I am a Samaritan woman. How can you ask me for a drink? (For Jews do not associate with Samaritans.) Jesus answered her, If you knew the gift of God and of who it is that asks you for a drink, you would have asked him and he would have given you living water....the water I give him will become in him a spring of water welling up to eternal life....God is Spirit, and his worshippers must worship in spirit and in truth. The woman said, I know that Messiah (called Christ) is coming. When he comes, he will explain everything to us. Then Jesus declared, "**I who speak to you am he**."*

When this woman goes back to her village she tells the people to come meet a man who told her the whole story of her life to that point. The townspeople of this Samaritan village follow the woman to where Yeshua is and invite him to stay with them. So he stays with them for two days. Afterward, the villagers tell the woman, "*We no longer believe just because of what you have said; now we have heard for ourselves, and **we know that this man really is the Savior of the world**.*" More narratives that speak of Gentiles are found in Matthew 8:5-13; 12:15-21; 15:21-28 and Luke 2:32.

More than a *Normal Man*: In John 6:16-21 he writes:

When evening came, his disciples went down to the lake, where they got into a boat and set off across the lake of Capernaum. By now it was dark, and Jesus had not yet joined them. A strong wind was blowing and the waters grew rough. When they had rowed three or three and a half miles, they saw Jesus approaching the boat, walking on the water; and they were terrified.

For more on this *More than a Normal man;* see Matthew 9:1-8; John 1:1-18 and 10:33-36.

Triumph over *Death* and the *Grave*: The narrative I share is found in John 19:38-20:20. I will only share the part that contains Mary Magdalene's perspective. Mary's amazing-too-good-to-be-true discovery is found in John 20:11-18,

Mary stood outside the tomb crying. As she wept, she bent over to look into the tomb and saw two angels in white, seated where Jesus' body had been, one at the head and the other at the foot. They asked her, Woman, why are you crying? They have taken my LORD

away, she said, and I don't know where they have put him. At this she turned around and saw Jesus standing there, but she did not realize that it was Jesus....Jesus said to her, Mary. She turned toward him and cried out to him in Aramaic, Rabboni! (which means Teacher). Jesus said....Go...to my brothers and tell them, I am returning to my Father and your Father, to my God and your God.

Matthew 22:31-32; John 11:24-26; 19:38-20:20 and Acts 1:22 also speak of Resurrection.

Not only does Messiah actualize death-to-resurrection but He teaches this truth through the death-to-resurrection in the seeds that farmers plant. If we are to understand what He means by His teaching of New Birth, in the New Covenant, we cannot miss this connection.

Rejected by the Jewish leaders and the people: Levi tells us of one such meeting that took place in the High Priest Caiaphas' home in Matthew 26:3-5,

Then the chief priests and the elders of the people assembled in the palace of the high priest, whose name was Caiaphas, and they plotted to arrest Jesus in some sly way and kill him. But not during the Feast, they said.

For more on Yeshua's rejection by the Jewish people and their leaders see Matthew 12:24-27; John 9:1-41 and Acts 4:1-12.

Gentile and Jewish conspiracy against him and the LORD; Peter speaks of this very thing in Acts 4:23-28,

Indeed Herod and Pontius Pilate met together with the Gentiles and the people of Israel in this city to conspire against your holy servant Jesus, whom you anointed.

Read also Luke 23:7-25; John 11:45-53; and Acts 3:13-18.

He forgives all who *Believe* and *Trust* in him; In John 3:2 we encounter a man who is part of the Sanhedrin and he comes to speak with Yeshua at night. Listen to his opening sentence,

*Rabbi, **we know you are a teacher who has come from God**. For no one could perform the miraculous signs you are doing if God were not with him.*

This leads Yeshua to speak of how one enters the kingdom of God. He then uses a story from the book of Numbers 21 to speak of how one plague was stopped while the people of Israel were en route to the Promised Land; here's John 3:14-16,

> *Just as Moses lifted up the snake in the desert,* **so the Son of Man must be lifted up, that everyone who believes in him may have eternal life.** *For God so loved the world that he gave his one and only Son,* **that whoever believes (trusts) in him shall not perish but have eternal life.** *For God did not send his Son into the world to condemn the world, but to save the world through him.*

Notice the parallels between the Son mentioned above and the serpent that Moses placed on the pole in Numbers 21. Matthew 9:2-8; Mark 2:7-10 and Luke 23:43 also give us more insight into his forgiveness of sin and redemption.

The **Branch, Root, Shoot, and Twig:** In the last book written by his loved disciple John, in Revelation 5:5, we read the following words concerning the long awaited Root of David, "*Then one of the elders said to me, 'Do not weep! See, the Lion of the tribe of Judah, the Root of David, has triumphed.'*" This descendant of Jesse and David is also found in Luke 2:15-24; Romans 15:8-12 and Revelation 22:16.

Beaten and **abused**: Matthew 26:67 tells us what happens to the prophet from Nazareth after he was condemned to death, "*Then they spit in his face and struck him with their fists. Others slapped him.*" John 19:1-3 adds to our above narrative by telling us what Pilate did to him; we read,

> *Then Pilate took Jesus and had him flogged. The soldiers twisted together a crown of thorns and put it on his head. They clothed him in a purple robe and went up to him...saying, "Hail, king of the Jews!" And they struck him in the face.*

For more on the abuse and beating of Yeshua see John 18:19-24 and 19:31-37.

Speaks in the **Name of the LORD:** In John 5:43 as Yeshua is speaking after healing a man at the pool of Bethesda he said, "*I have* *come in my Father's name.*" For more on his speaking in the Father's name see Matthew 21:9 and 23:39.

The **Shepherd** of the LORD: The Gospels speak of how many times Yeshua saw the people of Israel as sheep without a shepherd. In other words they were harassed with no one to protect or care for them. In John 10:11 he says, "*I am the good shepherd. The good shepherd lays down his life for the sheep.*" Matthew 9:36; 10:6; Mark 6:34; John 10:2-16 and Hebrews 13:20 also provide other shepherd references.

The **New Covenant** for Israel and the Gentiles: At his final Passover Seder in Matthew 26:28, Yeshua took the cup of wine, spoke the blessing over the wine and said, "*This is my blood of the covenant, which is poured out for many for the forgiveness of sins.*" I Corinthians 11:25 and Hebrews 9:15-20 also speak of this New Covenant.

Signs and **Miracles** done by Messiah: Matthew 9:35 tells us that, "*Jesus went through all the towns and villages, teaching in their synagogues, preaching the good news of the kingdom and healing every disease and sickness.*" Mark 5:41; Luke 7:11-15 and 7:20-23 also speak of his miracles.

Meek and **lowly**: In Matthew 11:28-29 Yeshua says, "*Come to me, all you who are weary and burdened, and I will give you rest. Take my yoke upon you and learn from me, for I am gentle and humble in heart.*" Matthew 21:5 also speaks of his humble character while quoting from Zechariah 9, when it says, "*Say to the Daughter of Zion, See, your king comes to you, gentle and riding on a donkey.*"

Messiah's **Mission** would seem to those watching to have failed. Matthew 26:56 tells us what happened at Yeshua's arrest, "*Then all the disciples deserted him and fled.*"

In John 20:1-31 we encounter one of Yeshua's women followers and two of his closest talmidim. When this woman and his talmidim encounter his empty tomb they don't raise their voices up in praise to God and thank him for raising their Rabbi from the dead.

This would have made great theatre but these people were not expecting their Rabbi to triumph over death and the grave. In fact, they never expected him to die in the first place, so death and the grave weren't on their radar screen of possibility. This is why even his talmidim missed the teaching and reality of His resurrection until after-the-fact. It wasn't just the leaders and people of Israel who misunderstood and missed this reality, His close talmidim totally missed this detail – making it seem like they did not believe or trust in His Word or Mission.

Even after 10 of his talmidim saw their risen Messiah, they can't even convince one of their closest friends and fellow talmidim that Yeshua is alive. When they tell him they've seen Yeshua alive, this is that talmidim's response in John 20:25, "...*He said to them, 'Unless I see the nail marks in his hands and put my finger where the nails were, and put my hand into his side, I will not believe it.'*" These men and women didn't live in a fairy tale world; they knew people didn't just pop back from the dead, which is why they were all shocked and had a hard time believing the truth that Yeshua had died, but was now alive. John 18:25-27 also speaks on this same subject.

In light of his death and resurrection, one of the most remarkable statements in the New Covenant Scriptures comes from this formerly unconvinced talmidim, Thomas. He gives a heartfelt admission when he sees the resurrected and living LORD. This man, who had been killed by the Romans, was now standing directly in front of him. If this wasn't enough, this, man who had died, and was now living, still had a totally fatal wound, yet Yeshua wasn't hemorrhaging, and he stood there in powerful strength. Is it any wonder that we read his declaration in John 20:28 "My Lord and my God!" While we do not physically see what Thomas saw – the resurrected Messiah in the flesh – in order to enter the Kingdom we must all come to the place where we see Messiah as LORD and God. Without acknowledging Him as God, we will likely never bow before Him, and without seeing Him as LORD, we will likely never yield our lives to His will.

This is the point called in the Scriptures, the Stone of Stumbling. Yeshua is the Chief Cornerstone, The Rock and The Sure Foundation. However, most of his generation stumbled over this fact of his life, which is Yeshua being El Gibbor, The Mighty God.

The **Spirit of the LORD** is the power behind Messiah. Matthew 3:16 speaks of what happened at his baptism,

> *As soon as Jesus was baptized, he went up out of the water. At that moment heaven was opened, and he saw the Spirit of God descending like a dove and lighting on him. And a voice from heaven said, "**This is my Son, whom I love, with him I am well pleased**."*

The writer of Luke in 11:20 says, *"But if I drive out demons by the finger of God, then the kingdom of God has come to you."* This above quote was spoken by Yeshua because he had just driven a demon out of man who was mute, as a result this man now spoke.

One man who was present at his Mikvah bath testified that he saw the Spirit of the LORD rest on him as he came out of the water. Later in a synagogue, recorded in Luke 4:18, Yeshua read part of the scroll of Isaiah 61:1, *"**the Spirit of the LORD is upon me**."* He said this referred to him; also see John 3:34.

Messiah and Atonement

As I write these words we're in the time period known as the Days of Awe, the solemn days leading up to the Day of Atonement.

The Hebrew Scriptures continually speak of one placing their trust in the LORD. First and Second Temple prophets also speak of the people of Israel and the Gentiles placing their trust in the LORD and in His Messiah.

Isaiah 42:1 speaks of Messiah bringing God's righteous Law to the Gentiles. Isaiah 42:6 speaks of Messiah being a Covenant for Israel and a light for the Gentiles. Trust is not a flippant thing, nor is it trust in someone who's unstable or not worthy of trust. Trust, as spoken of in Scripture, is reliance on, of being confident and sure in and of taking refuge within. This trust, solid refuge, sure and stable reliance can only be on someone who is true and authentic. We will look at this topic in more detail below.

At this point let me ask a question, "Would the LORD allow His Temple and altar to be destroyed without providing a way for sin to be atoned?" No, He wouldn't! At least, according to the Scriptures, it wouldn't make sense that the LORD would allow the Temple and altar to be destroyed without providing the means to atone for sin.

Remember, He told Moses that 'It was the blood that atoned.' And He never said that, at a later point in history, the shedding of the blood of sinless innocence would no longer atone. When a worshipper brought an animal to the Temple as a sacrifice for sin, an exchange took place. The person placed their sin on the animal through their touch and a transfer was made. As a result, the animal died in the place of the person.

As a result of this transfer, the person's sins were covered or atoned. Death came to the animal, being now the sinful one, but life came to the individual person, being now the blameless one. However, there was always a cost for this atonement!

With the Day of Atonement still on the calendar we must ask, "How does one atone for one's sins today?" Does repentance and following Torah alone really atone for one's sins? Or, are the Hebrew Scriptures still in play today, along with their requirements of shed blood in order for atonement to take place?

If repentance and following Torah brings atonement today, then why do some find it necessary to offer a rooster or a chicken or some other bird as an atoning sacrifice for their sin? Why do we have this great desire for flesh-and-blood atonement?

I suggest the answer to the above question is because today, flesh-and-blood still atones, just as the Scriptures tell us. However, it is now Yeshua's blood alone that atones for all time. Even as the Rabbis knew, when Messiah came, change would occur. One of the known changes would be in the Law itself.

John the Immerser (Baptist), a 1st Century CE prophet said of Yeshua in John 1:29, "*Look, **the Lamb of God, who takes away the sin of the world**!*" John the Immerser lived a life of solitude in the wilderness but through his preaching he turned many Jewish people back to the LORD and His Torah; these even included prostitutes and tax collectors. Crowds of people went to this man, confessed their sins and were baptized in the Jordan River.

As we saw in Isaiah 53, God the Father is the One who placed the sin of the people of Israel onto Messiah and He is the One to complete the exchange by placing the Righteousness of His Son Messiah onto those who Trust in Him. In this way, the Father – through the motif and actual reality of the sacrificial dynamic for atonement – caused the death of Messiah to become a substitutionary atonement for Israel's sins and the foundational reality of righteous standing before the LORD. And this atonement that came first to the people of Israel was also received by Gentiles as the Scriptures predicted and declared.

It was necessary for Messiah to come in the 1st Century CE with the Second Temple still standing, according to Daniel 9:24, "*to make an end of sin, and to forgive wickedness, to bring in everlasting righteousness, to seal up vision and prophecy and to anoint the most holy*." Messiah fulfilled all of these qualifiers in his life, sacrifice, resurrection and ascension.

As a result of Yeshua taking our place on the altar (the wood of the tree) as our lamb, and from our placing trust in His atonement that he provided, our sin is atoned. This is the Good News of the Scriptures!

Trust, a White-Knuckled Grasp on Reality

Before getting to the Conclusion I want to say some things concerning the word Trust. The word trust in the Scriptures is not a flippant term; it's a do-or-die term. Let me explain with three scenarios. I will use a rock climbing, snake biting, and exchange-offering scenario to demonstrate trust.

Most, I'm sure, have seen rock climbing walls; these can be inside or outside. A climber starts up the wall and can climb higher and higher. As the climber goes up the wall, they must use "rocks" to grip and aid in their ascent. If, for some reason, they lose their grip on the rock they may fall. However, they will not fall to their deaths, no matter how high up the wall they climb. The reason they won't die is because a rope is tied to their body and a "helper" lowers them safely to the ground.

The above picture where a helper lowers them safely to the ground is not the picture of a real rock climb. In a real climb, the climber must ensure that all the tools of their trade are in excellent shape. If during their ascent or descent their equipment fails, after the climber loses their grip, they may very well fall to their deaths. The reason this can happen is because they place all their trust in their grip, rope, skill, partner, etc. If any of these fail, more than likely their fall will be disastrous.

A climber who places all their trust in their equipment, skill or partner can be a good or bad thing that depends on a factor of reliability. If their equipment is in poor repair, their partner is inexperienced or their own physical condition is poor, their trust can be seriously misplaced; we might call this presumption. However, if all of the above are in pristine condition they will be able to accurately place all of their trust in each item or person.

Let me use another illustration from an above narrative that concerns the Israelites while they were roaming through the desert on their way to Canaan. This account is found in Numbers 21:4-9. As the people of Israel travel around the land of Edom they grow impatient and begin to grumble against the Lord and against Moses. Because of their grumbling the Lord sends poisonous snakes that bite many people. Many die, while many others are breathing their last breaths.

In the middle of the dead and dying, Moses appears before them holding a pole with a bronze replica of the serpent attached. Here's the trust part; when any of the dying Israelites look at this snake on the pole, they live.

Just as in a rock climbing scenario, this is no simple glance. This look is one of total trust; the person's life hangs in the balance. They're either all-in with their look or they are not in at all. If their look or trust is presumptuous they will die. When they look and place all of their trust on the snake on the pole, miraculously they live. It's easy to see in this analogy that the dying person does not bring life to themselves. These people do not place their trust in the serpent alone; they trust in the same God they grumbled against many minutes or hours before.

Scripture tells us here that each and every snake-bitten person who clung tenaciously in their look to the serpent recovered and lived, even though their snake bite was fatal.

This is the picture of Scriptural trust. There's nothing flippant or lazy about this trust. These people use every ounce of strength they have left in their dying body to turn and look at the snake. The energy used by the bitten person was rewarded with life and health, in the place of pain and death. Now we move to an earlier picture for our third frame.

When a guilty worshipper brought a spotless lamb to sacrifice for their sin many things were in play on this stage. This scene includes a human, priest and animal. As in my earlier story about Abel and Herbie, the death of this lamb cost the sin-offering person something. Later in Jewish history, they either took it from their flock or purchased one for the purpose of sacrificing it for their sin. Either way, cost was involved. But this lamb couldn't be just any lamb; it had to be spotless or without any kind of defect.

Next, the worshipper traveled to Jerusalem with this lamb in tow. Once they arrived at the temple, they brought the animal to be inspected. If it did not pass the test, it could not be used in a sacrifice of exchange. Once the animal was accepted, our next scene comes into view.

Here, the worshipper confesses all their sin as they place their hand on the animal. As a result of this confession, an exchange takes place and once again a high price is paid. The lamb dies in the place of the guilty worshipper. But the lamb does not die on its own; in fact, the guilty worshipper takes its life. The guilty one kills the animal, or to be more graphically specific, butchers the lamb. Essentially, the lamb pays the price and takes the death sentence for the sin of the person.

Next, the priest takes some of the lamb's blood with his finger and places it on the four horns of the altar. The rest of the blood is poured out at the base of the altar. All of the fat is taken and burned. This is how atonement is made for the worshipper. To be sure, it's not a neat and tidy scene as blood stains the worshipper, the lamb and the priest. It leaves a lasting reminder of the cost the innocent one paid for the guilty. Because the worshipper places their trust in this sacrifice of exchange, in the God who instituted these sacrifices, and in the blood of the spotless lamb, their sins are atoned.

This is why, when the prophet John, the one called the Baptizer, sees Yeshua approaching, shouts so loudly, the whole crowd hears and takes notice. His words, which are recorded in John 1:29, say, "Look, the Lamb of God, who takes away the sin of the world!" Yeshua, as Messiah, is our sacrificial lamb. We must place all our trust and existence in Yeshua Messiah using all of our white-knuckled energy, as we rely on his shed blood to take away our sin and bring us life even though we deserve death. This is the **Great Exchange**!

But there's more. As our High Priest, Yeshua continually intercedes for us before God to make our atonement sure! This atonement cost God so much yet His atoning Work provides life for all grasping onto Him with all their heart, soul and strength.

There's still more. Because of our trusting in Messiah's atonement of substitution for us something new has taken place. This new thing is that now we have a relationship with Yeshua. As a result of this relationship we gain an even greater advantage; we have an anchor, one that's completely reliable and sure. Now, because of this relational reliability if we ever fall while we're "climbing through life", someone else is holding the rope. It is the "Relational Anchor" of Yeshua which holds us secure; His Hold Will Not Fail! He is our solid Hope and our solid Trust! What Great, Great, Good News!

The Grand or not so Grand Finale

As a result of this atonement of substitution those who trust in Yeshua are no longer under the curse of sin and death because His Holy Spirit applies Yeshua's Righteousness to our account. I believe that David, in Psalm 32:1-2 speaks of this very thing,

Blessed is he whose transgressions are forgiven, whose sins are covered. Blessed is the man whose sin the LORD does not count against him and in whose spirit is no deceit.

The place where this blessing occurred is on the tree –Let me explain; we are reminded that the Scriptures say that anyone who is hung on a tree is cursed. Well, Yeshua was hung on a tree (cross) even though Isaiah 53 says he hadn't sinned. So, as a result of Him being THE Passover Lamb who took upon himself our sin to "give" us His Righteousness, he was cursed and bore our curse for us so that we might become His righteousness as explained in Romans chapter 5.

This is why Yeshua, while dying on the cross, speaks to God the Father with the following words found in Psalm 22:1, *"My God, my God why have you forsaken me?"* At that point in time, Yeshua had taken the curse we deserved upon himself; he thereby bore the sins of those who put their trust in Him. As a result of his being a curse and bearing the sins of those who put their trust in Him, a holy God looked away and forsook him at this very point in sacrificial understanding.

At least that's what those who stood there and watched him die believed had happened. Yet, as we saw earlier, God did not reject Yeshua's sacrifice of exchange; in fact, he accepted it fully as completely satisfactory to fulfill the requirements of His Sacrificial Law. It was Messiah's sacrificial death that provided our acceptance by God through this exchange on our behalf. His righteousness was given to us while he accepted, or bore upon himself our sin. What a great exchange!

But, as was said, this exchange came at a high cost – Yeshua died. Yeshua's dying was a high cost but His death was also the greatest victory for those who believe, trust in, and follow the LORD. As our substitute, he took our place which gives us entrance into His Kingdom.

I will put what Yeshua did in the language of Isaiah 53 to help us better understand what took place.

Who has believed our message and to whom has the arm of the LORD been revealed? [Yeshua] *grew up before him like a tender shoot, and like a root out of dry ground. He had no beauty or majesty to attract us to him, nothing in his appearance that we should desire him.* [Yeshua] *was despised and rejected by men, a man of sorrows, and familiar with suffering. Like one from whom men hide their faces* [Yeshua] *was despised, and we esteemed him not. Surely he took our infirmities and carried our sorrows, yet we considered him stricken by God, smitten by him, and afflicted. But* [Yeshua] *was pierced for our transgressions, he was crushed for our iniquities; the punishment that brought us peace was upon him, and by his wounds we are healed. We all, like sheep, have gone astray, each of us has turned to his own way; and the LORD has laid on him the iniquity of us all.* [Yeshua] *was oppressed and afflicted, yet he did not open his mouth; he was led like a lamb to the slaughter, and as a sheep before her shearers is silent, so he did not open his mouth. By oppression and judgment* [Yeshua] *was taken away. And who can speak of his descendants? For he* [Yeshua] *was cut off from the land of the living; for the transgressions of my people he was stricken. He was assigned a grave with the wicked, and with the rich in his death, though* [Yeshua] *had done no violence, nor was any deceit in his mouth. Yet it was the LORD's will to crush him and cause him to suffer, and though the LORD makes his life a guilt offering,* [Messiah] *will see his offspring and prolong his days, and the will of the Lord will prosper in his hand. After the suffering of his soul, he will see the light of life and be satisfied; by his knowledge my righteous servant will justify many, and he will bear their iniquities. Therefore I will give him a portion among the great, and he will divide the spoils with the strong, because he poured out his life unto death, and was numbered with the transgressors. For* [Messiah Yeshua] *bore the sin of many, and made intercession for the transgressors.*

Did you notice what verse 10 says? It says, *"Yet it was the LORD's will to crush him."* How can this be? Is God a sadist? No, the God of the Hebrew Scriptures does not gain pleasure by putting others, people or animals through pain, much less death.

What the Scriptures say at this point, I believe, is that the LORD was pleased in the obedience of His servant Messiah. He was glad that the sacrifice of Messiah caused all sin, past, present and future to be atoned. He was glad because His Messiah was THE Passover Lamb who took away the sin of His people and clothed them in His flesh of Righteousness to those who Trust in and follow Him.

I believe this is great, great news and shows the depth of God's love for us both as the Jewish people and as Gentiles. It also shows His great mercy and great patience. It also shows that what He speaks, He brings to fulfillment. This also fulfills His promise made to Abraham so many centuries ago – that his *seed* would bless all ethnicities. Through Yeshua, all ethnicities have truly been blessed by His Mercy and Grace.

Isaac's seed, Messiah gave a blessing to all people of the earth, starting with his own people, by atoning for their sins once and for all time. As a result of this one act of exchange, our sin has been covered and atoned.

I realize my effort may not convince you, and that's okay and your decision. The journey we've just endured is hard to take in during one sitting, so, take your time and let The LORD and His Scriptures work and accomplish their task.

My hope is that whether you are convinced, disappointed, mad, amused, grieved or otherwise, you will continue to look at the Hebrew Scriptures. I hope you will read them for yourself and ask the God of Israel whether or not Messiah has come. If you ask the LORD to show you and reveal the truth to you, I believe he will do just that.

Thank you for hanging with me as we journeyed through the pages of Scripture to search and see how Messiah brought blessing to the people of Israel and to Gentiles as well.

The fact that Messiah blesses all those who trust in him and brings peace to them is only the beginning of the peace and blessing Messiah brings.

Yes, this is only the beginning because Yeshua is going to return back to earth as a Mighty Warrior. He will set up his Messianic kingdom in Jerusalem and sit on David's throne after he triumphs over all his and Israel's enemies. Then, at that time, there will be worldwide peace just as the Scriptures say.

All the followers of Jesus, or Yeshua, his Hebrew name, were Jewish. These men did not have an easy life! In fact, 10 of his closest talmidim (disciples) died as martyrs.

The topic of this being a Jewish movement within Judaism is not something into which this book explored. However, we did broach, among many, the topic of trust in Yeshua (Jesus) as being required for our atonement. Suffice it to say that his talmidim followed the God of Israel, not some foreign god. These men followed the Torah of their Rabbi, just as Isaiah 42 declares. In fact, initially this group was called Followers of the Way; these men and women were seen as another Sect within Judaism.

Here's a relevant truth for today: Being a follower of Yeshua, who was a Jewish man, does not somehow make a Jewish person un-Jewish. In fact, the vast majority of his first century CE followers were Jewish. These followers went to Synagogue and the Temple, celebrated the Jewish feasts, followed Torah, and worshipped the God of Abraham, Isaac and Jacob. Did any of the Jewish followers of our above first three 1st Century CE Messianic Contenders become un-Jewish by believing and following in them?

My hope is that you will think deeply about all that we discussed and discovered during our journey. I also hope you will take the time to ponder how Yeshua fulfilled the words of the prophets, as shown in the New Covenant writings. Ultimately I hope you seek to follow Yeshua and His Torah while experiencing the Shalom that only Messiah can give.

Conclusion

At the beginning, I posited three things that I believed we've discovered to be true during our journey through the Hebrew Scriptures together. The three Scriptural truths I posited were: 1. God's choice of Abraham was specific, not arbitrary. 2. Israel's three-fold mission is to reflect God's holiness, be priestly intercessors, and proclaim God's glory. 3. The coming of Messiah brings life from the dead for Israel and provides the unmasking of truth for all humanity.

Messiah provides blessing for Israel and all humanity through his atonement on our behalf. This provides forgiveness of sin and a restored relationship with God. It is this forgiveness and relationship which is offered to all humanity.

It's the position of this author that the Hebrew Scriptures are true, reliable, and God's Words, written first for His Chosen People Israel and also for the whole world. As we saw above, these words point to a certain individual coming from the people of Israel, out of the tribe of Judah, and from the promised House of David.

Yeshua fulfilled the messianic prophesies of Scripture including ones that someone coming on the scene today could not fulfill, including being born before the destruction of the Second Temple. He alone had the ultimate relationship as Son to God the Father. He alone gave the signs from God to prove the authenticity of his claim as Messiah just as Moses had done. He alone, as the ultimate Servant of Israel, paid the ultimate price for sin, just as Daniel foretold. Yeshua willingly gave his life as an offering for sin. And his life's offering as our substitute was accepted by God.

It's my prayer and desire that you will avail yourself of his life, sacrifice and resurrection by placing your trust in what Yeshua has already done on your behalf as the Lamb of God per Isaiah 53, just as hundreds of thousands of Jewish people have done since the 1st Century CE. Begin to follow his Torah which he received from The Father. He has given this to us in order to bless each of us with freedom from sin, a clear conscience, joy unspeakable and Shalom as only Messiah can give.

Just how does one avail oneself of Yeshua's sacrifice of atonement? As the worshipper in 1st and 2nd temple times, we must confess our sin to God, believe that Yeshua's atoning sacrifice of exchange, did just that, atoned for our sins. Thank God for removing our sin through Yeshua. And last, we need to begin following His Word and Yeshua's Torah.

Being part of a larger community of trust is an integral part of growing and walking with the LORD. Looking into Messianic Congregations can be a good place to start. Much material, to help in your walk of trust is also available. You can find this material and even Jewish people to talk with, ones who have also placed their trust in Yeshua. These things are available through Chosen People Ministries and Jews for Jesus, two of many Messianic Jewish organizations.

I would love to hear from you, whether from a positive or negative perspective. As I said at the beginning I am wanting to dialogue with whomever has the desire to talk. If you have any questions or desire further dialogue please contact me at Godismypatriarch@gmail.com.

May you know the firm hope of trust in God that only Messiah can give; the firm clutch of God's hand on our lives.

Bill

Drawing of the Akedah by Jolie Barrios

Thanks Jolie for your beautiful depiction of the Akedah.